VIRGINIA TRANEL

Ten Circles Upon the Pond

Virginia Tranel was born and raised in Dubuque, Iowa, and graduated from Clarke College with a degree in English and Spanish. In January 1957, she married Ned Tranel and moved west, settling finally in Billings, Montana. Her essays have appeared in magazines and anthologies, including the Notre Dame Press anthology of best essays, *Family*.

Ten Circles Upon the Pond

Ned N. Tranel, December 5, 1933—East Dubuque, Illinois

Virginia Holmberg, December 10, 1933—Dubuque, Iowa

MARRIAGE: January 26, 1957, Dubuque, Iowa

CHILDREN:

Daniel Thomas, October 20, 1957—Colfax, Washington

Michael Joseph, March 3, 1959—Topeka, Kansas

Elizabeth Ann, October 18, 1960—Vermillion, South Dakota

Ned Anthony, July 13, 1962—Vermillion, South Dakota

Alane Patricia, May 13, 1964—Sheridan, Wyoming

Monica Joan, May 4, 1966—Sheridan, Wyoming

Paul Nicholas, October 11, 1968—Sheridan, Wyoming

Jennie Christa, October 2, 1970—Sheridan, Wyoming

Benedict John, November 16, 1974—Miles City, Montana

Adrienne Martha, November 10, 1978—Billings, Montana

Ten Circles Upon the Pond

REFLECTIONS OF A PRODIGAL MOTHER

Virginia Tranel

ANCHOR BOOKS

A DIVISION OF RANDOM HOUSE, INC.

NEW YORK

FIRST ANCHOR BOOKS EDITION, APRIL 2004

Copyright © 2003 by Virginia Tranel

All rights reserved under International and Pan-American Copyright Conventions. Published in the United States by Anchor Books, a division of Random House, Inc., New York, and simultaneously in Canada by Random House of Canada Limited, Toronto. Originally published in hardcover in the United States by Alfred A. Knopf, a division of Random House, Inc., New York, in 2003.

Anchor Books and colophon are registered trademarks of Random House, Inc.

Grateful acknowledgment is made to the following for permission to reprint previously published material:

Ruth Hamilton: Excerpt from the poem "Song for a Fifth Child" by Ruth Hamilton. Copyright © 1958 and renewed 1986 by Ruth Hamilton. Reprinted by permission of the author.
New Directions Publishing Corp: Poem "Stranger" from *The Collected Poems of Thomas Merton* by Thomas Merton. Copyright © 1949 by Our Lady of Gethsemani Monastery. Reprinted by permission of New Directions Publishing Corp.
Warner Bros. Publications U.S. Inc.: Excerpt from the song lyric "Cat's in the Cradle" by Harry Chapin and Sandy Chapin. Copyright © 1974 by Story Songs, Ltd. All rights reserved. Reprinted by permission of Warner Bros. Publications U.S. Inc., Miami, FL 33014.

The Library of Congress has cataloged the Knopf edition as follows:
Tranel, Virginia.
Ten circles upon the pond :
reflections of a prodigal mother / by Virginia Tranel.—1st ed.
p. cm.
1. Tranel, Virginia. 2. Mothers—United States—Biography.
3. Parenting—United States. I. Title.
HQ759 .T734 2003
306.874'3'092—dc21
[B] 2002034102

Anchor ISBN: 1-4000-3121-4

Book design by Iris Weinstein

www.anchorbooks.com

Printed in the United States of America
10 9 8 7 6 5 4 3 2 1

For Ned
and our children
and our children's children

One bird sits still
Watching the work of God:
One turning leaf,
Two falling blossoms,
Ten circles upon the pond.

One cloud upon the hillside,
Two shadows in the valley
And the light strikes home.

—from "Stranger," by Thomas Merton

CONTENTS

ACKNOWLEDGMENTS • *xi*

The Binding Problem • DANIEL *3*

Missing Mountains • MICHAEL *37*

Loving as Fast as You Can • ELIZABETH *68*

All Day, Every Day • NED ANTHONY *100*

While the Blossoms Still Cling • ALANE *131*

Backward Against the Stream • MONICA *161*

Beneath the Snow, Spring • PAUL *194*

The Squeaky Wheel of Happenstance • JENNIE *225*

The Presence of Absence • BENEDICT *256*

On Being a Ten • ADRIENNE *288*

ACKNOWLEDGMENTS

The people who brought this book into being are named in its pages: Ned, whose goodwill sustained us through the rearing and the writing; our daughters and sons, who taught me wonder and perseverance and the joy inherent in purposeful work; their spouses and children who enrich my life as they enlarge our family circle, and my sister-in-law, Betty Tranel, who strengthens our entire family with her constancy and caring. I'm grateful, too, to my community of readers, writers, and confidantes: Donna Davis, for her careful reading and enthusiasm; the Soapweed Sisters' Salon—Sheila Ruble, Danell Jones, and Francesca Lees—for their thoughtful comments; Nancy Englert for her unflagging friendship; and the five Unitarian women who quest with me every Thursday over dinner. My appreciation to Jim Bellows, who read the early essays and encouraged me to contact agent Sterling Lord, whose belief in my work has made all the difference. The editorial touch of Judith Jones at Knopf has been gentle and discerning. I wish I could thank all of the probing minds that fed mine during the lonely mothering times, writers whose work inspired me and kept me going.

Ten Circles Upon the Pond

THE TRANEL FAMILY, SUMMER 1980

Back row, left to right: Paul, Elizabeth, Ned,
Ned Anthony, Michael, Daniel
Front row: Alane, Jennie, Virginia with Adrienne
on her lap, Ben, and Monica

(COURTESY CETRONE STUDIO)

The Binding Problem

DANIEL

Traveling should be easy now. Our youngest child is three. No one is in diapers; everyone is capable of verbal communication, which complicates decision making but should preclude sudden eruptions on the upholstery. We're a happy, companionable family traveling from Ashland, Montana, to Houston, Texas, where my psychologist husband, Ned, will attend a conference on learning disabilities: eight children and two parents, sufficient numbers to justify our gas-guzzling Travelall in the midst of an oil embargo, plus enough clothes, equipment, and illusions to last twelve days. We're eager to get away from winter and Watergate's bad news and are looking forward to touring the Johnson Space Center, seeing the Gulf of Mexico, and, although no one has said it aloud, being unashamedly white for a while.

Two years have passed since we moved from Miles City, seventy miles north, to the house we built high on the hill above Ashland and the Tongue River. Our dining room windows frame the sunset over the Cheyenne reservation, the long-shadowed beauty of shale hills drenched in red and gold. Because we chose to live and work in this community, we enrolled our children in St. Labre Indian School rather than the public school where other white children go; we attend Sunday Mass at the mission church, a stone structure designed as a teepee buttressed with a Christian cross; at games, we sit on the Brave side of the bleachers and cheer against teams our children once played on; our kids invite school friends home for meals and weekends; this past Christmas season, Blake and Tony, two young Cheyenne brothers with no place to go, spent the holidays with us.

Still, the morning sun glares on our pale skin. Each day our children walk down the hill to school and learn more about the meaning of prejudice. One afternoon, our eight-year-old daughter, Monica, wide-eyed and breathless, was chased home by jeering Indian boys. *Hey, white girl, watch out. We're gonna get you.* During preseason football practice, our oldest son, Dan, lived with the team in a dorm. Rest remedied the brutal physical regimen of two practices a day but not the emotional strain of constant confrontation. He learned to be vigilant and tried to avoid fistfights with verbal tactics.

Reality is taking a toll on the romantic illusions that brought us here. Disturbing daily sights deepen the ache of isolation: a woman sprawled drunk at noon on the sidewalk in front of the bar; a young girl tucking a pinch of tobacco inside her lower lip; a man living in an abandoned car near a tangle of bushes by the river. A few days after we moved into our home, a group of giggling people emboldened by alcohol knocked on our front door to announce their hunger. Did we have food? I invited them in and opened the refrigerator to the woman. She searched the shelves, found cold boiled potatoes, and sliced them for sandwiches. A skinny, pockmarked man squatted on the floor next to Monica and joined her in a game of jacks. Another morning, a lone man drove out of his way to our house to ask if we had a little money for gas.

The issue isn't racial. What we're concerned about is exposing our children to a reality too grim for them to process. All children, not just ours, need time to make sense of their own lives before they can understand the predicaments of others. And teenagers need a circle of peers with whom they can entrust their dreams. Dan's sole confidant is Rick, a smart Cheyenne kid who plays the guitar and sings Jim Croce songs and is committed, as are many of the talented young, to spending his life here, helping his people.

This trip is supposed to be a vacation from coping. It's even supposed to be fun. But the car cruising so merrily down the road through the Crow Indian reservation is a cage on wheels, vibrating with punching, crying, bickering, all to the beat of hard rock. The driver of the vehicle is sixteen-year-old Dan, bright-eyed with a brand-new driver's license and bushy-headed with an Afro hairstyle. Intelligent, too, skilled and trustworthy. Furthermore, argued his father this morning, this highway driving will be good experience for him.

Risking a carful of people, though, is not a good experience for me. The blaring radio is rattling my confidence. I'm two weeks pregnant and still without symptoms (unless the dim-wittedness that lured me into this car is hormonal) and demoted to the "way back," the third seat where the youngest children ride, happily wrestling, playing reckless games of Slap Jack, looking out for things beginning with

C that, when spotted, grant the observer the right to pinch someone. Hard. Preferably an unsuspecting napper. I glare at the untamed hair and the head bobbing to the rhythm of "Born to Be Wild." Is he noticing the gauges that tell facts about oil and brakes and gas? When he glances at the road, does he actually see it? Or has he escaped into the teenage never-never land of noise?

"Car!" someone shouts.

"Stop it!" I shout louder, meaning this car, this trip, and maybe even the direction of our lives. But certainly, the radio.

It takes three more shouts before my husband, the window passenger in the front seat, turns his head. "What?" Ned repeats my message to Dan, whose disgruntlement bristles in the rearview mirror.

"Huh? Down?" Dan's eyes round in disbelief. "Off? All the way off? Aw, Mom, c'mon. Be reasonable. It's Steppenwolf."

I gesture toward three-year-old Jennie, whose head is flopped at a forty-five-degree angle as she sleeps open-mouthed against Elizabeth's shoulder, then mime my words to facilitate lip reading. "Off. Or I drive."

Dan looks to his dad for an ally. Ned responds by reaching across Mike, in the center seat, and pressing the radio's off button.

"Jeez," Dan grumbles. "You guys spoil everything."

Mike, who'll be fifteen in a week and has planned our return trip to include a sentimental stop in Kansas, where he was born, unfolds a map at arm's length. "Over there is where Custer and the Indians fought." He frowns. "Actually, it wasn't really a fight. It was a massacre. Depending on how you look at it."

How you look at it depends, of course, on your ability to see. "Would you mind lowering the map, Mike?" I ask cheerfully. "It's blocking the windshield." My reputation as a wet blanket has been escalating ever since we pulled out of our driveway. Fifty miles ago. Which means one thousand six hundred and fifty miles to go. Why am I here? I wonder for the jillionth time. *To know, love, and serve God and be happy with him in heaven* comes the rote catechism reply, but it won't do. This is an existential challenge. Am I a self-determining agent responsible for the authenticity of my choices? Or an unconscious accessory to an ordained plan? My track record is incriminating. It began in Dubuque, Iowa, on a frigid January morning in 1957.

MY WEDDING VEIL drifts over my face as, on my father's arm, I float down the aisle of St. Columbkille's Church in a gown of *peau de soie,* walking toward him, the dark-haired, restless man I don't know. At least, not in the biblical sense. I mask my eagerness by looking to the left of the altar where that other Virgin gazes back, a serene, blue-mantled statue inviting me with open arms into her mystery. My dad hands me over to Ned, an age-old property trans-action, but I'm blissfully unaware. The nuptial Mass, cele-brated by Ned's older brother, a priest, the binding vows to love through sickness and health until death do we part, the blessings and music blur by. And then I'm kneeling alone at Mary's feet to pray, a bridal custom I connect vaguely to virgins and vessels and acquiescence. But a pru-dent move, too, given Mary's role in Catholic tradition as mediatrix of all grace, a kind of funnel for God's blessings, a religious version of the maxim "The hand that rocks the cradle rules the world." As the mother of God, surely her hand has power. So does her left foot, deftly restraining a coiled snake, mythology's symbol of male fertility reincar-nated as Christianity's tempter. Unaware of the serpent's former reputation, I stare into the blunt eyes and recall my

7

seven-year-old self, veiled for my First Communion, kneeling in this same church before this same Virgin for whom I was named. I thank her for guiding me from veil to veil.

As we exit the church, friends bolster our fertility with a deluge of rice. The reception is a pleasant nuisance of well-wishers and cake and photographs. At last, I'm sitting beside Ned in the royal blue Chevy sedan he bought last week for $150. In the backseat are all of our possessions, packed for the two-thousand-mile trip to Pullman, Washington, where he'll begin work on a doctorate degree in psychology at the state university and I'll work in the accounting department at a job utterly unrelated to my interests or my college degree in English. My parents wave to us from the front porch. My mother dabs her eyes and says something to my dad, probably one of the proverbs she uses to explain idiosyncrasies and provide moral direction. "Birds of a feather flock together," she said to my brother when he brought home a friend whose character she questioned. "An idle mind is the devil's workshop," she told my sister when she found her daydreaming over her dusting assignment. "Familiarity breeds contempt," she warned when I went steady for the first time. Today, she might be saying, "They're young and haven't learned how life's corners must be turned."

"Still wet behind the ears," I imagine my dad responding as he puts an arm around her shoulder and swipes at his own eyes with the other hand. They shiver on the porch and eye the sign friends have tied to the bumper of our car. Trailing down the road behind us are three scrawled words: HOT SPRINGS TONIGHT!—code words for the longing of couples of that culture who'd lived out the lyrics "Love and marriage, love and marriage go together like a horse and carriage." Simply imagining the joy of consummation made brides blush and grooms sing a different tune: "Tonight, tonight, won't be just any night, tonight there will be no morning star."

Two right turns and we're on our way, naive newlyweds in a blue sedan streaking down the snowy highway like bold strokes on a white canvas. For all we know, those right turns were wrong, and, like artist Robert Motherwell, who claimed to begin each canvas with a series of mistakes, everything ahead of us would be a matter of correction.

"How far did you go the first night?" I once asked a newly married friend, meaning miles on the map. Her cheeks flamed. She stuttered, then smiled. "Well . . . we went, well, all the way . . . of course."

All the way across Iowa's hibernating cornfields we honeymoon. All the way across the blanketed wheat fields and sand hills of Nebraska. All the way across Wyoming's snow-swept rangeland, as white as my cast-off bridal gown. In Idaho, we climb into the pure, driven snow of White Bird Hill, where snowflakes swirl like a bridal veil, blinding us to the turns and twists in the road ahead. We put our faith in a mysterious blinking light tunneling north and follow a snowplow all the way to our destination—Pullman, Washington, a quaint town erupting from a sea of wheat. We open the door to an apartment rented over the telephone, three dingy rooms in an old house perched on a steep slope across Main Street from Washington State University.

We close the door behind us with a sigh. We've escaped the Korean War, the leaden winters and sticky summers of the Midwest, the obligation to plant roots in soil we consider unsuited to our fantasies. Ever since the college summers when Ned followed the wheat harvest through Nebraska and Montana, he's imagined his future on a sunny hilltop in the West. And now his dream and his name are mine.

While I yawn over tedious forms at my desk, Ned studies the behavioral patterns of rats and mice for insights into human conduct. My drowsiness is not entirely boredom. Somewhere in the Hot Springs of our honeymoon fantasy, probably in the real place of Rock Springs, Wyoming, our first child has been conceived.

One afternoon, as I'm walking home from that dreary desk, two dogs romping in an empty lot catch my eye. They sniff and growl and paw. They dance and skitter. The male rears up on his hind legs and thrusts toward her. She pauses, then sidesteps and drops him on all fours. Again and again, the anxious male tries to mount her; again and again, the jittery bitch leaps away. Finally, she surrenders to his pursuit, slides to a stop, and receives him. I walk faster, feeling found out, besmirched, unable to deny the essential similarity of the mating dance. But I know, too, the enormous difference between this animal frenzy and human lovemaking, an act that can, indeed, help create the ingredients of a loving relationship: trust, consideration, patience, and hope. I run the three blocks to our apartment, trying to outdistance the Victorian attitudes I meant to leave in Iowa's fenced fields. I'll need this animal instinct, along with Dr. Spock, to care for my first child.

"Hell, that's impossible," says my dad, when I call home to report our good news. His quick calculating has left him six days short of nine months and as astonished as the Virgin Mary before the angel Gabriel. Or perhaps what he finds impossible is imagining me, his strong-willed youngest child, as a mother. A vagabond mother, moreover, traveling cross-country again that summer according to her husband's career demands. A willing, eager vessel for a child destined to be a vagabond, too—conceived in Wyoming, quickening in Deadwood, South Dakota, waking me with middle-of-the-night heartburn in Savannah, Illinois, thumping my ribs at Craters of the Moon National Park in Idaho in September as we drive back to Washington State for another school year. A month before my October 20 due date, we settle into married student housing, a converted army barracks where our upstairs apartment has an extra bedroom and all of our neighbors have children.

ELIZABETH SHIFTS under Jennie's weight, scowls at the front seat, and jolts my consciousness with a question. "When do I get to drive? Or do the boys get to sit in the front seat for this entire trip?"

"You're only thirteen. And we've only been on the road for an hour. We'll switch places every two hours." I'm impressed at my impromptu diplomacy. The trouble is, no one in the front seat is paying any attention.

"Danny drove when he was thirteen."

"The tractor, maybe. Six miles an hour around the field."

"Oh, huh! Sure. Mom, you know better than that. He drove the pickup when he was eleven. And the car. Dad let him drive whenever he wanted. Just because he's a boy."

I exhale impatience. "He didn't drive on the highway with the whole family in the car."

She exhales disagreement. "He gets to do everything. Just because he's the oldest. Big know-it-all."

"So ask your dad if you can drive," I suggest, calling her bluff. In fact, I'm as aggravated as she with the smug trio up front. I thought women had the right to vote, and I'd cast mine against a sixteen-year-old driver.

"Dad!" she demands over and over until he finally hears. "Mom said I could drive when we get to the ocean."

"I'm driving," snaps Dan.

"We'll work it out," Ned says patiently, predictably, enigmatically.

"The Gulf of Mexico isn't the ocean," says Mike.

"Who asked for your opinion?" growls Elizabeth. And then she grumbles to me, "Why didn't you have me first?"

Mike brandishes the map. "It's not an opinion. It's a geographic fact."

Elizabeth glowers at the mountains streaking by.

"I wanted to practice on boys," I tell her. "So I could give you the benefit of my experience."

I'm not being entirely facetious. I knew nothing about children in 1957 except that I wanted some. Six boys and a girl, I told anyone who asked. No one recoiled in shock or wondered at the odd ratio or saw it, as I now do, as reflective of a patriarchal system that preferred sons, those potential priests and doctors and lawyers through whom mothers might gain vicarious power. My first daughter, despite her present sullen state, changed my mind and heart.

"There's no denying it, the first child affects you more profoundly," my daughter, Alane, our fifth child, will say years later as we watch her four-year-old son instruct his two-year-old sister to growl louder if she wants to be his pet brontosaurus. It's not that you love the first child more, we agree, but that the first anything is inevitably more fascinating thrilling impressive. First day at school. First watch. Date. Apartment. Car. Rocket to space.

SPUTNIK! SPUTNIK! SPUTNIK's gone up. It's October 4, 1957, and the world is agog at the news: the first man-made satellite is orbiting the earth! The Russian feat causes near pandemonium below. A month later, the Soviets pick up the pace by orbiting *Sputnik II,* an eleven-hundred-pound capsule carrying a small dog. With the amazement comes a frenzy of American self-criticism. How did U.S. technology fall behind? nervous newspapers ask.

The X ray my doctor holds up fascinates me more than any headlines. He points out the disproportionate head, down low in my pelvis, the strip of backbone, the curled-up legs, the tiny dark commas that are fingers and thumbs. "See this?" He grins. "Your baby's sucking its thumb!" What I see and understand for the first time is that the child inside me is real and must come out. I've had no Lamaze, no get-acquainted stroll through the hospital's maternity ward. Nor is my earthly mother nearby to console me. That night, I finger the rosary beneath my pillow and whisper childhood verses to my heavenly mother, the woman in blue.

Paranoia clutches the collective American unconscious. The Russians are superior. Surely planning to attack. On their way right now. *But so is my baby. My baby is coming! Ned, where are you?* The nurses have banished him from the room. I'm alone and frightened. Then the terrible rending of transition, two opposing forces battle for power, the infant thrusting toward light and my body holding on, desperate to claim some fragment of my original being. *It's coming! Ned! Hurry. Where are you?* I hear his footsteps in the hall, running toward my room. *No, sorry, sir, you can't go in there. We're taking her to delivery now.* I'm alone again. *Push. Push. No, stop. Don't push.* I'm fully opened to push out my child, but a mask is clamped over my face and I'm sent into an ethereal world where I become a better patient, more amenable to pulling and cutting and stitching. Not until evening, when the ether has worn off, do I see our son. His forehead is bruised, his skull dented and blotched from the clamp of instruments, but he's more spectacular than any satellite orbiting the earth. At high noon on his "impossible" due date, our first child has landed in our life.

My mother comes cross-country on the train, through

the Dakotas where she claims there is nothing, nothing at all; through Montana where there is even less; over the mountains and across bridges that straddle terrifying canyons to Pullman, Washington, to help me out for a week and meet the baby who enfleshes her unspoken words about human sexuality. When he is a week old, we baptize him Daniel Thomas, even though *Sputnik* might be more appropriate. The Russian word means "traveling companion," and this newborn babe has logged more than eight thousand miles with us.

We orbit in amazement around the son who has become our world. On the first Christmas morning of our marriage, we wrap him in a blanket and place him under the tree while we snap a photo. He is our gift. If we've cheated ourselves of bonding time as a couple or altered through pregnancy the process of getting to "know" each other physically or burdened ourselves with premature responsibility or failed to consider the real cost, we're blissfully unaware.

The task of guiding this precious life to maturity is both thrilling and daunting. Every twitch and grunt and grimace fascinates us. The first burp. Coo. Smile. Giggle. "He turned over." *Looked like an accident to me.* "No, no, on purpose. He twisted and tried until he did it!" He's amazing! He's sitting up! He's incredible! We're incredulous, too, at the fierceness of our love for him. And surprised by our utter vulnerability. We hover and warn and cheer. He is our *Sputnik,* traveling with us everywhere. On Sunday afternoons, we tramp the back roads of western Idaho, introducing him to the delights of nature, but *his* nature is our delight. We watch and worry and applaud. In June, he travels with us to Topeka, Kansas, where Ned begins a year's internship with the Menninger Clinic and I can peaches and make a home of another converted barracks. Late in the afternoon, like an eager pup waiting for his master, our son takes up watch at the front door; when he catches sight of his dad, he bounces up and down and babbles. Now he's circling the room, holding on to the sofa, the chair, the table. He's taking his first step, arms waving, flying straight to me. He's remarkable!

NO WONDER he's driving.

As we skirt the beauty along Colorado's Sangre de Cristo mountain range, the car becomes a cacophony of ill will. I consider giving up, returning home, but logistics unnerve me. Would I go Greyhound? Hitchhike? Take the car with a select crew? If we split up, would the boys go on with Ned and the girls retreat with me? Elizabeth would balk at that scenario. Along with her equality agenda, she's brought suntan lotion, a swimsuit, and a plan to acquire a tan. Besides, we're halfway there. I huddle in the backseat, a pawn of the front-seat patriarchy: copilot husband, teenage tour guide, and Afro-haired driver born to be wild. Where did I go wrong?

These thoughts bring me up short. Is it instinct that determines our direction? Carl Jung said the first half of life is a "state in which man is only a tool of instinctive nature." Children, he claimed, are "driven unconsciously in a direction that is intended to compensate for everything left unfulfilled in the lives of their parents."

My parents' parochial Midwestern lives were innocent of words like "unfulfilled" and "unconscious" and "compensate." My dad's message reflected a life spent in manual labor: *Get an education.* He and my mother worked and saved money and paid the bills and went to church and raised children begotten almost mysteriously. "Your father never saw me nude," my mother told me the day before our wedding, the way an athlete might boast, "I get up at dawn to run." Then she handed me a yellowed pamphlet lauding marital modesty, her sole direct communication about sex, but an explanation, too, for the dark closet she undressed in, the flannel nightgown she wore to bed. Maybe her generation's awe of that subject was a way of saying that the mechanics of sex aren't the issue so much as the attitudes woven into the fabric of each day, the respect shown for the body's functions and feelings, how children are bathed, diapered, and toilet trained, how a man and woman live together, if they treat each other with kindness and respect and enjoy each other's company. "Actions speak louder than words" would have been the proverb here.

What was unfulfilled in her life, I wonder, this woman named Anne Marie Cox, who at age thirty-seven became Charlie Holmberg's second wife and moved into a home with another woman's furniture and youngest child, an eight-year-old boy yearning for the mother who died when he was three months old. A year later, her own son was born. Perhaps she was overwhelmed by her complex obligations as wife, mother, stepmother, and youngest sister, protector of home and family and dignity, magnet for the multitude of relatives who dropped in. Maybe at times she wanted to give up. Instead, she made soap and fed clothes through the wringer of an old washing machine and canned vegetables and told me tragic tales of infant deaths, motherless children, widowed men. I learned that my aunt Bertha's mournful eyes reflected the loss of four infants; that my uncle Tom's turn from God began when his young wife, mother of nine children, died; that my father turned *to* God when his first wife, also named Anne Marie, died suddenly and left five children. I found out that among the children of my mother's twelve siblings, I am the third Virginia. The first was struck and killed by a car when she was seven years old; the second died a few days after her first birthday. I'm the one who lived.

But Jung has lured me on this scenic turnoff, and here I am, prying up rocks from the past when I ought to be paying attention to the pavement ahead. I peer over the four squabblers in the middle seat and meet Dan's accusing eyes in the rearview mirror. *Killjoy,* they say. *Spoilsport. Party pooper. Mom.*

So who cares what he thinks? But the honest question is, Why do I care so much? Because he's my firstborn child? Because I gave him the best of me, all the energy and enthusiasm of a first-time mother amazed at the grace in his every grimace? Or because I gave him the worst of me, too, the skewed perspective of ignorance and inexperience?

I think of the frantic March midnight in 1959 in Topeka when we called our neighbor, then bundled up our sleeping sixteen-month-old son and sent him off with her while Ned rushed me to the hospital. Twenty minutes later I gave birth to our second child. A few weeks later, I arranged this infant son on the bed for a snapshot, but it was years later when I opened the photograph album and saw for the first time the little boy standing on the other side of the bed, forlornly sucking his thumb as he gazed at his new brother.

"Don't you ever pick that baby up?" my mother asked that June on a balmy day in Iowa as Danny tottered over the lawn of my childhood home. We were visiting for a few days on our way back to Pullman, Washington, where Ned would continue course work toward his doctorate. *Baby?* I was carrying him in my arms, three-month-old Mike. Danny was a big boy.

He was a bigger boy the following June when we returned to Dubuque to spend the summer. In the fall, we moved to Vermillion, South Dakota, where Ned had taken a job teaching in the university. Danny became the biggest sibling in October 1960, two days before his third birthday, when our third child and first daughter was born.

Once again, my mother came to help. She did around-the-clock laundry, made peanut-butter sandwiches, kept track of shoes and schedules, read Mother Goose, and cuddled little boys. "Your other two babies," she called Danny and Mike, to my chagrin.

When she returned to Iowa, I needed ten more hours in each day and another set of arms and legs. Unable to "pick that baby up," I hurried him up. *Danny, can you help me with this? That's a big boy. Hurry up now. Be good. See what Mike is doing.* Three-year-old Danny encircled two-year-old Mike in protective arms. *That's a good brother. Can you help him into the car?* Always rushed, I switched lines in the grocery store, jiggled keys when the checker chatted to the bagger, scolded sluggish stoplights and lethargic drivers. I dragged children down the aisles of grocery and hardware stores and into fabric shops where a bored Mike learned to hate gingham on bolts. He instinctively resisted rushing, and thereby earned a reputation as a dawdler, a dreamer when, in fact, he was simply behind schedule—our schedule.

Danny's firstborn inclination to please us made him easy prey to the pressure of our harried days. *Hurry now. It's time for nursery school. Hurry. It's time for kindergarten. Hurry up, please, it's time to pack up your teddy bear and gather up your toys. We're moving to Wyoming. Hustle. Help me with these boxes. Can you open the door for your little sister? Don't cry. You're a big boy. You'll like the West. Just think, you'll be in first grade.*

"He's only five," said the principal of the school in Big Horn, Wyoming. "State law here says children have to be six by September fifteenth to start first grade."

I told him our son already had been in school for two years, nursery school and kindergarten. What would he do at home all day? He had so much enthusiasm and energy. Surely, the board could be persuaded.

To our delighted relief, the board said yes.

Like most parents operating under the influence of *Sputnik,* we thought our son needed to be in school, where his days would be structured and his learning goal-directed. The intense competition of Soviet-American relations had spilled into every aspect of society. Experts analyzed and compared school curricula and teaching methods and declared American children ill equipped for the space age. Children shouldn't fritter away time doing activities merely for fun. They must learn to compete, achieve early, and grow up fast. Never mind yesterday's "early ripe, early rot" philosophy. Forget that the essence of genuine education is not to become powerful over others, but to stimulate curiosity and strengthen intellects to recognize what's good and true and worth working for. The race to the moon made runners of us all.

Ironically, social change threatened the existence of childhood just when we'd begun to know more about the needs of children: to be nurtured—to have time and space to explore, physically, intellectually, emotionally, and spiritually; to be bonded—to have loyal role models in whom they place their trust; and to be safe—to have a secure base from which to stray, across the room, the yard, the world. Children grow and learn better when social demands are balanced with time for self-expression—art, music, drama, and play—and when they have time to investigate and imagine, free of organization and judgment and the opinions of others. Play, pure and unbridled, nurtures creative minds, but now play was sent to summer camp to specialize in competitive sports. Instead of kicking the can for the heck of it, kids were coached to kick a football for the winning point. Playing baseball on the corner lot, shooting marbles, climbing trees belonged to yesterday. Kids were told what to want, their questions answered before they were asked, watches given to them before they could tell time so at least they'd know when they were falling behind. Ned and I never did swallow this philosophy whole and, a few children later, debunked it entirely, but it affected schools and sports and parental attitudes, and it curtailed any Huck Finn traits loitering in our first son.

"I can't keep him busy," said Dan's fifth-grade teacher. "I gave him two hundred words to define and memorize. Half an hour later, he was back, asking if I had anything else hard to do."

"He's a great kid to coach," said the seventh-grade football coach of our just-turned-twelve son decked out in football regalia. "Eager to do his best. Willing to work hard."

The following summer, 1970, as we prepared to move from Wyoming to Montana, where Ned was already working and searching for a suitable house, twelve-year-old Dan became the "man" on our sixty-three-acre place, in charge of animals and chores and helping a mother pregnant with her eighth child. One afternoon, I watched from the kitchen window as he herded cows toward the barn. Just as he shooed them through the gate, two or three looped back and ran off. Over and over, he circled and shouted; over and over a few escaped. When I went out to help, I saw the tears streaming down his face. And I also saw a child overwhelmed by the task of a man.

In the fall, after we settled in Miles City, Dan entered eighth grade at Sacred Heart, a Catholic school in the throes of the latest educational fad, self-paced learning.

Teachers served as mere guides parceling out assignments to children who accomplished them at their own pace. Dan thrived on it, but it was a short-lived experiment that deprived too many kids of support and direction.

As the oldest of eight, Dan was seldom seen without a younger sibling in his arms, or riding on his shoulders, or trailing him down the street where he cut grass for hire, or to his room where he listened to Harry Chapin on his new stereo: "The cat's in the cradle and the silver spoon; little boy blue and the man in the moon. I'm gonna be like you, Dad, you know I'm gonna be like you." But that summer, when he went to Wyoming to work on a ranch, he went alone. He was thirteen. My instinct—that bitch I met in the field before his birth—howled that he was too young. My heart said don't let him go. But I didn't pay attention to either one.

In ninth grade, he played on Sacred Heart's victorious Fighting Irish football team; sometimes before games, his stomach hurt. A few times, he vomited. As a junior at St. Labre and quarterback on the Brave team, his job was to rouse team spirit, memorize the offense, and call the plays. In the middle of a Friday evening game, as we watched from the bleachers, he collapsed. I sat beside him in the small plane that whisked him off to a hospital in Billings, 120 miles away. I tried to calm him, but all the while I sensed something awry other than a physical injury.

Fear, the neurosurgeon said, after an examination and overnight observation. Tension. A pseudo-seizure, psychologically based, a way to cope with stress. It was something he saw in bright young athletes trying to play everyone else's game: coaches nervous about their careers, fathers bragging and wagering on the sidelines, girlfriends and classmates cheering from the bleachers, lackadaisical teammates. "Get that quarterback," Ned shouted from the edge of the field. "Throw the ball," yelled the coach. "Catch it," screamed the crowd. "We want a touchdown," shrieked the cheerleaders. "Nothing wrong with him," said the doctor, "other than too much pressure."

This event plunged Ned and me into an examination of our parenting and the responsibility we'd thrust upon our son simply because he was oldest and willing, a kind of family quarterback who carried the ball down strange fields for the younger kids to follow, who blazed trails and provided practice for inexperienced, well-meaning parents whose unwitting egos were tied up with his achievements. Dan's diligence and firstborn inclination to identify with us more than with his siblings fooled us into treating him differently. But acting grown-up behind the wheel of a vehicle doesn't mean a child is ready to take over monthly payments or maintenance.

Now here we are, bound together on the road to Texas with Dan's aggrieved eyes accusing me from the mirror. I plead guilty. We expected too much too soon from him, not because we didn't care, but because we didn't know. Fortunately, kids have an uncanny ability to recognize the difference. They forgive faults but hate phonies. When adults continually put their needs before those of children, all the cell phone "I love you"s in the world won't convince them. But love that's real makes leeway for mistakes. If I'm to be a trustworthy parent, I have to treat my children with dignity, which means respecting their developmental stages, which means it's time for this born-to-be-wild driver to become a passenger.

"Ned, are you ready to take a shift behind the wheel," I ask, "or shall I?" I'm risking, I suspect, a simultaneous shift as pariah of the Travelall. But all this tiptoeing around others, trying to keep them fed, clothed, contented, and safe without ever alienating their affection is what has landed me, and a lot of other women, in the backseat. I shush the protestors; Ned tells Dan to pull over, and I unleash the law: If we're going to keep on, we need to get along; we have to modify personal desires for the sake of family harmony; each person, regardless of age, musical preference, or personal belief, has to keep the group welfare in mind. Ned chimes in with his famous "contribution speech," which boils down to "give, don't just take." And then he walks around to the driver's side.

"So is this a democracy after all?" Mike wants to know.

I hear a trick question and hesitate.

"No," says Ned, shifting into gear. "It's a family."

"It sure sounds like a democracy," Mike says, "and that means we get to vote."

"None of you are old enough." My reply suggests the crux of the issue. Maybe the irritant on this trip hasn't been the teenage driver but the deferential parents.

From here to the eternity of Houston, we muddle through. We arrive at our hotel, a ragtag crew attracting dubious glances as children whirl Frisbees and run laps around the lawn. That evening, ill at ease over my mutiny, I volunteer what's expected of me—to stay in with the proletariats while Ned takes the four oldest off to the Astrodome to see Tony Orlando and Dawn. Television dwells on Patty Hearst, the nineteen-year-old woman kidnapped a couple of weeks ago by the Symbionese Liberation Army (SLA). The SLA is demanding that her grandfather, William Randolph Hearst, distribute two million dollars' worth of food to California's poor. I'm in no mood for this food bank army unless it's liberating me. The kids clamor for *Midnight Special,* any old reason to wait up. But I'm past patience with everything raucous.

A little feminism is a dangerous thing. Drink deep or taste not of liberation's spring. Adapting "Mrs." to "Ms."

implies autonomy, but resentful dependence can simmer on: it's *his* fault I'm a pregnant plebeian penned up in this room; *his* fault there are hungry poor people and fat California millionaires; *his* fault I'm not among the chosen ones at the Astrodome; *his* fault I spent three fretful days in the backseat of a Travelall. I want the shelter of *his* arms, but not the constriction. What I get is a secondhand rendition of "Knock Three Times" when the jolly concertgoers return.

The next day dawns in a universe of possibilities. We tour the Johnson Space Center and come away dazzled. All this human ambition—the striving for the stars, the yearning to achieve and learn and try harder and explore, the playful minds that imagine more than they can know, the disciplined minds that test what's been imagined—puts us in a state of awe. Maybe science will answer via satellite the human pondering that nags us through every journey: Why am I here? Where am I going? Does it matter? Is there anybody out there who cares? Will we make it safely home? And if, indeed, we are "fallen" creatures, is it possible that God began like Motherwell, blundering deliberately so that he might hand us the brush?

Before we return north we make the promised sojourn to the Gulf of Mexico, where the sun soothes any leftover surly spirits and the sand makes castle builders of us all. The waves wash enthusiasm over grouchy souls until it no longer seems to matter who drove or how we got here. What counts is that we came and arrived at this place together.

We drive home via Kansas, taunted by repeated renditions of this week's DJ favorite, "Seasons in the Sun," and plummet back into the reality of the reservation in mid-March, land bleak with winter's remnants, snow worn out from whirling across fields and slamming against fences, people worn out from clinging to the margins of society.

While our NASA-enlightened kids indulge in a model-building spree, gluing together models of rockets and missiles and lunar landing devices, my days once more become a long response to the needs of children: opening doors, drawers, jars of strawberry jelly; reading Little Bear stories; investigating odd silences, silencing obnoxious noise, spreading peanut butter on bread, blankets on the lawn for noon picnics, myself across the day, wondering if there will be enough of me to cover a twenty-four-hour span.

In November, our ninth child and fifth son, Benedict John, is born.

My nights are fragmented. I'm lying in bed, nursing my infant and drifting in and out of sleep, when I alert to the sound of the front door opening. I recognize Dan's footstep on the stair. I've been worried about him, his restlessness, the wall he's built around his life. He's seventeen, and a year from now he'll be in college, thousands of miles away. I have no perspective, no way of knowing if he'll ever come back, literally or figuratively.

He's at the top of the stairs now, pausing outside the bedroom door, calling softly, "Mom?"

"Dan? Yes, I'm awake."

He opens the door a few inches, sighs, shuffles from foot to foot, and says he doesn't know what to do. Maybe he should just quit the team. "Why play when nobody will pass me the ball? When they treat me like I'm not there."

"They" are the Cheyenne and Crow kids who resent white intrusion on the basketball court, one of the few arenas where they've felt the thrill of superiority.

Another sigh. "It's just not fair. The trouble is . . ." He's speaking slowly, thinking aloud. "I've never quit anything before. Not even football last year." Rather than quit the game after that traumatic Friday evening, he learned to play it. Ned, remorseful that his paternal zeal may have figured in Dan's collapse, taught him to expend his pregame nerves in physical work. One Saturday morning, they transported the top half of a collapsed windmill to our yard and erected it there, a haunting reminder of our quixotic striving. Before another game, they hauled home a cast-off wrought-iron fence and reassembled it around our yard. By kickoff time, Dan could see and touch what he'd accomplished; the symbolic achievement of downs and goals began to lose their power.

But how shall I console him now? Shall I remind him that sometimes quitting is the only way to win? Shall I say what Ned would if I jostled him awake: We'll work things out? I tell him finally, "Try to get some sleep, Dan, and we'll talk about it in the morning."

I hear another sigh and then his footsteps retreating downstairs to the room he shares with three brothers. I imagine him lying in bed next to six-year-old Paul and listening to the rhythm of his brothers' breathing until at last, he drifts into sleep, his fears on hold until tomorrow. I slide my hand under my pillow, groping for a rosary no longer there. And then I miss her, the woman in her outmoded mantle with her foot upon the snake.

Tomorrow never comes. Dan is gone from the hallway, from his room, from our house. He graduates, strips his posters from the walls, jams his clothes into a suitcase, and goes off to the University of Notre Dame to grow a beard and study psychology. The valedictorian of St. Labre's graduating class, a Notre Dame honor scholar, he's lost in a strange Midwestern world of white students.

Time travels like a whirlwind through our house, carrying off my children and my good intentions, leaving me behind to survey what's left undone: clothes waiting to be mended, gardens waiting to be tended, questions waiting to be answered, the echo of my seventeen-year-old son shifting from one foot to the other in the dark hall outside our bedroom door as he asked for direction. "Mom, I don't know what to do."

THE INFANT LYING next to me that night when Dan stood wondering in the hall is now seventeen and the driver of our van. We're returning home to Montana from Iowa.

"Hey, Dad, where do we go right?" asks Ben, turning his head toward the bucket seats behind him where Ned and I ride, pretending to mind but secretly enjoying our role as irresponsible old fogies. In the other front seat is thirteen-year-old Adrienne, who in Elizabethan fashion has rabble-roused through South Dakota for a turn at the wheel. Her dad has been teaching her to drive. Experience has told him that by fourteen she'll no longer listen to fatherly advice.

"Huh? Who?" mumbles Ned, rousing like a bear from hibernation. We've reached the frayed edge of Ashland, where we've promised to show our youngest two children the house high on the hill where we once lived.

We've been in Iowa City visiting Dan, his wife, Laurie Hall, and their two blond daughters, Thomasin and Courtney, at their farm south of town. Since completing his doctorate ten years ago, Dan's been working as a neuropsychologist in the Neurology Division of the University Hospitals. He's thirty-four now, and his Afro has disappeared along with most of his hair. He took us through the clinic, pointing to charts and diagrams and maps of the brain. The child who'd grown up working seemed to be at play, a curious explorer wandering the labyrinthine ways of the human mind. Like a delighted little boy showing off a new electric train, he fingered a model of the human brain and explained to us the focus of his research—synchronous multiregional retroactivation—the term his scientific team uses for their theory of how the mind works: different sensory modalities provide information to different areas of the brain, and these fragmented pieces converge to give us the experience of a "whole." I teased him, saying that it sounded like another name for family reunion. He snickered and replied, "Maybe that's why it's called the binding problem." He knows my pride in him, but he also knows that I sometimes fail to worship at the altar of science.

Yesterday morning, as we got into the van, he gave me a sly smile and a few paper-clipped pages. "I know you have certain ideas about this, but this article brings up some important issues."

I raised an eyebrow at the title: "Environmentalists: Ban the (Population) Bomb." "Is this a fantasy of retroactive birth control?" I asked. "Or a plot to shun me at next year's family reunion?" We have a little game: his mind stands guard like a cat under a tree while my words flutter birdlike among branches. Sometimes an errant one swoops low. He bats. Other times they fly wide circles and tantalize his scientific grounding. He snatches. He makes menacing jumps toward wisps of thought. He pounces on wild generalizations, intuitive theories. He hungers for clarification. I quote books I've read, none of them with footnotes.

Ultimately, we retreat in mutual respect—the cat to curl up on the grass, the bird to rest in the tree. But this time, he'd caught a wing, and I fell wounded. This wasn't a game; it was an indictment of my life.

As we whizzed past fertile cornfields, I read: "Ask

almost any environmentalist the underlying cause of the world's major environmental problems and the answer is likely to be—too many people." The coordinator for population affairs in the U.S. State Department declares that "overpopulation is not a stabilizing factor, whether it be political stability, developmental stability, or environmental stability."

A mix of anger and dismay gripped me. My son had turned on me. I felt compelled to justify my life, to explain my choices to him, to rebut his Malthusian attack. I wanted to tell him about the idealism of my youth, the honeymoon that gave him life, but his face would take on the skeptical look science trained him to use. He'd tilt his head as if to turn his brain a certain way, arranging the critical input receivers for the best filtering of information.

We crossed South Dakota accompanied by Phil Aaberg's homage to the plains, piano music that Ben chose according to a compromise that evolved over the years—the driver picks the music; the parents set the volume. But while left-hand arpeggios rolled like the land and Aaberg's right hand sang of larkspur and cottonwoods along the creek, my thoughts rumbled like thunderclouds.

I'm trapped. I've done the deed. I fantasized about the cultural ideal—two "replacement" children. Which would I choose? Undoubtedly Dan claims firstborn exemption from his own advice. Michael is the second child. Two sons. I visualized life without the third child, Elizabeth; the fourth, Ned Anthony. Surely two talented, generous adults couldn't be classified as environmental problems.

Suppose Ned and I had spent our first five married years nurturing relationship rather than children. Our children then would be Alane and Monica, in real life numbers five and six. Never again could they complain of being "neglected middle kids." What if there were no seventh child, Paul, with his nurturing heart and subtle sense of humor?

I want to tell my scientist son I'm glad for Paul—for all my children—but I would sound callous, unconcerned about ozone depletion and global warming. Is this the despair priests feel? Their life's work considered not only obsolete but downright dangerous?

Aha! Priests! he would say. *The church told you what to think and do.* I can't deny the comforting shelter of that cultural cave where candles, flickering and dancing to the chant of litany, lulled me to acquiescence. Even as the national birthrate declined, we kept having children. Isolated in the foothills of the Wyoming Big Horn Mountains, far removed from the strident unrest of the sixties, I spent my days making bread, sewing, pushing strollers, reading Dr. Seuss, answering simpler questions:

"Why do caterpillars have sticky yellow stuff inside them?"

"Why would anybody trust a snake that talked?"

"Why do I have to nap and she doesn't?"

Let others wrestle with dilemmas about war and race and justice. Did the survivors of that decade emerge with anything more than memories of smoking pot or having awesome sex with someone whose name they've forgotten? I tell myself I'm not sorry I ignored that tumult.

But I don't want my son to see me as a mindless slave who bore children as a means to eternal life. I wanted each one. Each revealed a new dimension of life. I liked seeing my days from that broadened perspective.

Or was I simply rebelling in a socially acceptable way against my mother's overprotective tendencies? I moved far away and set up a life of challenge, thus proving my independence—no need to be a "flower child." Or perhaps

I was trying to empower myself through a greedy use of the limited options available to women then. Or embodying society's ideal, and my church's theology, of woman as mother, the oblivious January bride kneeling before the Virgin.

Or maybe it came down to this: I was the child driven to compensate for what was left unfulfilled not only in my parents' lives, but in the lives of aunts and uncles, too. Fruitfulness was my remedy for the aging and death that hovered over them. My recompense for my mother's dark closet and flannel nightgown.

Was it *all* unconscious reaction? Was there no element of rational choice?

"WHERE DO WE go right, Dad?" Ben repeats into the rearview mirror. I see him taking mental notes to spin into a story to tell his siblings at the Christmas table, the tale of chauffeuring Mom and Dad from Iowa to Montana. *They were conked the whole way. Every so often, one of 'em would rouse and ask if I needed a relief driver. No, I'd say, then off they'd go again to slumber land.*

Ned leans forward and points. "Just past that sign for St. Labre." We fall silent as we drive past the post office, the grocery store, the bank, the bar with its crumbling sidewalk where, a few weeks ago, Blake, the carefree boy who once stayed with us through Christmas, was found dead, stabbed at age twenty-two for a little whiskey in the bottom of a bottle. Or for no reason at all. Nothing has changed. Everything has.

We reach the intersection. I look one way and see a strange conglomeration of motives, days of mistakes and miracles, years of confusion and grace. As in the ether-sedated birth of Dan, much of that time remains chaotic, dark, mysterious. Not until six hours after he was born did I see him, touch him for the first time. So it goes. Six hours become six years, sometimes six decades, before we understand.

I look the other way and see the promise and reality of my children. As in the unmedicated birth of Adrienne, it is the excruciating awareness that deepens the joy.

Adrienne strings questions together, trying to connect herself to a family history she wasn't part of. "That's where you lived? Way up there?" She looks up, wide-eyed. "And that's the hill Paul rode his Big Wheel down the time you guys forgot him?" It's a story we'll never live down, the Sunday we hurried off to Mass and left behind five-year-old Paul, who pedaled frantically over sharp shale to catch up.

"Danny hauled your stuff down *this* hill in a dump truck when you moved to Broadview?" Ben asks incredulously as we wind past ponderosa pines up the narrow, steep, rough road. He appreciates the feat because recently he served as our prime mover from one house to another in Billings.

Ben, nine months old when Dan left for college, is now the biggest brother. He towers over Dan and flaunts thick, curly hair before his oldest brother's balding pate. Amiable Ben, baffled by Dan's intensity, challenges it. During holiday hockey games, he thwarts Dan's competitive bent by stealing his stick. When Dan industriously washes dishes in the kitchen while the rest of us linger over coffee, Ben picks him up physically and hauls him protesting back to the dining room. Ben rebuffs Dan's farewell handshake with a gruff command: "Give me a hug, you bastard." I don't take the epithet personally; it's brotherly love.

As we drive slowly past the two-story house that's now a group home for Cheyenne children, my brain stages a full-fledged family reunion. Sensory information converges into the sweet scent of July watermelon, children somersaulting on new-mown grass, the brilliant stillness of August when the hillside seemed lost in thought, grasshoppers clickety-clicking through sleepy September afternoons, the sighing ponderosas. A young boy watches us from the front step with dark-eyed curiosity, shrugs, and ambles off. Four or five children burst out the front door, grin and wave, then romp after two small dogs nipping and chasing each other along the wrought-iron fence. Near the edge of the hill, we stop and walk, crunching pine needles beneath our heels. The windblown ponderosas clinging to shale as if it were solid rock recall the struggling heroes of my mother's stories.

Ben gestures south, toward the land stretching away below. "That looks like a prehistoric ocean floor."

Ned tells him that the sandstone formations were once a barrier island along the coast of an inland sea, that geologists compare them to the sand now accumulating along Galveston Island. This prompts me to tell the story of our long-ago family trip to the Gulf of Mexico, which goads Ben and Adrienne to wish they'd been along.

"You were," I tell Ben. "In utero."

Adrienne pouts. "I missed all the fun."

"Watch for snakes," I call as they sprint ahead. My reminder echoes over the coulee and the years.

This memory incites another. More proof for Dan and his research team. I think of the afternoon I saw a bull snake twist up the trunk of a pine tree. I watched it wind around branches and through stiff needles to its destination, a nest of baby birds. Flinging its head into the nest, the snake grasped a newborn bird and devoured it. Another thrust of its head, another baby gone. Instinctively, I went to get my son's bow and arrow. I planted my feet and settled the bow, as I'd learned to do eons ago at Girl Scout camp. I aimed and drew. *Thwack.* The arrow tumbled to the ground. Another try. *Thwump.* I traded the bow for a long-handled rake, but there was no dislodging the thief. Bird by bird, the snake emptied the nest while the mother bird flew frantic circles overhead, crying out in beseeching chatter.

I am that bird. Dan's questions wind like a snake around my life, intruding upon my nest of certainty. What I fear from the jaws of the snake is judgment, my firstborn's negative judgment upon my choices.

Today's attitudes ask me to squelch my hard-earned joy in my children, to see them as some giant oil spill or destructive path slashed through a rain forest, to see myself as the perpetrator of an ecological crime. Yet Dan's concerns are real. For a multitude of reasons, human communities can self-destruct, and do.

We spend our energies on a dream and awaken to find it disdained. Is the dream the problem, the blurry, unaware, unconscious, hidden-away pieces that direct our lives? Or the awakening to another perspective? *Where did we go right?* It's a song Dan sings when he comes home toting his guitar.

When I see Dan's fascination as he touches a plaster corpus callosum, when I observe his compassion for our world and its welfare, I wonder: Did it germinate long ago as he leaned over to teach Alane how to tie her shoelaces or boosted her into the tree house when other siblings shut her out? Or when he lifted Paul to his shoulders for a "high sky ride," or gathered a group of brothers and sisters for an afternoon of fixing fence? Or memorized two hundred words too fast? Or when, as a restive high school senior, he taught math to restive fourth-graders? Or when he took his own hard-won football lessons to Notre Dame, where he captained an interhall team that played "for fun"? Or learned to use manual work to temper his anxiety but not his ambition, the yearning that rightly leads to achieving something beyond oneself? I imagine a trace of wistfulness in his eyes. His questions may not be about *my* life, after all, but about *his*.

Perhaps he wishes he could have his season in the sun, too, as I did, without worrying so much about dangerous ultraviolet rays. The article he handed me may be a plea for understanding, his way of explaining why his choices are different from mine. Now I realize what we *both* clamor for: respect for the sincerity and context of our choices.

Each of us, standing alone at the edge of uncertainty, tries to balance beliefs and desires. Then, swallowing hard, we lunge, hoping our decisions will bring satisfaction. My desires pulled me to necessary places where loneliness, isolation, prejudice roused me awake. These desires were, in a sense, *my* environmental truth, planted in me for a reason. If I had ignored them, I might have stumbled through life unaware. My children have challenged me to pay attention and to overlook, to dig in and to let go, to call them by name yet know they aren't mine, to live life as process, sons never finished, daughters never solved.

Dan, exercising his rights as firstborn, has confronted me with another truth—the binding problem, the genomes and experiences fragmented in my body and brain: a demure Virgin restraining a snake; a piece of warm raspberry pie; a couple of dogs in a field; a six-year-old reading aloud *The Cat in the Hat;* the scent of starch and sterility in the dark convent laundry room I scurried through on my way to piano lessons from an old nun with sour breath; *Sputnik* orbiting a hospital television screen; the repeated line of a song, "I'm gonna be like you, Dad, you know I'm gonna be like you"; lists—words to memorize, groceries to buy, things to be done, things that can't be undone; a black-and-white photograph of my mother in a modest, old-fashioned swimsuit; three letters addressed in my dad's childlike hand to Mrs. Ned Tranel; a medal-laden purple-and-gold letter jacket from St. Labre. Scraps, images, and events all waiting in my flesh for a sign.

For a moment, I'm disheartened. I want to shed my past and choose my turns. I want assurance that I've lived a conscious life, worthy of the scientist's respect. But I treasure far more this hilltop full of questions and the irrational love of a son.

Missing Mountains

MICHAEL

The telephone rings just after daybreak, ominously early for an ordinary call. We've lived in this house for ten months now, but I continue to wake disoriented. My glance goes straight to the window, a habit learned during more than seven years of country living. Is it snowing? Blowing? Sunny? Gray? The shade is drawn. We have neighbors now. Miss Snell, who reads the day away in the bay window of her yellow Victorian house, and in the red-shuttered cottage across the alley, a thirtyish couple and their young daughter. Their infant son died of SIDS. The mother didn't tell me when, but the tears rimming her eyes said time didn't matter or always heal. Immediately, I think of my two sons who are not upstairs with the younger children, sleeping where they belong.

My husband, Ned, answers the phone. Something has gone wrong. I see it in the muscles tensing across his back. I hear it in the tightening of his tone. "They're still up there? I'll come right away." He hangs up and turns toward me.

The call is from Dorothy Dow. She and her husband, Jack, own a ranch west of Big Horn, Wyoming, where our two oldest sons, Dan, thirteen, and Mike, twelve, are living and working this summer. The Dow ranch is not far from our place, the sixty-three acres of irrigated land in the foothills of the Big Horn Mountains and the ranch house where we lived until last fall. It was the first home we ever owned, where we lived the longest, where we imagined growing old. We haven't sold it or even put it on the market. Maybe we'll go back someday. For now, we're renting a sprawling old two-story house on an ordinary street in an ordinary Montana town. Ned is a clinical psychologist with the Miles City Mental Health Center. I'm full-time mother to our eight children, ages ten months to thirteen years.

Now two of those children are lost in the Big Horn Mountains. "Not lost," Ned says, tempering my Irish penchant for imagining the worst. "Still up there. Dorothy said they were still up there." He phones a friend, a pilot who owns a small plane. They arrange to meet in fifteen minutes at the airport. He dresses quickly and explains.

At two yesterday afternoon, Jack Dow dropped off his own son, a twenty-one-year-old Vietnam vet who recently returned to the family ranch, and our boys at the top of Goose Creek canyon. This was their Sunday treat on a brilliant August day. A chance to be in the mountains they'd been looking at all summer. A break in the routine of ranch work. They planned to fish their way down the canyon and meet Jack at the campground at dusk. "The trouble is," Ned says slowly as he pulls on his jeans, "they didn't show up." He buttons up a flannel shirt that anticipates brisk mountain air. "Jack waited well past midnight. No sign of the boys. He's flying over in his plane now to get a closer look."

My mind rushes to thoughts of high-altitude hazards. Bone-chilling nighttime temperatures, sudden storms, lightning, dangerous rapids, bears. Our sons are as resourceful as any ranch kids, but mountains are brutally unpredictable. Our outings there have been family affairs, occasional ski trips, more often afternoon picnics on easy summer meadows. Even on idyllic days I tucked parkas and mittens into the trunk, and often enough we needed them.

Fear drains through me. I stare at Ned and conjure up scenarios. Perhaps Dan, in a burst of teenage bravado, took his own path and is wandering alone while the other two look for him. Or Mike, stopping every few feet to examine up close the trees and animal tracks he'd been imagining from a distance, has fallen behind.

"Did they have coats?" is all I can think to ask.

"She wasn't sure. Dorothy wasn't sure. She didn't see them leave." He looks out the window, then adds confidently, "Jack will spot 'em." But his hands tremble as he fastens his belt, and he takes the steps two at a time.

I berate myself for ignoring my mothering instinct. Why had I agreed to a plan I'd never been comfortable with? Why had I allowed our two sons to go off to work for the summer?

Fall through winter, school and sports schedules helped our family adjust to town life. But as the snow melted and buds unfolded on greening branches, troubling images of summer haunted me. How would I keep a houseful of energetic kids busy from June to September? Not simply busy. Using up time wasn't the point. In the country, we'd built a life involving real work—hay to stack, gardens to weed, fences to paint, animals to birth and occasionally bury. That meant a grave to dig and a stick cross to mark it. Their reward was undistracted play. Beneath the shelter of the windbreak sat an enormous sandbox where they turned sand into hills and hills into mountains. Each spring they transformed the yard into a rodeo arena, with ropes to define the chutes, old brooms for horses, and five-gallon cans for the barrel race. They camped overnight in the wilds beneath the willow tree. They rode horses and bicycles and Big Wheels and kicked a ball around. On this town street, our neighbors, wary ever since that October day when the moving van unloaded enough beds for a boarding school, would be up in arms at the sight of five bicycles, two trikes, a scooter, a pogo stick, and a rusty wagon parked by the front door. A yard considered large by town standards would be a summer prison to country kids accustomed to acres of space. Here, the grass took an hour to mow, another to trim. Here, the trash disappeared magically from the curb every Friday morning. There would be no need for the Saturday-morning ritual that required a tractor and wagon and every kid in the family to transport junk to the dump situated on the farthest reaches of our land. In the country, poor television reception made a three-program-per-week limit easy (*Walt Disney, The Waltons, Red Skelton*). In town, for lack of anything better to do, our kids would waste their curiosity watching TV rock groups or wandering the amoral streets of the seventies.

Not that Miles City aspires to big-city vices. It's a prairie cowtown of quiet neighborhoods and hardworking families, the plain sister to western Montana's mountain towns. The sister who's friendly and honest and, except for an infamous brothel and the annual ruckus of the spring Bucking Horse Sale, virtuous. Filtered through mountains and plains and traditional people, coastal fads fizzle out. In fact, landlocked culture sometimes lags so far behind the avant-garde that it ends up ahead, never having subscribed to trends now being rejected.

But we were like bears hibernating in the dark of our pastoral ideals. We awakened to the glaring reality of the seventies, and it frightened us. Ostensibly mature people were talking about doing their "thing." Teenagers swayed to music celebrating drugs and heeded advertising peddling identity as a Calvin Klein label. The peer group was not a civilizing influence. Something had to be done.

The April phone call was strategic. *Jack Dow on the line. Looking for a good hand. That oldest boy of yours . . . Dan? . . . Think he could he come down here and work for me this summer? Room and board and a hundred a month.*

Dan was flattered and eager. His work habits were being noticed. He was able and versatile and willing. He could build a straight stack and wire a taut fence. He could drive a tractor, rake hay, ride a horse, milk a cow. He'd move irrigation tarps, cattle, or mountains for the approving nod of a man he respected. Until this summer, that man had been exclusively his dad.

Ned viewed Jack Dow's proposal through his usual optimistic lens. Here was an opportunity for Dan and a partial solution to the dilemma of adolescent male energy and a town life that didn't suit us.

But the prospect of our oldest son working away from home all summer troubled me. Dan's fervor made him easy prey for a way of life that revolved around the sun's energy, not that of a thirteen-year-old boy. He would be tired and hungry and homesick. His absence would complicate long summer days in town when I anticipated needing his sibling leadership. Furthermore, this plan would thrust twelve-year-old Mike, a notorious daydreamer, into the ill-fitting role of "eldest child."

Our second son was our first lesson in biodiversity, that of children. Dan, who arrived at high noon on his due date, is green-eyed, blond, and compulsively punctual. Mike, whose due date was uncertain, is dark-eyed, brown-haired, and wound by an internal clock that ticks along to the rhythm of Emily Dickinson's words: "It is easy to work when the soul is at play." This admirable attitude puts him at odds with schedules. From time to time, after a barrage of reminders to "hustle," his frustrated father has gone off without him, but the lesson didn't take.

Ever since our move, Mike has been pining for the unexplored vistas left behind in Wyoming: the lawn opening to the foothills of the Big Horn Mountains; the shadowy fantasy world beneath the lilacs where he played cowboys and Indians with his younger brother Ned Anthony; the irrigation ditch where they caught frogs and sailed boats and mixed muddy concoctions in coffee cans; the elaborate burning ceremonies he staged at the Saturday dump site. He even missed chores previously considered oppressive. A month ago, when we visited our Big Horn place to check up on things, he milked the dairy cow for old times' sake.

So we devised a summer plan that included him. For the first two months, Dan would work at Dow's by himself, and Mike, although he hadn't been spoken for, would join him for the last three weeks. By August, Mike's idling imagination would be ready to shift into Dan's higher gear, and Dan's intensity would need the tempering of Mike's whimsical ways.

Now both boys are missing. Missing in the mountains.

My worrying intensifies. I see my bloodied sons in the clutches of a maddened grizzly; I see them tumbling into the angry current of a mountain stream, being slammed against rocks until they finally disappear. I see them shivering through a bitter night without coats or food. I see a glassy-eyed hermit/cannibal wandering along and doing them in.

When I retrieve the milk from the doorstep, I notice the woman across the alley opening her door. We wave to each other, but I regret the connection. She is an omen, reminding me of a reality I don't want to consider.

I go through the routine of breakfast, filling bowls with Rice Krispies and cornflakes, pouring milk to the designated height, and demonstrating to five-year-old Monica that her squat juice glass holds as much as Elizabeth's tall, thin, tippable one. All the trouble of measuring fails to change her mind.

I am a mere physical presence, unsure if I can survive another hour of uncertainty, another hour of feigning confidence in front of the children who are here at the table, spilling milk and squabbling as if this were an ordinary day. I avoid the word *lost* when I explain to them that their dad has gone to meet their brothers, who spent the night in the mountains.

I pray to the God of my childhood who has control over every slip of the foot, each hair on our heads; I pray to my parents whose vantage point in eternity may give them some advantage; I pray to the fickle mountains. "Be gentle with my sons," I beg the mercurial spirit of peaks and valleys.

The telephone shrieks like a cruel siren: *Dan and Mike are missing. Your sons are lost in the mountains.* Dorothy Dow tells me that Jack has landed after flying over the canyon. "He didn't see them," she says. "But that doesn't necessarily mean . . ."

A groan escapes me. I ask if Ned is there. Their father's presence will be the compass guiding our sons home.

"Not yet. But Jack is going over again." I bite my lower lip and listen to her reassurance. "Bert knows how to get along up there. They'll be okay. And I'll call you as soon as . . ." Her voice drifts off, making a lie of her optimism.

A vise of terror grips me, threatening to crush my hope. I recall the recent news story about a young boy lost for days. I imagine his mother, the agony of waiting through the search. But he was found, alive and sleeping in the shelter of a log after an unlikely hike upstream. *Miraculously* found, the article said. Dan and Mike aren't young children. They're strong. Healthy. Almost men. And Bert is a man. But other stories haunt me. Stories about both boys and men. Stories without miracles.

At least you have your other children, people foolishly say to parents when they lose a child. As if children are interchangeable; as if those remaining will expand to fill the void in a parental heart; as if, because she has a daughter, the woman across the alley no longer grieves for her infant son. The story of the shepherd who anguished over one lost sheep is truer to the present turmoil in my gut.

When Mike was not quite three, he was ill with an intestinal bacteria that refused to respond to medicine. After a bout with diarrhea and vomiting, he began to run a fever. His eyes seemed to grow larger and darker as they sank deeper into his pale cheeks. He was hospitalized on the brink of dehydration. When the nurses tied a net over his crib to keep him inside, he howled and clawed like a frightened animal. The next morning, when I went into his room and saw him lying quietly in his pen, a cage of fear closed around me. Had he given up? We had two other children at home. I was three months pregnant with our fourth child. But this little brown-eyed boy, Michael Joseph, born in Topeka, Kansas, at 3:20 a.m. on March 3, 1959, was our beloved, one-of-a-kind, irreplaceable son.

The other children are solemn. They pretend to play, but they're listening to the sounds of my worry. The pacing and sighs. The dash to the window when a car door slams. I see an intrepid Miss Snell reading beneath the unlit lamp in her window. Something like envy flashes through me. Holding fast to her book, she lives out her solitary days inside the walls of her family homestead, impervious, it seems, to lost children and shattered mores.

Across the lawn, near the red cottage, the mourning mother leans over a bed of petunias blooming defiantly in summer's heat. Daily, she kneels in front of them, tending them, touching them with the gentleness of a mother wiping milk from her baby's lips, smoothing down a cowlick, buttoning up a coat.

Children are too young at twelve or thirteen to go off to work for the summer. By trying to protect our sons from one danger, we've exposed them to another.

At the sound of light rapping, I rush to the front door. Dana Sue, the blue-eyed five-year-old from across the street, asks for Monica, who is towing an old blanket through the kitchen toward the back door. Come to my house, begs Dana Sue, an only child, and we'll play Barbie dolls in the attic. Monica's eyes shine with delight.

My instinct says, "No. No to Dana Sue. No to Barbie. I want you to stay at home. Your brothers are lost." But I can't shackle my daughter to my dread.

The telephone rings. I stare at it.

"Can I go?" Monica pleads.

I've been telling myself no news is good news. Now I must answer the phone and learn the truth.

Monica tugs on my arm. "Well, can I?"

I look at her without comprehension and pick up the phone.

"Good news!" Ned shouts as if he had no telephone. I sit down, gratefully weakened by relief. "They're okay," he says, over and over. "Dan and Mike are fine. They're here with me." He tells me they walked out of the mountains this morning and called the Dows from the first house along the road. Now they're in Dorothy's kitchen making up for the meals they missed. *Let all the earth shout for joy.*

"We caught fifteen trout, Mom," Mike blurts into my ear. "But then . . ." He sighs. "Then we lost every single one." He moans. "Oh, man."

"You should see Mike," Danny gloats when it's his turn to talk.

"You will, soon," Ned assures me. "I'm bringing him home with me. Seems the place he picked to sleep last night was a bed of poison ivy."

Dan, shivering next to him all night, somehow avoided the poison ivy's wrath. He's primed to go the distance alone, willing to keep on picking up rocks from the hay-field in order to hear Jack pronounce the field "a pleasure to mow."

Monica tugs on the telephone cord and pouts. "C'mon, Mom."

"Can she come over?" chimes in Dana Sue. "Please? Just for a little while?"

"For an hour," I say against my inclination. I watch Monica cross the street, imagine her following Dana Sue up the narrow steps toward that dim attic and blond doll. But even that dreary prospect can't stop my heart from singing at the good news of my sons.

AN HOUR LATER, a grouchy Monica returns from her stint in the dark and runs straight to the yard to join Alane in her tent, a hodgepodge of blankets pinned to the clotheslines.

Three hours later, Mike is home, too. His eyes are swollen nearly shut. Red blotches cover every inch of visible skin. His spellbound siblings gather to admire him. They address him as Frankenstein and summon their friends to come have a look. He basks in his status, the mythological hero who has gone forth on a life-threatening journey and returned, scratching, to tell the tale.

THEY WANDERED the stream all afternoon, delighting in the mountains, their rare leisure, and the excitement of catching fifteen rainbow trout. As evening approached and the light slipped away, Bert picked up the pace. They had five miles of rough terrain to walk and a creek to cross before they reached the campground at the agreed-upon time, eight o'clock. The canyon narrowed, forcing them to scramble around rocks and trees. They fished less and less and walked faster. Now the canyon was two sheer walls and a rush of water without a bank. They would have to climb out, up a shale slope, then, harder going, up steep rock to the top. The shale shifted and pitched Dan and the fish toward the water. He saved two fish, but their nerve was gone. They eased back down, creeping over a ledge, sliding on scree, down, down. Now Mike lost his footing and tumbled toward the racing creek.

"My brother saved my life," he told his wide-eyed audience. "My brother Dan."

The sun dropped below the canyon walls. Headlights flashed below; the Dows were still waiting at the trailhead. They would have to go on, without flashlights, half walking, half crawling through the treacherous dark. They managed two more miles, to within a half mile of the campground, but they were still on the wrong side of the creek. Dan spied a crossing, and set out. Midstream, he slipped and fell; the current caught him, viciously tossing him against rocks as it carried him off.

"All I could do was stand there and watch my brother die," Mike said to the rapt faces around him. "But then, there he was, crawling out, fifty yards downstream."

It was two in the morning now; the headlights were gone; their trout were gone; Dan was soaked and cold; they couldn't continue. They found a soft place to lie down and shivered there without jackets until dawn. When they woke, they saw their mattress: a dense cushion of poison ivy. A plane circled. They waved and shouted, but it disappeared. They started walking downstream again and soon spied a fallen log, nature's bridge to the other side. They scrambled over and landed moments before a black bear lumbered through their traitorous bed. But they had crossed to safety, to the trail and the campground and the road, to civilization, a house, people, a phone, and a shower.

Ignorance truly is bliss. If I had known last night when I woke to the sound of a restless child, if a veil had lifted to show Mike lurching toward the water or Dan thrashing around rocks, I would have been the one sure casualty.

WE'VE LIVED in this house in Miles City a full year now. There are advantages to being in town. Biking on pavement, summer swim classes in the Tongue River, milk in clean cartons set into insulated boxes on the doorstep instead of plunked into the sink in a manure-splattered bucket, the newspaper delivered at the front door each afternoon, the ease of running to the grocery store for a few items versus an exhausting stock-up trip to town. I delight in impromptu chats with neighbors, spontaneous movies, evening study groups, a library within walking distance, a parish school that introduces us to parents who are struggling, as we are, to raise children who will make kind, wise choices. And I find solace in Miss Snell's abiding presence in the window across the lawn.

She's turned on her reading lamp. Beneath its glow, I can see her profile, the stern English nose, the prim bun fastened at the nape of her neck, the slender hands holding the habitual book. It's only noon, but the day's gone dark. Heavy pewter clouds hang in the Halloween sky. Tonight's treat seekers will need a layer of warmth beneath their ghoulish garb.

Last year, our kids came home stunned from their first trick-or-treat adventure in town. Goodies came fast and easy. Their makeshift costumes—an oriental bed jacket, an old tweed overcoat, a cast-off formal—were considered clever in the country but curious in town. In the country, their dad drove them to a drop-off point on a gravel road. Collecting treats required a brave hike from light to light, one fraught with tumbles and spilled sacks. Because so few kids knocked, people were friendly. And wise to them. "Hi, Alane," an old man greeted the surprised little girl beneath the sheet. "Take an extra popcorn ball, Elizabeth, since you waited until last." Finally, as imagined goblins hovered, they dashed toward their waiting dad, who brought them home, thrilled and chilled to the bone. They sat on the living room floor and dumped out their reward: chocolate bars, homemade cookies, gum, popcorn balls, taffy apples. Gravel, too, and grass and a few twigs.

In town, no one had asked them to come in. No one speculated over their identity or inadvertently called one of them by name. There were no giddy tumbles in the dark that made the candy sweeter.

This year, they're trick-or-treat pros. City blocks are a cinch; an hour in the right neighborhood will produce enough M&M energy to keep them running in high gear all winter. Their costumes are spread out on their beds. Each child has mapped a different route and handpicked a companion. No more of this all-in-the-family trooping about. They've discovered bottom-line efficiency.

· · ·

YEARS LATER, when my children are grown and I'm shopping alone in a cavernous mall on Halloween, I will puzzle momentarily over lines of costumed children snaking slowly from store to store. In front of each store stands a clerk methodically dropping a packaged portion into a gaping bag. Sadness will be my response. These kids, necessarily anxious over razor blades embedded in apples and drugs laced through cookies, will never know the heady delight of an imagined world where children and mischief and goblins prevail and captivated adults surrender sweets.

THE AUTUMN DAYS dwindle, along with the Halloween candy, toward winter. Our Big Horn place is for sale now, but our hearts tarry. Before we can let go of it, we must find another place we can call home. A house in town won't do. We need a *place,* a protected space where memories strong enough to survive time and disillusionment can take root in our children. We want a place where they can linger in the contentment of childhood and mature from the inside out like Iowa's sweet, juicy, tender, thunderstruck, vine-ripened tomatoes, so different from insipid hothouse fruit. This is the slow ripening we want for our children. We imagine it happening only in the country. And we stubbornly imagine the country in terms of green fields with a mountain view, not the dry sprawl of brown land surrounding Miles City where we live and work.

Ned's desire for a rural setting is natural. He grew up in northwest Illinois on a farm encircled by oak-covered bluffs. His family worked the fertile fields, swam the muddy creek, and raced their horses across the pasture toward home. There, through lush summers of morning dew and nightly cricket song, through indulgent autumns and sharp winters that honed nature to its essence, he learned about cows and weather and land and cooperation and making do. He spent his college summers following the wheat harvest as part of a crew of custom cutters. There he learned about space and freedom and the American West that promised young men cloudless skies.

"Out where hearts are a little truer, out where skies are a little bluer, out where the west begins," Ned printed in a boyish hand on the postcard he sent from western Nebraska three months after we met. Was this the romantic illusion that lured us west later on?

Or was the frontier slogan "Go west young man, go west" part of the illusion, too? The promise of a wilderness where you could be footloose, a rugged individualist escaping troubles and tedious responsibilities, even history itself. Where you could shrug off the psychic burden of family and community and tradition.

Maybe we imagined breaking free of the measured yards and mores of the Midwest and our families, the predictability of euchre games in the kitchen every Saturday evening and roast beef dinners in the dining room every Sunday noon, the confinement of an Iowa landscape as neat as a sheet of graph paper—cornfields, farmhouses, roads, and towns, in every square section a school. Maybe we were fleeing a world tainted by McCarthyism and constant international emergencies. Maybe we were distancing ourselves from the wounds festering in our culture and genes: the whiskey reeking on the breath of one uncle; the odiferous pipe of another, the alpha male of family memories who pontificated in our Sunday living room; the silence that fell on our table whenever my mother corrected my dad's manners; the exhaustion my dad exhaled with a self-pitying sigh to the teenage me: *Someday you'll be sorry for your ingratitude;* the religiosity evident in the pictures on the walls and the jar of holy water on the pantry shelf.

Certainly, the western landscape reflected the unexamined longings of our youth. It was our Eden where we could imprint upon the children we would have, each little tabula rasa, our version of "the good."

WE FAILED. Clearly, we failed. Instead of escaping the world with our children, here we are plunged into the center of it because of them. We care about everything. Neighbors and schools and churches and movies and politics and fashion and books and friends and music and teachers and other families and petunias and cars and newspapers and disease and war and football schedules and orthodontists and the price of tennis shoes and weather and the backyard barberry bush and the yellow paint peeling from Miss Snell's sunstruck house. Now what?

Now the environment, that's what. The earth itself has made the list of worries. Pictures of oil-slicked birds and hills ravaged by strip-mining are in the daily news. As a species, we've been operating under the arrogant assumption that we're the apple of some eye, but the game is up: we're trespassers, tramplers, plunderers. In our lust for "the goods" we've forgotten the good. We're asked to volunteer this time, to tiptoe out without a trace, chanting, "Mea culpa, mea culpa, mea maxima culpa." Large families first, please.

The truth is there are simply too many of us to live in a house on a city block. We're unwilling, unwieldy neighbors. The front yard sports a blown-up water bed mattress—an ingenious trampoline but a hideous lawn ornament. Kids come from miles around to bounce on it. The side yard is a beaten-down baseball diamond. The grass has given up. The neighbors ogle us with eyes that suggest we should, too. We're defenseless, exposed to every random influence that comes down the street, knocks on our door, and asks for one of our children.

Ned resorts to the survival strategy he learned as a child: solidarity. Sticking together saved his family when his forty-two-year-old father died of cancer. Ned was four then; his seven brothers and five sisters were between three months and seventeen years old. His mother circled the wagons. She taught them to rely on God, each other, and the land. At night, they prayed the rosary together on their knees in the living room; by day, they tilled the soil, put up hay, milked the cows, weeded the garden, and picked wild raspberries from the tangled abundance on the hill behind their house. They played checkers and King of the Hill and established the ritual of homemade ice cream with all its trouble and mess—chopping ice from the creek, packing it in salt, churning churning churning.

Ned marshals our family for Sunday Mass. We say grace before meals and prayers at bedtime. He takes our kids outdoors for group activities—raking leaves, biking, building outlandish snowmen, ice skating, shoveling walks. Indoors, he challenges them to chess and checkers and his version of Monopoly, in which he's always the banker, eager to make risky loans and excuse minor debts because he believes the way to win is to keep everyone in the game. Solidarity: it's not a philosophy derived from competitive capitalism but a strategy devised when one has only a memory for a father.

But binding ties are out of vogue.

Dan, an awkward freshman, is walking around town holding hands with a sophomore, a girl two years older and five years more sophisticated than he. He pulls the telephone into the closet for mumbled midnight conversations.

Eleven-year-old Elizabeth is running with a pack of savvy peers and shunning the naive siblings at her heels.

Alane rushes in bright-eyed from second grade, prefacing every remark with a quote from the enthusiastic young nun who is her teacher. "Sister says . . . Sister says . . . Sister says . . ." Last week, Sister said she was quitting the convent.

Spirited, rowdy Monica has turned into a pale, sedentary attic dweller enamored of the treasures in someone else's house.

Every evening at the dining room table, our nine-year-old son, Ned Anthony, counts the money he made peddling afternoon papers in the miasmic Main Street bar. He and his ten-year-old friend have discovered that drunks tip generously, as if bringing forth from their pockets the forgotten coins of boyhood innocence. My son's hazel eyes glint with greed at these easy profits, but I worry about the effect of his daily trips into the sour smell of adult disillusionment.

I compare my own paper-carrying experience. For thirty-five cents per week, I delivered a segment of my brother's route, a side street where houses were far-flung, dogs were mean, and one toothless old woman kept a yard full of geese. It was there, gingerly picking my way toward the front porch, that I learned the meaning of "loose as a goose." My brother was exploiting me. He admits it now. But I didn't care. At four p.m. every afternoon, I was the neighborhood's first paper*girl,* bolting down the boulevard on my red bike, flinging the world's fate onto porches and an occasional roof. My son is a grasping capitalist plodding on foot into a dingy bar.

But Mike, Mike is the child on my mind when I waken during the night. He's nearly thirteen. His dreamy-eyed backyard puttering is interspersed with glances into the mirror. Posed questions: a stern frown; an arched brow; a shy smile, all asking the same thing. Who's there? Who are you? What do you want?

One Mike answers by befriending kids on the margin, kids who, for one reason or another, are rejected by their classmates. The lonely, chubby boy who has trouble reading aloud in class but talks nonstop in our kitchen after school; the freckle-faced kid who, according to the whispering, had a seizure on the playground last year in the middle of Red Rover. Since then, only Mike, the guileless new kid, has called out "Red Rover, Red Rover, send Chuckie right over."

A second Mike sits by the window strumming his guitar and gazing at the globe we gave him for Christmas, a gift meant to nurture his geographic interest and role as family tour guide. Periodically, he stops and gives the world a spin as if it were a roulette wheel offering him a chance to escape. Other times, he closes his eyes and taps his fingers, imaginary drumsticks that play along to Three Dog Night. He's saving up to buy a drum. He wants to join a group. And travel. The globe has boomeranged.

And there's the subterranean Mike who explains life by digging into the meaning of death. The obsession began a few weeks ago when he noticed an area of loose linoleum in the pantry floor. He pried it up; a wooden ladder dropped down into a dark hole. He scrambled for a flashlight and shone it onto a shallow dirt basement, the secret world of every child's dreams. Elated, he gathered up toys befitting this netherworld: trucks, cars, and G.I. Joes. Siblings stood at the edge and dropped everything down to Mike, their courageous leader, the first to descend.

But crouching in the bowels of the earth is making them morbid. The usual thrust of their play, road-building and domestic scenarios, has taken a dark turn. For weeks now, Mike has been masterminding funerals. Military funerals. In this bleak basement, they bury their G.I. Joes, those sturdy, loyal survivors of years and years of backyard warfare. While Mike shakes a mournful tambourine, another child buries the soldier whose arms are broken off at the elbow; then the fellow with no feet; next, the headless hero whose existence is pure miracle; and finally, Capty, the handsome, blond, singularly intact officer in the smart blue captain's uniform. But there is no *requiescat in pace* in this cemetery. No sooner do they bury these ill-fated men and erect stick crosses on their graves than they promptly dig them up. Day after day, the tambourine issues its death rattle, and the soldiers go into the ground only to be disinterred moments later.

In December, we gather around our Advent wreath, light the candles, and sing the traditional song of longing and waiting: "O come, o come, Emmanuel, and ransom captive Israel." But our kids, their faces melancholy in the flickering candlelight, express other longings: "C'mon, c'mon, Emmanuel, and find poor Capty lost beneath the house." Somehow, sometime, between interment and resurrection, Capty has disappeared.

Brashly, I proffer to my Ph.D. psychologist husband my uncredentialed diagnosis of these dismal underground doings: Mike is homesick. "You can take the boy out of the country, but you can't take the country out of the boy," I tell him, repeating my mother's prescient comment to me before I married Ned.

Mike is not so much a country boy as a boy who needs to work out his fantasies outdoors. He needs space and freedom to dig holes and build mountains; he needs solitude to wonder at his work. And he needs time to ponder the work of nature going on around him. Why does the wind tilt the cottonwoods eastward? Who causes the summer clouds that catch on mountain peaks? What mysterious thing is destroying the backyard willow branch by branch? Why won't Wyoming tomatoes turn red before the frost? Does everything depend on sun and moon and stars and rain? He longs to know. Because above all, at least above ground, he's a boy who shall not—will not—cease from exploration. Below ground, though, he's gloomy. Depressed, I tell my husband. Our son is depressed.

Ned considers all of this, then suggests that Mike's death fixation may be connected to his budding sexuality. A child's emerging sexuality automatically raises questions about death, the clinical psychologist before me is saying. I roll my eyes at the "automatic" aspect. When kids ask about sex, Ned insists, they're asking about the meaning of life. If we didn't die, we wouldn't need to reproduce. Simple as that. Sex=life=death=sex. *Le petit mal,* the French say, to describe orgasm. Little death.

Now I'm really worried. Bad enough that the burrowing beneath the kitchen is funereal. This theory smacks me up against the scary possibility that sex is creeping into the underground mix. I'm doomed to go down there and crawl around on my knees to supervise. No. I refuse to be mother to a bunch of cockroaches, skittering about in dark basements and neighbors' attics. No matter what the diagnosis, we've got to get our kids back into the daylight, into the healthy country air where we belong.

"GOOD NEWS," Ned says, his voice edgy with excitement. "I'll tell you the details when I get home." Uncharacteristically, he's calling from his office in the middle of a February afternoon. He's told me only that he's had an interesting offer. One that might mean having a place in the country again. All through the after-school feeding frenzy and the restless predinner gloaming, all through the precious confusion that is our meal together, I wait, surprised by my patience, which is more a requirement of common sense than any proof of virtue.

At last, the older children are occupied with homework and the younger ones are in bed, if not sleeping. Ned and I sit down at the kitchen table. His quick glance at me is cautious; he fidgets, meaning he's anxious that my interpretation of good news may collide with his. The objective news is this: He's been offered a position as psychologist with the Cheyenne Indian Mission Board, an enterprise of the Capuchin Order. These priests and monks operate St. Labre Indian School in Ashland, a tiny Montana town on the edge of the Northern Cheyenne reservation.

We could buy land there, Ned says; we could have our own place again, this time on top of a 350-foot hill overlooking a sweep of pine and sky and space, the Tongue River meandering through fields and meadows below, our children outdoors playing in the sunlight again, taking care of animals again—cows, horses, maybe even sheep—our all-American white kids going to school with Cheyenne and Crow Indian kids, a cultural intermingling that intrigues us.

People caution us. Some say the reservation is a lie, a lockup for Native Americans, a way to isolate them from the mainstream, a place to put out of sight what we want out of mind. Others arch an eyebrow and keep their opinions to themselves.

A site visit confounds the decision. From the hill above the Tongue River and the mission school, the hill that would be ours, we watch the disappearing sun streak the sky with blue, lilac, gold, and crimson. We are not looking across green fields toward the Big Horn Mountains, but across sprawling, unkempt shale hills toward a blaze of setting sun. Ashland is a ragged, isolated town seventy miles south of Miles City on a gravel road. My body takes notes:

a *gravel* road, a *ragged, isolated* town. The effects of social and emotional isolation are strewn everywhere: junk piled in front of shabby reservation houses; drunkenness; despair; the solitary woman staggering down the road with a half-empty whiskey bottle, a young girl trailing behind; a chaste landscape sullied by the human condition. Is this a place to drop down roots, or drop out?

A FEW CHRISTMASES ago Santa brought Mike a set of Lincoln Logs. Promptly, Mike situated himself and his gift on the floor in the doorway between the kitchen and living room. This strategic building site allowed him to be involved in the activities of both rooms. He went to work, fashioning a magnificent fort complete with elaborate turrets and towers. He added a lookout platform and a drawbridge for a make-believe moat. As he settled the last log into its niche, someone rushed from the kitchen and stepped into the center of his creation.

In the same way, we set down our dreams in a particular space and time. Now we're straddled in the present, a strategic but vulnerable position where family and world, shelter and risk, past and future, converge. Our search for a place of security has brought us to a place of choice. We've inoculated our children against dreaded physical diseases—polio, diphtheria, whooping cough—but we don't know how to protect them morally and intellectually. How do we strengthen their minds and hearts without exposing them to every imaginable pathology? Even if we could, *should* we sequester them from the world? A family, after all, is not a fort.

But here in this arid wilderness, on top of this raw shale hill where pine trees cling and rattlesnakes surely prowl, we could have land again, a chance to build a home that fits us. No more adapting to rented houses with awkward kitchens and stingy yards and sidewalks leading to disenchantment. For a while longer, we could shelter our family from the frenzied world while they learn lessons only the land can teach.

The logic is intact, but my knowing gut will not be squelched. Neither will our children's needs dissolve. The whole enterprise feels risky. Moving would require our children to adjust to yet another house, another bedroom, another school, this time an Indian school where they would be immersed in a culture of remnants and fantasies, where they—*we*—would be in the minority. Moving would mean living for the first time on dry, yucca-covered hills where Mother Earth seems peevish and hard-hearted, not at all the fertile, receptive mother of mountain-fed pastures and green Midwestern fields. Green: the color of spring, the color my young mind connected to growth and hope as Sunday after Sunday I watched a green-vestmented priest go through the miraculous motions of death and resurrection. Green: the color Wallace Stegner says you have to get over if you plan to stay in the West. I tell myself the evening show of colors will sustain me. The view from this hilltop will be enough.

What we will begin to see from our new home on the hill is that much of what we blamed on town life and seventies mores was a developmental stage. Our children were growing up. We couldn't contain them in our house or yard or even in our hearts. They were never ours to begin with.

FIFTEEN YEARS LATER, Mike is daydreaming as he drives home through the darkening canyon of Timpanogos National Park southeast of Salt Lake City, Utah. Perhaps a whiff of tangy evergreens merges man and boy, taking him to a pine-covered hill in Montana and back to the shifting inner and outer landscape of being a thirteen-year-old again. He sees the black-eyed Cheyenne girls with their inviting smiles; the sullen boys with their cornered glances and daily invitations to fight. An ominous rattle rises from the shadowy ground as he and his brothers climb the evening hill toward home. Two rattlesnakes, one above, one below, announce their territorial rights. Which way to go? Killing the snakes means more mice in the barn.

He flinches at the memory of his sideburned fifteen-year-old self in ground-dragging bell-bottoms and elevator shoes, sneaking off in the family pickup to visit a girl forty miles down the road. Twenty miles out, the pickup shudders and plops down like a mule on its haunches; the left rear wheel wobbles away and lands with a thud in the pit of his stomach. What to do? Getting out of this fix means getting into another at home.

The muscled kid in a purple-and-gold football uniform still impresses him, though. He's the center on St. Labre's team hiking the ball to Dan, the senior quarterback. These two brothers are the only white Braves. Mike is the only white Brave on the debate team, too, standing behind the podium in his "hip" leisure suit to argue against South Africa's apartheid policy.

Or maybe he's wondering what became of Yurii, the enormous Russian army-style storm coat that he named and wore for subzero chores. The first Christmas Eve after Mike's marriage, when his usual place on the sofa was empty during the gift-opening, Yurii showed up, propped there in memoriam by a lonely brother.

Or maybe Mike is remembering himself as a novelist behind drawn shades typing the tale of a drummer in a teen rock group. Did he hear his dad muttering outside the closed door? *That's not healthy, being locked up inside all summer.* Alas, the subterranean sex-death theory had come to pass. The Mike of drumming and testosterone and football and cool clothes had murdered the Mike of mountains and Yuriis and mud mixing and pensive play outdoors.

But he resurrected. Miraculously, out of the adolescent tomb of self-absorption, he rose. From the fifth-floor window of his dorm at the University of Notre Dame, he marveled at the world again. The mountains were missing and the hazy sky was wrong. But there was some sort of organic experiment going on and *Homo sapiens* was a crucial participant. In graduate school at the University of Iowa, he began imagining his role in the planet's mysterious mission. The following summer, he and his wife, Jane Ahern, sat on the shore of Yellowstone Lake reading Roderick Nash's *Wilderness and the American Mind*. James Watt was the Secretary of the Interior. His rapacious antienvironmentalist policies incited in Mike and Jane a desire to do work that would promote understanding and concern for the natural world. They chose the National Park Service as their instrument.

NOW, AS HE FOLLOWS the winding road along the mountain stream, Mike, the incessant drummer, taps the steering wheel to the rhythm of the woods. A torrent of melted snow crashes through the canyon and races impetuously toward the thirsty lowlands.

Just as he crosses the bridge that brings him home, a shadow darts through his thoughts. A man. A man is running along the edge of the roaring creek. He stops, alarmed, and leaps away again, hurdling bramble like a frightened deer. Mike parks and hurries after him. The man turns and looks toward him with eyes blinded by terror. "Help, oh, God, please help," he cries out, and waves his arms toward the creek. "My son . . . my little boy . . ." Mike follows his gesture but sees only the white wrath of water hitting rock. The man collapses onto his knees, head in hands, moaning, then looks up, shakes his head, as if try-ing to awaken from this nightmare. He points upstream. "Up there," he gasps. "He fell in. Up there."

Mike radios for park rangers to help search for the boy. As he tries to calm this young father, a man about his age, he looks up to see the face of his own daughter, Kelsey, pressed against the window as she waves in welcome. There is nothing of comfort to say. Only the agony of waiting and imagining. Nearly a week will pass before rangers find the small body tangled in branches near the shore.

Every day, on his way to and from work, Mike drives past this memory. Each time, he sees the frantic father run-ning, crying, calling. But always, the answer is the same. Unfathomable silence.

THE FOLLOWING WINTER, a car careens through swirling snow down the wrong side of this same road. Jane, driving up from the opposite direction, takes the curve in her Explorer. She glances at three-year-old Kelsey strapped into the seat next to her, then into the white wall ahead. Two circles of glaring light burst through. She swerves, the Explorer slides off the road, clatters through the trees and across the rough residue of snow and brush. It slams to a stop, flips, and lands upside down, caught on a fallen tree and suspended over the edge of the icy creek. Jane and Kelsey are belted inside, unhurt beyond the terrible fright.

"If it hadn't been for that log," Mike tells me later, his thought trailing into the aching memory of a frantic father crying for his little boy. My remembering goes back further, to Mike sliding on the scree of Goose Creek Canyon. If it hadn't been for Dan, he might have fallen into the creek. And Dan, who did fall in, might have been found later, like that little boy, a body in a tangle of branches, if it hadn't been for—for what? Who determines these outcomes? The awful, capricious Other of the mountains? The untamed desires that urge us to conquer places within shouting distance of death? There is nothing of comfort to say to my son. We both know that any one of us could be swept away at any moment from everything we cling to.

But instead of retreating to civilization, Mike and Jane go deeper into the wilderness. They move to Alaska to work in Denali National Park. It's as if something in their hearts tells them that the only way we can save ourselves from the raging current is to leap into it.

"THERE'S A BLACK BEAR crossing the road in front of me," Mike says. The delight spilling into his cell phone tells me he's at work but his soul is at play. He's en route from Denali to Anchorage, a four-hour drive he makes often as park planner. Much of his work takes place in the complicated margin where wilderness meets domesticity. When Congress passed the Alaska National Interest Lands Conservation Act in 1980, the park tripled in size, from two million to six million acres. Not everyone was ready to cede their turf. Land considered personal recreation territory was suddenly public domain to share and protect. Snowmobilers grumbled. Loggers saw poles going to waste. Quandary easily became impasse. How much buzzing and bustling is tolerable before breeding and feeding patterns are disturbed? Would a train facilitating human travel be detrimental to that of animals?

Now, in early August, Mike calls to tell me it snowed three inches in the park last night. The road, permanently heaving from frost, is slippery. But, well, what else is new. "This is Alaska, Mom." His next words crackle with static and noise, then a shout: "I'm going to lose you here. I'll call you when I get through this—" And he's gone.

This is reality. Cell phones and caribou. Roads and moose and e-mails that say, "Kelsey and I saw a lynx this morning. Awesome, since they're very secretive." Unlikely connections. Sudden separation. Wilderness and civilization and the wonder of being in the world. "This is Alaska, Mom." His words speak the same awe that shone on his face when he built roads in the shelter of the Big Horn Mountains or watched a wet calf slide from its frenzied mother; when he came home from school, an eleven-year-old boy bearing the thrilling news that this was the first Earth Day; when he coped with boring chores by imagining himself on a mountaintop; when he illuminated with a flashlight the possibilities of a dirt basement; when he uncovered pieces of the past on a parched shale hill—a sun-bleached, handmade oar, arrowheads, a fossil imprinted by palm leaves; and when he crouched in the damp dark of Timpanogos Cave to position a small container under a tedious drip of water. It was as though nature oozed narrative for his thirsty mind to absorb, but slowly, spacing each drop with wonder.

I WONDER AT my son. More to the point, I wonder how it is that I, daughter of the mundane Midwest, am mother to this man with his wall full of maps and heart full of questions. I ventured the sidewalks of a single neighborhood, jumping rope, roller skating, playing hopscotch; I scurried for shelter when it thundered; my wilderness was called "Uncle John's Woods," where our family tramped for walnuts every fall; my encounters with nature were embedded in acts of defiance, not exploration. When I was seven, I spent summer afternoons picking clover, not for its sweet fluff, but to tie it into a chain to barricade the avenue, my sister on one side of the street, I on the other, challenging cars to break through our innocence. When I was ten, I packed a suitcase and left home, apparently planning to stay awhile on the branch in our backyard cherry tree. Long enough, at least, to measure my mother's anguish. When I was twelve, I hiked to Catfish Creek with three eighth-grade friends, not to marvel at the sluggish brown water, but to smoke Lucky Strikes. The hole we dug in that black, teeming earth was not out of curiosity, but a place to bury the unfinished pack so that week after week, we could return like criminals to the scene of our rebellion.

My cowardly heart hungers for home, but I've been handed a vagabond's life. "Farther on, Babouscka, farther on," was the promise given to the old woman in the Christmas story I read year after year to our children. Babouscka chose to stay by her warm hearth rather than journey into the cold night with three men searching for a child beneath a star. The next night, concerned that she had squandered her moment in the light, she sets out with a lantern alone, knocking on doors, asking, "Is he here? Is the child here?" But no, the answer is always, "Farther on, Babouscka, farther on." And so she goes on. Watching the stars. Wondering at the choice that keeps her wandering through the years.

Mike would smile at my ruminating. Maybe Babouscka's taking a scenic detour, he'd say. Think of the adventures she might encounter on the way, the fascinating people she might meet. He'd cite examples from the drive-away map on his wall, trace with his finger the color-coded lines of routes he took on various college breaks, remind me that returning a dropped-off rental car to its point of origin was his chance to explore an unknown road.

Wonder is part of the deal humans make with the world. It lures us into the night to follow stars; it leads us up a mountainside like that well-sung bear, to see what we can see; it takes us into Texas in a rental car; it pulls us into the wilderness of genes and cells and synapses; and it brings us back home again, past the raging current that has carried off a child, through the room with an empty crib, into a tended place in our own hearts where the garden and the wilderness, gratitude and reverence, are one.

Loving as Fast as You Can

·

ELIZABETH

Pinned to a felt board on the wall in this room my daughter calls her own are swatches of fabric, deep navy blue interspersed with white, emerald green, and a watercolor print in shades of red. Elizabeth is working out a design for a baby quilt, her gift for each child born into the family. This one is intended for the baby her brother Ned Anthony and his wife, Dana, are expecting in late December 1999, four months from now.

"What do you think, Mom?" she asks, gesturing toward the arrangement.

Ah, music to a mother's ears, a parent's highest achievement, a child, *this* child, sincerely wanting to know, *Mom, what do you think?*

She moves a few squares around. "Does it need more navy? Is there too much white?" She stands back and assesses. "It would help if I knew if the baby is a boy or girl."

"The pink and blue thing? But that's not supposed to matter anymore."

"Mom! You know better than that."

I'm not sure I do, but it sounds as if I should. So rather than expose my fuzzy thinking to her clarity, I say, "I have noticed some slight differences between sons and daughters." On second thought, I do know better than to propose what's *supposed* to matter to this daughter with her passion for the *heart* of the matter.

"Slight differences?" She laughs. "Try oceanic." Growing up with brothers and now mothering her own sons has taken a toll on her perspective. So has the fact that she was born the same year as the Pill and matured in the midst of feminist anguish and angst. "But we'd better stay on task," she says. "Before we're inundated with noise and boys."

"Do you have a pattern book?" I ask.

"Lots." She points toward a shelf holding a collection of brightly bound books. "But I want to come up with my own design." She smiles. "With a little help from my long-term consultant."

She means me, although my influence in that role has waxed and waned according to her project and developmental phase. Currently, her consultant is distracted by the eclectic collection in this room. On her desk, beside the briefcase plump with legal documents, is a stack of books, children's stories by Roald Dahl, *Philosophy of Law, Parenting with Love and Logic, Prisoners of Men's Dreams.* Strewn about the desk are more books, an open box of crayons, a large sheet of paper with a child's watercolor version of the Beartooth Mountains, a box of Wheat Thins, the latest issue of *Bon Appétit.* Maybe women *can* have it all, I think. Maybe there is a workable pattern for our female lives. Wedged among the quilt books, I notice other titles and begin to read them aloud. *"Your Child's Health. Regional Italian Cooking. Letters of Virginia Woolf. Lettere dal Carcere."*

She repeats the last title, revising my Spanish pronunciation to Italian.

"*The Yellow Wallpaper and Other Writings* by Charlotte Gilman."

"That was written in the late eighteen hundreds," she says. "She thought child rearing should be done by trained professionals, not left to maternal instinct."

"Why not supplement maternal instinct? Train mothers to rear children. Fathers, too. *Teach* them, rather. *Train* makes me think of a dog-obedience class."

As if on cue, a ruckus stirs outside the window, the incomparable sound of approaching children.

Elizabeth fastens a square of white atop a larger one of green and hands me some pins. "We'd better get busy. Our window of opportunity is about to close."

I set watercolor red against the green, hesitate, then take it away and say, "You realize I've never made a quilt like this. Are you sure you have the right consultant?"

"It's just a matter of playing with design."

Playing with design. Is that what she was doing as a child when she dressed herself in mismatched plaids and odd color combinations? At times, I thought she was playing with me, testing my ability to endure embarrassment and ignore amused glances. Had I been raised with fewer ribbons and curls, I might have been tempted to lay out her clothes on the bed each night. Had she been more compliant, I might have succeeded. I was in charge of the clothing that went into her childhood dresser drawer, but from age two on, she was in charge of the combinations that came out.

A noisy battalion marches to the door and stops. Barking dogs. Rambunctious boys, Elizabeth's three sons campaigning for attention. Eric, nine, wanting his Roald Dahl book, John, eleven, wanting food, Ben, thirteen, wanting a ride to swimming practice, all of them wanting in, wanting to know what's going on in this room where their mother is sequestered with her mother, irrefutable proof that she was once Elizabeth, the girl, the child, the infant, the fetus swimming in utero.

Swimming that June morning in 1960 as we drove cross-country in our aging sedan with a homemade box trailer, container of all our earthly belongings, bumping down the road behind us.

I KNEW NOTHING of *The Sound of Music* when I took down the curtains in our apartment as we prepared to leave Pullman, Washington, and the friends with whom we'd shared the carefree indigence of graduate school. But the musical had been presented for the first time in New York a few months before, so it's possible I was operating in the aura of Maria, the nun-turned-nanny who fashions curtains into children's outfits. In any case, the cotton panels had plenty of wear left, and I needed maternity clothes.

I felt inventive and clever as I pressed and cut and sewed the fabric into the outfit I folded into my suitcase a week ago. I imagined myself wearing the smock and slacks when we pulled up to the two-story white house on Grandview Avenue in Dubuque, Iowa. I saw my mother's anxious face melt into happy relief as she hurried onto the front porch and down the steps to greet us on the sidewalk, claiming Danny and Mike from the backseat, marveling at how they'd grown, saying with her eyes that her real concern is for her own baby, pregnant for the third time and her oldest child not yet three. But there I'd be, fresh as a daisy in my new blue maternity outfit, dispelling her fears with my well-groomed serenity.

Instead, here in Fort Dodge, Iowa, two hundred miles from the enactment of my fantasy, I feel like a frump. What my mother will see is what I'm suddenly sure everyone in this café sees: a pregnant woman wearing the fabric that hung for a year over the drafty bedroom windows of our campus apartment.

"Can you tell my clothes were curtains?" I whisper across the chrome table to Ned as I pour milk on Danny's Cream of Wheat. He leans to hear over the hubbub of our two young sons, then hands the half slice of toast he's just prepared to Mike, who transfers the jam to his chin with one lick.

"Curtains?" Ned repeats, heedless of the resemblance between me and the window decor above his pillow all year. If I'd asked him to name the drainage of every river on the continent, he would have sailed through the list, but he flounders in matters of style. Yet, without his talent for selective concentration, he wouldn't have finished the course work toward his doctorate in psychology and we wouldn't be on our way to spend the summer in our home-town. Nor would we be looking forward to September, when Ned will begin his first real job, teaching psychology at the University of South Dakota in Vermillion. There, we will have a regular income and a regular house and, in mid-October, our third child.

On this mellow morning in June, that baby is blissfully unaware of being transported as a window display through Iowa's small towns, arriving at last in the kitchen of my childhood home. My dad lures Ned and our sons to the garden with the promise of red raspberries straight from the patch. Alone with my mother, I confess my clothing ruse. Her lighthearted laugh surprises me. A wary woman with a keen dignity, she cares what people think, a trait that curtailed my girlish whims and probably accounts for the abashing bolt that struck me in Fort Dodge. She's as well groomed at home as away. Today, she's wearing the usual neat, starched housedress; every wave of her silver hair is in place. But it's her strenuous Irish soul that responds now. "Where there's a will, there's a way," she says. It's an aphorism I've heard since I was two, first as a lament over my strong-willed ways, and later on, as a statement of her belief in the power of effort and ingenuity and resolve.

She describes her own confinement, as pregnancy was called then, when she had neither maternity dresses nor spare curtains but sequestered herself in make-do clothes. She said she often stood at the front door feeling alone and left out as she considered the world beyond.

Years later, as I fan through a catalog with a vast array of maternity apparel—bib overalls, swimsuits, business suits, evening wear—I find myself speculating about what my mother might have chosen. Would she have dressed up and gone out or lingered, yearning and uncertain, at the door?

SHE'S IN MY kitchen now. It's October in Vermillion and my mother and I are sitting together in the breakfast booth. It's not really *my* kitchen. This spacious two-story house on the edge of campus belongs to a middle-aged professor and his wife who rented it to us while they're away on sabbatical. When they return in June, we'll be hunting for another home, but in the meantime, we're heirs to amenities representing years of work and marriage. Comfortable furniture, a dining room with an elegant table, a complete set of china in the hutch, tablecloths, silverware, small pans and large pots, a washer and dryer, stacks of sheets in the linen closet, a row of boxes labeled CHRISTMAS ORNAMENTS on a storage shelf. I imagine a ceiling-high, fully decorated tree sparkling in the living room and, beneath it, our bright-eyed, pajama-clad sons waiting for Santa. Swaddled nearby will be the stubborn child now in utero.

I'm five days overdue. We arrived in this house on Labor Day in summer's final splurge of heat. Now oaks and elms have littered the campus with color, and my predicted "labor day" has come and gone. My mother's loyalties migrate between mother and wife. Apprehensive at leaving my seventy-nine-year-old father home alone, she allotted two weeks for this mission of mercy, and I've already used up one.

Meanwhile, Ned pedals to and from the university every day on his first bike, one he bought secondhand and taught himself to ride. On weekends, he boosts Danny onto the carrier in back and perches Mike in the basket in front and off they go around the campus, without gears or helmets or even any warnings from me. Biking is not yet a sport burdened with technique and safety regulations but simply a way to navigate the terrain of each day.

That terrain is giving me grief. "You're limping," said my mother when we met her train. I explained that my baby's head had dropped against the sciatic nerve in my left leg, that walking shot pain from my hip to my heel. A week earlier, dressed in my maternity best, I'd climbed four flights of stairs and stood for two hours with Ned in a reception line welcoming new faculty members, typically a man with a wife now eligible to belong to a group of wives. Mine was called Psych Wives. The next morning as I trudged, lame and miserable, through the neighborhood in search of our two wandering sons, I regretted the exercise of will that sent me up those steps.

"I'M SO GLAD! Now you have your girl!" cries my mother over the clatter of two small boys when I telephone the news from the hospital midmorning on October 18. *Now you can be contented,* she may have been saying. *Three is enough.* Children who grow up, as she did, in large families with meager resources know the somber side of unbridled fertility. But what I heard in her words was a recognition of the mother-daughter bond, the particular energy that flows between a woman and the child whose body was begun in hers and now reflects it. And what I felt was wonder at that reality: now I had my girl.

My mother adds a week to her visit, then boards the train ambivalently, wishing she could stay for the baptism on Sunday, wishing she could stay for the laundry and dishes and dusting. She leaves behind pies, neat stacks of folded diapers, and a trail of advice: *Don't try to do it all. Let the house go. Rest when your baby does. Remember, she'll be as happy as you are.*

On October 30, we baptize our newborn Elizabeth Ann, a name that evokes staunch role models, both familial (my paternal grandmother, my mother) and biblical (mother of John the Baptist, mother of Mary).

Elizabeth *is* happy, an exquisite, dark-eyed, tranquil baby. Therefore, I must be happy, too. And I am, in an abstract sort of way. But the demands are more and harder than I imagined. I'm the only one at home who can open doors and cans, who can make sandwiches and any sort of sense. I spend twenty minutes looking for shoes, buttoning coats, and finding caps so that Danny and Mike can play outdoors, and in ten minutes they're back, beating on the door, wanting in on the schemes being contrived by the females inside.

One day, as I sit on the sofa breast-feeding Elizabeth, three-year-old Danny climbs into the far corner, pulls up his shirt, and begins to nurse his teddy bear. Across the room, Mike sucks his thumb and ponders the bundle always in my presence, being fed, burped, changed, bathed, carried about, delighted in.

Other days, my sons roam off in search of a world before pink. And I'm fastened in nervous bondage to the window and the infant in my arms. This Eve, this strange creature my sons ogle and speculate about, has disturbed their patriarchal paradise. With no forewarning, aside from a few mysterious comments about something growing inside me, I've brought home a wailing red creature that they're expected to welcome and cherish.

Three is the hardest number, some sage at the university advises Ned, who brings the news home to me. I'm in the bathroom crying when I hear him open the front door. It's two weeks until Christmas. Danny and Mike are on a pre-holiday rampage that I tried to avert by unpacking our nativity set and offering it up to their restlessness, twenty or so gaudily painted plaster figures: Mary and Joseph, a disproportionately large infant (the son of God, mind you), three Wise Men, a weary cow, a few goats, a flock of shepherds and two sheep. Now the cow has a crumpled horn, the goat's hind legs are broken, a shepherd is lost, and I've just hung up from a blatant, futile phone call to Santa, informing him that he can skip our house this year. "Just skip it," I hissed into the phone. "No one is being good."

In retrospect, I suspect our sons were simply being children, noisy and squabbling, clamoring, clamoring, clamoring. But I needed a night out, or maybe a night *in*—in a peaceful place like the Bethlehem of Christmas song, where I could lie in deep, dreamless sleep while the silent stars went by. Instead, this miracle occurs: Our two-month-old daughter begins to sleep through the night.

After the holidays, after the wreaths and remnants have been tucked back into their boxes, after Danny and Mike are napping on schedule again and my nerves have begun to heal, I pull up the bassinet close to the dining room table and coo intermittently to my baby while I type Ned's doctoral thesis. On a Smith–Corona manual typewriter, I tap out one original copy plus two carbons. Next summer we'll return to Washington State University, where Ned will defend the surprising findings of his research: extraverts cope better with isolation than introverts. This is information I ought to be factoring into our plans. We're talking about moving west and finding a place in the country to raise our children. Ned's work will be the deciding element, though, not my psychological profile. I'm doing what I've been groomed by my church and culture to do, facilitating other people's lives. But every typing mistake entails meticulous erasing and correcting, and I catch myself growing impatient, muttering aloud, feeling put-upon.

The typing project is barely finished when I begin the next, another move to another house across town. Settled deep in the shade of tall elm trees, the two-story yellow house has four bedrooms upstairs and one bathroom down. Across the road is a large park with swings, a sandbox, a jungle gym, a place for our children to locate their play. Their wandering days are over, and, therefore, so are mine. The bathroom's location will have something to say about that the following winter when I begin trekking up and down according to the demands of a fourth pregnancy. But first, Ned and I and our three children trek the twelve hundred miles to Pullman and return with his Ph.D. and our hopes in his hands.

In January, a few days after Mike has recovered from the intestinal infection that hospitalized him, fifteen-month-old Elizabeth is vomiting and running a fever and losing weight. We're in the car on our way to the hospital again. When I look down at the lethargic child in my arms, an awful reality strikes my heart: now I might lose my girl. All week, we watch and worry and hope. And then she's better. On our fifth wedding anniversary, our daughter is well enough to come home. Ned and I celebrate with dinner in a restaurant, then hurry to the hospital to claim our gift.

With the birth of our fourth child in July, the infamous issues of dealing with three are resolved. More precisely, the problem shifts to Elizabeth, who is twenty-one months old and sister to three brothers.

"MOM! I MEAN IT. I need a ride to swimming practice." The tussle outside the door escalates until Elizabeth opens it and her three boys tumble in. The labs, Jake and Roxanne, strive for entry, too, but their wagging tails and enthusiasm threaten to destroy an already tenuous order. Elizabeth shoos them outside.

"I'm gonna be late for practice," grumbles thirteen-year-old Ben.

"You'd better get moving then," Elizabeth replies. "Your bike's in the front yard. Right where you left it yesterday."

"Aw, Mom, I'm tired. And after swimming, I'm wet. Why do you have to be so mean?"

"Benjamin, it's a beautiful summer afternoon." *Case closed,* she's just said.

Eric snatches his book and grins. "*Big Friendly Giant.* Just what I wanted." He gives his mother the thumbs-up.

John moans in agony and rubs his belly. "There's nothing to eat anywhere. How come we never have any food in this house?"

Elizabeth puts an arm around his shoulder, looks into his suffering brown eyes, and runs through the list of abundance at his fingertips. When she says the word *pizza,* he lights up and bolts toward the door, where he stops. "Mom, did you notice we're almost out of dog food?" And then he's gone.

Ben tries again, this time turning sad, dachshund eyes on me. "Do you think my mom is being fair? I bet you never made *her* ride a bike everywhere."

"She rode a horse," I tell him. He groans and clears out. The story he's about to hear won't help his cause—how Elizabeth at twelve found a summer job waitressing in the Ashland café and then, because her independent temperament required independent transportation, rode her horse down the shale hill and tied it up behind the café while she served hamburgers and coffee for two dollars an hour. "Mom never waits on me," said Ben the last time he listened to this tale.

She closes the door, then opens it far enough to call after Ben, "Come straight home from swimming."

"It's not my fault you had to grow up in the country," he fires back.

She rolls her eyes.

"And we thought we were doing all of you a favor by hauling you off to the boondocks. Although, I'm not so sure of that anymore."

She reassures me that she loved our place at Big Horn, and longed for it when we moved to Miles City, where everything changed. "Our space, our activities. The smells and sounds." And then, knowing my concern over all that upheaval, she says, "But I had friends. I liked that part."

We conjecture about that little group of girls—Lisa and Julie and Nancy. Elizabeth imagines Lisa as a stay-at-home mom. And she's heard Julie is a veterinarian. Nancy is a medical technician in Billings. In fact, they ran into each other at a birthday party recently. "One of those canned celebrations," says Elizabeth. Birthdays, it seems, are now a business enterprise. Kids play miniature golf, bowl, frolic in the amusement park. "People don't have time to make cakes anymore," she says. "I got on that train for a few years. Until I realized the kids weren't enjoying it. So this spring I got off. But it took a while to adjust. Twenty-four hours, to be exact. You could probably hear Eric wailing at your house."

"Apparently, he got over it. He seemed perfectly happy at this year's party." I mean the usual gathering of grandparents, uncles and aunts, cousins, and two or three special friends for brunch and birthday cake.

"He had a great time. And worked like a little beaver to get ready. Made the piñata. Frosted the cake. Set up lawn chairs. "

When I point out that her perseverance obviously paid off, she shakes her head. "Believe me, when he was howling and saying how much he hated me, I began to think I was taking the whole thing too seriously. Why turn a birthday party into fodder for therapy?" She sighs, picks up a white square, trades it for navy, then stands back to gaze at the pattern emerging on the felt board. "I'm not sure what to do next," she muses aloud. "There's just so much . . ." Her words trail off.

"Green?" I venture, assuming the quilt to be the subject of her unfinished sentence. Dangling phrases are my forte. But wavering has never been Elizabeth's way.

Why did you come to meet me? she asked as a child when she got off the kindergarten school bus in the middle of the day and found me waiting at the cattle guard. To me, the ground blizzard that had turned the quarter-mile walk to our house into a whirling white journey to nowhere was reason enough. But to a six-year-old girl who felt quite capable of finding her way alone, my presence was an affront.

I'm convinced she absorbed confidence in utero, the parasite fetus taking everything it needed, leaving me depleted and turning to pattern books while she has a room *and* a mind of her own.

But I may be taking more credit for her fortitude than is my due. Her brothers appreciated that virtue, too, and devoted themselves to schooling her in it.

TODAY IS ELIZABETH'S First Communion day. She hasn't started an argument or uttered a confrontational word since the nine of us got into the car in the country twenty minutes ago. It's a feat as rare as this Wyoming day in June and as wondrous as her white dress and veil. Sitting next to her in the middle seat are her sisters, Alane, five, and Monica, three, spellbound by her pure silence. But the three brothers in the backseat are taking advantage of their eight-year-old sister's uncommon docility. They taunt her with words the way they might test a lethargic snake with the toe of a boot.

As we approach Sheridan and the church, eleven-year-old Dan is prying into the domain of her First Confession. "Did you confess to Father yesterday how many times you've been lazy?"

"Yeah," chimes in Ned Anthony. "And, and how many times . . ." He sputters to speechlessness. He's almost seven and senses he belongs in his brother's camp, but this older sister has come to his defense before and will again, he knows, if she sees justice jeopardized. Besides, she's the one who discovered the intriguing hideaway in the corner of the front yard where sumac and willow and dwarf oak abound. These bushes form playhouse walls that Mother Nature regularly redecorates, painting leaves from green to gold to blazing red, all for the sake of the children inside. In that deep shade, Elizabeth and Ned Anthony store treasures found on an ordinary day—a feather, a few tiny bones from a bird, a cow's horn, and smoke bombs, something so precious and rare that they must be kept carefully and used judiciously. They're not sure if smoke bombs are dried horse turds or toadstools, but they make a magnificent black cloud when stomped upon.

"Lazy is a Deadly sin," ten-year-old Mike informs his sister. "And if you didn't tell it, you can't go to Communion."

"Elizabeth's conscience is not yours to examine," I say, and rescue my hat from the clutches of eight-month-old Paul, who's in my lap and trying to pick the roses blooming on its brim.

"What's conscience?" asks Ned Anthony.

"I saw her take a can of root beer to her room last Friday," says Dan.

Now here's a real crime, say the triumphant eyes of all three. Elizabeth has violated the Seventh Commandment, as well as a house rule. Pop was something we doled out as a treat on special occasions—a Fourth of July picnic in the backyard, during a special Sunday night TV program, or when Ned and I hired a baby-sitter and went out for an evening. Pop, went our reasoning, was essentially junk food, like potato chips and candy bars, that ruined appetites and teeth. Allocating money for it strained common sense and our tight budget.

"Does everyone have shoes on?" Ned asks, trusting this distraction will get us fight-free to the door of Holy Name Church, a block away. Clusters of white dresses and suits are already visible on the steps. Elizabeth fixes her eyes, if not her mind, on that goal. This pacifism is at odds with her history and her natural tendencies. Ordinarily, her self-appointed task as a passenger in the car is to incite her brothers to riot. Her methods are subtle and nonspecific. Trouble smolders underground for miles, with sporadic outbreaks and mysterious scufflings that build into a nasty eruption like the one last month when we were returning from Flagstaff. The search for culprits led straight into her blameless brown eyes.

"Okay. Into the backseat," Ned told her. She climbed back and sat down in haughty bliss in the depths of the Travelall as if she'd been given a choice box seat while the rest of us were jammed into general admission. "Now turn around," said Ned. For two hundred miles through the Wyoming sagebrush from Baggs to Buffalo, she rode backward, setting a family record that still stands. For someone prone to carsickness, it was an impressive accomplishment.

The feat was also noteworthy for Ned, who may have been tempted to capitulate, as fathers supposedly are wont to do, to the doe-eyed innocence of his first daughter. But the women who brought him up—his mother and five older sisters—embodied female stoicism. He's told me the story of the day he came into the kitchen and caught his mother crying at the sink. She clutched her index finger and claimed she'd cut it paring potatoes. During those precarious years following her husband's death, tears were a luxury she couldn't afford.

When we pull up to the curb in front of Holy Name, Elizabeth anchors her veil with her right hand, clasps her white prayer book with her left, and exits with dignity. Safely out, she turns, wrinkles up her nose at her tormentors, and sizzles to Ned Anthony. "See if I ever give *you* any more pop."

"Are we gonna stop at the candy store after church today?" is the question uppermost on the minds of the other children scrambling from the car. They're trying to determine the impact of this occasion on our routine. Specifically, will there be a payoff for sitting still through the songs and ceremony?

"Sure, we'll stop," Ned answers as he comes around the car for me. "The candy-store man is counting on us."

Perhaps the white-haired man who presided over the glass case full of suckers, Tootsie Rolls, Cracker Jacks, and bubble gum at the corner news store did count on us, not for economic viability but for the light that children bring to dimming days. Certainly he beamed when ours burst in every Sunday morning after Mass. He waited in patient amusement while each child agonized over how to get the most for a dime. Whenever some miscreant hung back in a cloud of remorse, the old man's shoulders drooped and he cast baleful glances at us.

Stopping at the candy store was the reward our children connected to churchgoing. My compensation as a young mother, penned up and pent up from a strenuous week of child care, came when I lined them up at Mass, often wearing dresses and coats and caps I'd made for them. Ushering young children out of the house with clean faces and a shoe on each foot left me frayed and irritable, but if a man behind us patted a crew-cut head shorn by Ned the night before and asked if it was "fuzzy or bristly," or a woman smiled at me and said, "What a nice family," my spirits soared.

This was precisely the peril some feminists warned of— mothering full-time tempted women to mistake a relationship for a career. And to see children as blocks of marble to be chipped into perfect shape. Still, there were tasks to be done and lessons to be taught, and even if I couldn't call it my work, it seemed to be my responsibility.

Ned opens the car door. Just as I lift Paul and turn to get out, Paul throws up. Not the ordinary overflow of a recently fed baby, but a spewing sufficient to alter our plan. Ned takes over in church while I'm confined to the car, mopping up and drying off, keeping one eye on the geyser threatening in my arms and the other on the communicants as they proceed in somber double file along the sidewalk toward church. Each child stares straight ahead, palms pressed together, fingertips pointed upward, a flawless performance that testifies to weeks of rigorous Saturday morning sessions with a stern nun. Despite Vatican II and all the talk of open doors, this could be my First Communion day, with its emphasis on proper church etiquette that confused acting good with being good.

There's Elizabeth now in the homemade dress she declared "the best in the whole world" as she curtsied this morning before the bedroom mirror. The dress was made of dotted Swiss, a simple A-line style with puffy, wrist-length sleeves on which I'd tacked embroidered daisies. She'd touched one, then hugged herself and giggled. I secured her veil, and we admired our accomplishment in the glass.

The delight she took in her dress established a tradition. Each of her four younger sisters received First Communion in a dress sewn especially for her. As I sewed, they hovered, asking questions that popped into their heads, trivial queries that have befuddled theologians and caused schisms throughout history. *Is God's body really in the bread? Do we actually eat Christ's flesh? Is the wine really his blood? Or is it all pretend?* Explain mystery, in other words. Talk about reality beyond experience and language. What I said was that Christ is in the people. That their presence and faith is the body we call Christ and celebrate in the form of bread and wine. It's a theological point not well published, perhaps because most people don't worry too much about the chemical composition of the host. Or perhaps because understanding it modifies the power of the priestly role.

In 1986, as I sewed the last communion dress, more mundane questions bothered me. Was all this sewing and fussing a seduction, a quasi-entrepreneurial activity that deceived me into thinking I had choices, opportunities, power? While I spent my time searching through pattern books and sewing dresses for a ritual a woman wasn't worthy to perform, Wall Street whirled with mergers and takeovers and acquisitions. And the Singer Company announced it would stop making sewing machines.

As the row of chastened children slowly passes our car, Elizabeth slides her eyes toward me. I smile. She winks. My steadfast daughter, a confessed thief in communion clothing, has stolen from this solemn occasion one sweet moment for me.

Paul is bouncing and babbling. His stomach has made apparent peace with its contents and the worst of the evidence is gone from my pale blue linen suit. I venture up the church steps, open the heavy door, and tiptoe into a dark so sudden that everything is foreign. Instead of the humdrum of English, I hear the music and mystery of Latin. Instead of my daughter, I see myself in communion dress, shepherded into the front pew by the anxious nun who prepared us and now intends to collect her due. When the priest elevates the host at consecration, I turn around, searching for my mother, hoping she may have left the bed where she's confined with something called the "change of life." Instead, I meet Sister's icy glare and whirl around, trembling. This becomes the remembrance of my first bread.

My eyes have adapted to the darkness. I see my daughter kneel at the communion rail, then tilt back her head to receive the host. She stands, eyelids down, and walks toward her seat, but as she turns, she opens her eyes and glances over her folded hands. We're a church length apart, but she sees me.

THIS IS THE ROOM Elizabeth calls her own, but the evidence indicates otherwise. The books and projects that are hers are entangled with the business of her boys. Like dandelions, children gradually take over their surroundings, a cradle in the corner of the bedroom, a high chair, a set of blocks, coloring books, and the next thing you know an entire shelf in the refrigerator belongs to the cardboard polar bear brought home from kindergarten. And one day you catch yourself, as I did, absentmindedly rearranging butter and eggs around a child's work of art.

Today's culture confronts parents with a more ponderous predicament—making room for their children while juggling the content of their days. Work is something most people need and want to do, but there are no social policies to address the associated parental issues: the biological bond between mother and infant, the young child's need for constancy and caring.

Considerations of this sort were on my mind the autumn day in Helena as I watched from the gallery of the capitol's legislative chamber. Elizabeth stood below, right hand held high, as she was sworn into the state bar: "I, Elizabeth Tranel Halverson, do solemnly swear . . ." The dress she wore, had made for the occasion, spoke of another pledge. She was five months pregnant. But nothing in this event considered that event. Mothers are left to do their swearing in the kitchen or in the dark of night when they're summoned from sleep for the third time.

The child in utero the day she took her oath as an attorney was born four months later; three months after that, Elizabeth began to work part-time while continuing as a full-time nursing mother—physically complex, yes, but plenty of women were doing it. Then the day came when her regular child-care person canceled at the last minute and Elizabeth frantically called around for a substitute. As she made arrangements, reality struck: she was preparing to leave her baby with someone she'd never met. Confounded by her heart, her will began to lose its way.

"You were saying there's so much to do. . . ." I prompt her with the sentence she left unfinished.

"Every so often it hits me. . . ." She circles the room with her eyes. "In another seven or eight years, this will be all over. My cubs . . ." She smiles. "I guess it's time I quit calling them that. My guys will be gone. But this . . ." She looks down at her briefcase and starts over. "I like my legal work. But it's hard to keep it at a level I can sustain and still pay attention to things here. Last week just as I was leaving my office to take a deposition, the swim coach called and said Eric was complaining of a terrible headache."

"So did you call Jim at his office?"

"He was in trial. I'm the one on call in emergencies. One job has to be the main one." She looks up and sees my question. "That's the way we want it. And I'm glad Jim's willing to take financial responsibility. Some men aren't anymore."

As we consider the quilt design, we speculate about the effect of Jim's traditional Montana upbringing on his perspective. And how my choices have influenced hers. And how her own experiences have shaped her philosophy, that pragmatic blend of feminism and tradition that I admire.

She thrived in the atmosphere of a women's college but was irritated by the feminist nun who wasted time ranting about white male writers. She wanted to *learn* about them, partly because she'd need the information at test time. She spent spring semester of her junior year at American University in Washington, D.C., and worked as an intern with the Free Congress Foundation. On the anniversary of *Roe vs. Wade,* her office participated in the Right-to-Life march. The January morning was cold, and Elizabeth wore pants. "Dress for the weather," Ned had drilled into her during those years of driving country roads. But her attire that morning brought a reprimand. As an intern representing this group, she should be wearing a skirt. This incident prompted her to step back and examine the coexisting ideas: why couldn't she take a stance on abortion as a female wearing pants?

I tell her now that her sons are lucky to have her strength to bump up against.

"Sometimes I feel more like a target for their frustration." She relates an incident from the other evening. John was watching TV and a pop singer, a teen idol whose name means nothing to me, cavorted across the screen in a see-through leotard. Elizabeth made a snide comment about her singing talent. "You're just jealous," retorted eleven-year-old John.

I laugh. "Well, what woman wouldn't like to keep her twenty-year-old figure?"

"And be the object of male desire. And make a few billion in the process. But now I have these boys to raise. And I see how tender and innocent they are, and I wonder if there's any hope of . . ." Her tone drifts into that lonely confusion again. ". . . of just giving them enough time to grow up."

We talk for a while about her concerns. She describes the usual parental struggles. The steady round of decision making over mundane problems—chores and overnights and what's in the news—seeming trivia that, in fact, matters a great deal. It's here that parents help kids see the issues and appraise them and come to conclusions they're willing to act on. Here that they encourage sons and daughters toward actions that are just and good. Here that children are taught to wait and work for what they want because doing so gives them a sense of purpose and something to believe in. And the joy that comes from obtaining it hones their desire for good.

She brings up contemporary complications. The affluence and busy schedules that make it easy to confuse parenting with purchasing. But a deluge of stuff, too much, too soon, only blunts enjoyment, the way junk food blunts hunger, and adults are left puzzling over their child's ingratitude or their teen's growing ennui.

There's a trend, too, of relying on education when modeling and mentoring would be more effective. But the immediate concern for this mother trying to guide three sons past the shoals of adolescence is the media's vicious use of violence and see-through sex. Gratification as a substitute for meaning plays out in the lives of too many young people as casual sex, with no connection to love or commitment or marriage.

"Casual sex," I say, "What an oxymoron."

Elizabeth puts down the fabric she's been holding, sits down at her desk, and looks at me. "What worries me is—what happens when kids have seen and done it all? When there's nothing left to imagine?"

Here I am, her long-term adviser, caught between my parochial upbringing and the moral free-for-all of my children's world, which I want to understand, not merely judge. Although what's the point of growing old if judgments are synonymous with narrow-mindedness?

I trot out the story of my dating years, when my mother issued curfews, always earlier than any of my friends'. When I was late, she turned on the porch light, a glaring reminder of my transgression, as well as a damper to dallying embraces at the door. Inside, I'd find her sitting in the dark by the telephone, as if anticipating an emergency; or if she was in bed next to my sleeping dad, she'd be propped up on pillows and wide awake, a hand resting on her heart, which was racing with worry over a subject she never mentioned. Even so, her distress told me there was something at stake here. And her Victorian approach at least allowed me to imagine and yearn and make connections between my desires and my future.

Now, sex has been hauled beneath the glare of media lights and turned into a kind of spectator sport, lovers like boxers in a ring, no punches withheld. Either way, the intent seems the same: to deny the power—and therefore, the anxiety—connected to an act that is a mysterious matter of life and death.

This exchange lingers in my mind through the afternoon. What I know, but don't go into, is that imagination is at the heart of empathy. *What is it like to be in that person's place?* Empathy, in turn, is the emotional skill at the core of morality. *How do I respond to others in a way that is fair and true?* The question is mind-boggling: What *would* happen if there were nothing left to imagine?

"You may have stirred up more questions in John than you realize," I tell Elizabeth later on.

She lifts her chin and says, "But it was true. She really *couldn't* sing." This is the tone that reveals the part of her that doesn't give up, the part that withstood brothers.

EIGHT-YEAR-OLD Elizabeth often lies on the braided rug in the living room, listening to our records, singing along with *Finian's Rainbow, Oklahoma!,* Nat King Cole's "Papa Loves Mambo." Her favorite is *The Sound of Music.* She's enamored of the Austrian family with its stern, loving captain and confident, spunky governess in charge of the large, happy crew. They're like us. They have seven children and mountains in their background, too.

"How do you solve a problem like Maria?" she sings on the afternoon following her First Communion. She's stretched out on the rug enjoying her status and the quiet that happens only when the younger children nap. On the stereo in the background, a chorus of nuns sings along.

I'm in the kitchen leafing through my recipe book in search of an inspiration for yet another meal when we've just finished cleaning up the kitchen after the last one. If I didn't believe that coming together at the table involved more than refueling our bodies, I'd be tempted to give it all up. But supper will be simple. Brunch is our Sunday feast, the same every week: we come home from church and get busy, whipping eggs and cheese into a casserole for the oven, lining up strips of bacon in the frying pan, stirring batter for pancakes, pouring orange juice, preparing the table. Today, we covered it with a white tablecloth, lit Elizabeth's baptismal candle, and set it in the center. Everything else was the same: the chatter and complaints, the squabbling and laughing, the crying, the spilled blueberry syrup to mark the occasion.

Dan slams the back door, sticks his fingers in his ears, and grimaces as he comes into the kitchen. "Send Maria outside," he says. "That'll solve her problem." This is our family solution to most indoor troubles. Outside is where restless natives, rambunctious children, bedraggled mothers, frustrated fathers calm down. Outside is the place to take your temper for a walk, to figure things out, to find quiet, privacy, respite. Outside is where children can follow their bliss and discover a dust bomb. Outside is where Ned is now with the older boys, cultivating the recently planted corn.

Corn on the cob is a treat in any climate, but in Wyoming it's the prize for a race won with the elements. More often than not, corn that's supposed to be knee-high by the Fourth of July is striving to reach an ankle before frost. Ned, Midwestern farmer at heart, plants it anyway and urges it along with plenty of water and optimism, and when all goes well, the afternoon comes when he calls helpers into the backyard. While they husk, I bring water to a boil and at dinner we know the delight of timely effort infused with hope and crossed by good luck. Elizabeth expressed it best the summer she was three, when she sat next to her dad at dinner. Gripping an ear of tender, fresh corn in her fists, she chewed earnestly all the way down the cob, stopped suddenly, and looked up at him. "You're the best daddy ever. You plant everything I like. I love you as fast as I can."

Loving him, she'll correct him gently later on, when she's a mother and an attorney and he asks her if she's going to work today. "Yes," she'll say, "at home," her way of reminding him how long it takes to break cultural habits, how easily we fall into the familiar language that limits work to what's done in the marketplace.

"Don't you *like* children, Maria?" Elizabeth asks now, in a British accent, of no one in particular. The answer comes in Maria's voice. "Oh, yes, Reverend Mother! But, seven?"

Dan swings open the refrigerator door and stands meditating before the shelves.

Elizabeth is on her feet now, whirling and singing: "'Girls in white dresses with blue satin sashes, Snowflakes that stay on my nose and eyelashes.' Mother! Listen to this!" she calls into the kitchen and then sings: "Girls in white dresses with sleeves full of daisies."

I laugh in reply.

"Babes, pipe down. Who told you you could sing?" growls Dan. "Babes" is her sibling nickname.

The singing stops. Elizabeth appears in the doorway, lifts her chin, and looks at me. "Reverend Mother? Have I your permission to sing?"

I'm not right for this role, but I know my line. I've heard it at least three times within the last hour. "Yes, my child."

Then, with as much spunk as any Maria could muster, Elizabeth tells her brother, "I have been given permission to sing."

He shakes his head, slams the refrigerator door, and turns to go out. "I give up. I'd rather watch corn grow than listen to her." I watch him retreat up the same road where, a few years ago, he pulled this younger sister in a wagon, queen of the parade he and Mike were staging. But that was pretend, and she reigned by default.

FOR A REASON I can attribute only to temperament or fall-out from the Garden, most of the conflicts flared between Dan and Elizabeth while Mike rooted for male victory from the sidelines. As a teenager on his way out for the evening, Dan left her with a list of prohibitions: Don't touch my stereo; don't listen to my tapes; don't go into my room; don't even think about it. His warnings continued to the door, but no sooner had the car disappeared over the first hill than Elizabeth was in his room playing a forbidden song.

Were girls allowed to goad boys without reprisal, Dan wanted to know when he returned and found his records disturbed and I poured cold water over the revenge heating up. Why shouldn't an older brother trounce his younger sister when she eavesdrops on phone calls to his girl? was the adjunct issue Mike proposed. The aggravation always astir within this society was ameliorated by the presence of other siblings, but never fully resolved until later on, when Providence stepped in with a sense of humor: two daughters for Dan, one for Mike, and for Elizabeth, three sons.

Between teenage Elizabeth and her younger siblings, though, there was generosity and affection and admiration. She gave them stuffed dogs and bright-eyed bears. She rocked the baby. She made bright batik banners and French braids and luxuriantly frosted birthday cakes. And she also made *them* very, very mad. Their rage was provoked primarily by her imperious style as person in charge on those occasions when Ned and I went out. Leading a pack of insurgents through the evening safely and off to bed on time was a fearsome responsibility. Like sovereigns throughout history, anxious over owning more power than authority, she devised shrewd ways to maintain control. They could watch TV if they scratched her back; they could have a Pepsi if they delivered food and drink to her.

One summer evening, they staged an uprising, refusing to serve, calling her Reverend Mother, calling her Queen Elizabeth, calling her Babes-Sir. She sent them outside and locked the door behind them. They spent their time and wrath digging a grave—for *her*—just outside the family room window where she sat alone, reading and feigning serenity while dark clods of dirt and darker clouds of thought smacked against the glass.

Calling her Reverend Mother was their mistake. That was my role. She was Maria, dancing across the meadow as one of the children but vested with the captain's authority, a governess with permission to sing. Two years later, in college, she was Nurse Ratched.

That was *not* a role, Dan and Mike advised their fellow students at Notre Dame when their sister, a freshman at St. Mary's, the women's college next door, was cast for that part in the university's production of *One Flew Over the Cuckoo's Nest*. But it was their word against her brown eyes. The truth was that her older brothers were now a direct channel to other Notre Dame men and suddenly more asset than liability.

Elizabeth was in her element. She felt nurtured and challenged and intellectually regarded. She felt cared for. "Not coddled," she explained, lest I imagined her becoming a moral wimp. "But considered."

The panty raids in vogue were both spectacle and opportunity, she gloated to her sisters at home. Guys were plentiful and eager but restricted from girls' rooms by parietals, a source of great complaint, but a boon, too, because young people were given leeway and time to venture into relationships tentatively, with less risk of violating their emotions by making physical commitments without psychological ones.

Despite the pleasures of college, Elizabeth held fast to the dream that began in high school. She would spend her sophomore year in Rome. In 1979, before e-mail and international telephone rates, Europe was a formidable distance. And she would be the first to go. "Sometimes I think I'm a thorn bird, throwing myself up against things to see what will happen," she wrote to me that spring. "But I don't think I could stand myself if I just coasted along. At times, I get feeling so lost, I wonder if I'll ever have a niche again. Anyhow, I had a good cry (only the second time since I came here). Now I'm fine."

She worked through the summer as a waitress. Between shifts, we assembled her wardrobe, clothes meant to be hand-scrubbed and dried over a railing, styles that would facilitate her desired immersion into Italian life, dark wool skirts and corduroy jumpers. As we sewed, we imagined her life across the ocean. One day she looked up from the hem she was sewing to watch eight-month-old Adrienne crawl full-speed toward the fabric dangling from her lap. "She'll be walking by the time I come home."

"CITTÀ DEL VATICANO" said the postmark on her first letter home: "I don't understand why anyone would want their own room, especially in a foreign country. The other kids think I'm lucky. But it's the first time in my life I've had a room alone and I'm terrified."

Her siblings scoffed. Was this the hard-hearted Elizabeth who'd locked them out for the sake of being alone? But as her letters arrived, they read on. They laughed at her description of the short Italian lady pulling a huge dog down the frenzied street; they learned about gelato and Caravaggio and Bruno, the bus driver. She said she was speaking Italian more and relying on gestures less. One night she dreamed she came home to a mother whose hair had turned completely white. She knew then that she'd been away a long, long time. She was homesick.

> You know, Mother, I came over here thinking I was going to prove to everyone what a tough cookie I could be—I never cry or miss anyone and I can finance this whole cruise because I worked so hard all summer. Well, now I know I can't do any of this alone—I need you and Dad and everybody to help me. I need to live with some crazy roommate to keep things in perspective. I'm not going to pretend to be a rock any more! I love Rome—but there are always times of loneliness no matter where we are.

Sundays were the worst. She missed the rowdy ride to church, the noisy brunch afterward, riding her horse bareback on sunny afternoons. She missed the little kids, Jennie and Ben. She missed the baby, Adrienne.

"What I miss most of all," she wrote in late October

after her nineteenth birthday, "is talking things out, knowing I could always get good advice whether I wanted it or not. I feel like such a transient. Where is home? I have to jump out of the nest and go build my own, but it's scary. At times I feel like I'm about 4 years old—totally ignorant about life. I'm 19 so I should be more independent and strong. But as they say, Rome wasn't built in a day. I'll be o.k. when I'm 20, right?"

Telephone calls were inconvenient and expensive, so we began exchanging cassettes, flying our recorded voices back and forth across the Atlantic. But my thoughts kept fast-forwarding to Christmas and the empty place at the table. I would have to toughen up. Her absence foreshadowed the norm, not the exception. But she promised to send a special tape. She would record it before she left for her holiday travels and mail it in time for Christmas Day.

After dinner and White Christmas pie, we set the recorder in the center of the table and there she was, telling us about the places she'd visited so far: Paris, London, Germany, Austria. "Salzburg was so amazing. The mountains made me want to yodel like crazy. I'm so anxious to see you all again but I can't believe how happy I am. Tomorrow! Tomorrow!" And then she began, not to yodel, but to sing, "*Buon Natale* means 'Merry Christmas to you.' *Buon Natale* to everyone. Happy New Year and lots of fun." Suddenly, Ned pushed back his chair and left the table.

"What's wrong with Dad?" someone whispered.

"He looked like he was ready to cry."

"He *was* crying."

"Dad? No, he wasn't. Dad doesn't cry."

Dads *don't* cry, not at the table, not on Christmas night, not when they've been brought up in a house where tears are blamed on paring knives.

In January, she wrote from Madrid that Christmas had been hard, not at all like those she knew. "When you're on your own, responsible for every meal, every mile, you realize how much your family did for you. If I didn't think this year was worth the pain, I'd be home in a flash. But I'm honestly truly happy."

In April, just before she left Rome, she wrote:

I really want to just fit in again with all my (hopefully) valuable experiences. The family has been my support all year and I know I can depend on it to help me adjust again. But I want more than anything to slip into my place and fill it naturally, as before. Anyhow, dearest Mom and Dad, I want to tell you one thing for sure— there's no way I could EVER have come over here without your unending support and confidence.

The homes she missed and imagined in college are both in Billings, ours across town from hers. The child who flew away first is the one who returned to settle down.

"BEAR?" CALLS a man's voice from the front door. Elizabeth's husband, Jim, is home from his office and walking toward her response: "I'm in my room."

"Bear" is what he calls the mother of their sons. Jim Halverson is a native Montanan. He knows the traits of bears, the fierce instinct of the female to protect her cubs, the brute instinct of the male to kill them. There is nothing to be feared here. This is a nest, not a den.

All Day, Every Day

·

NED ANTHONY

hat are they *thinking?*" asks a friend when I tell her that my son, Ned Anthony, and his wife, Dana, parents of three young sons, are expecting a fourth child. The exasperation in her tone stops me short, like a child caught in the bold act of trimming her own hair or applying lipstick to the bathroom wall, the aghast parent demanding reasons—*What are you doing? Why?*—the child shrugging and sputtering until she's sent off to her room and told not to come back until she can explain herself, which should take care of her for a decade or two.

I'm caught with the evidence of my bad example. Before I've come to any conclusions about my own life, I'm being asked to defend my children's choices. Fortunately, I'm prepared. Ever since that first, devastating indictment on my life's work, my son, Dan, has kept the argument going with regular reports on the Earth's carrying capacity. One year I'm guilty, the next absolved. The latest forecast is in my favor. All I need to do is state the reference: *Nature,* August 2001, and the title: "The End of World Population Growth."

My friend dismisses me with an annoyed shake of her head. I swear I'll quit hanging out with Unitarians and academics with their fretting intellects, but first, I indulge in one last flash of my own. "Maybe they're counting on Providence, like Goethe," I suggest, and summarize the statement tacked above my desk: the moment one definitely commits and begins, Providence moves, too; all sorts of things happen to help that otherwise wouldn't have occurred.

She rolls her eyes upward and exhales an impatient sigh.

"Okay, so they're careless Catholics, not thinking at all," I say, reading her mind aloud.

But knowing this son, I know better. He's neither careless nor Catholic. At least, not the practicing sort. Somewhere in the quest of his twenties, he took a hiatus from churchgoing. A typical, perhaps even an essential thing to do, if faith is to mature. Pause became pattern. He could no longer accept the metaphor of the shepherd and the sheep, the meek flock following along out of tradition and obligation. Religion, he said, was getting in the way of his spirituality.

I was having trouble with that myself. The combination of feminism and Vatican II made dissidents of the most devoted Catholic women. But the peril in the metaphor came clear one morning in the early seventies when I was awakened at an outrageous hour by the aggravating bleat of sheep. There, huddled near the pasture fence, was our flock of lambs, pathetically crying across the barbed wire to their anxious mothers, while ten yards to the north stood a wide-open gate none of them had sense enough to seek.

Sheep are stupid, I thought, not meek. The analogy may have applied at one time in history, but now it was obviously a tool used by peevish cardinals to keep an educated flock in check. Nearly thirty years later, I wonder: Is it possible that those lambs *saw* the open gate but were immobilized by fear? Maybe the mothers bleating on the other side were encouraging them to make a leap of faith and set out. But what of the maverick in the flock, the lamb I watched wander off? Who'll guide him through the gate?

"I'M NOT GOING all day every day, that's for sure," announces six-year-old Ned Anthony, tossing a Red Chief tablet, already tattered, on the kitchen counter. He's just come home from his first day at first grade and I've greeted him with the standard parental question, "How was school?"

His answer threatens my aplomb. His three older siblings clamored for the classroom. When other parents expressed frustration with a reluctant student, a smug satisfaction spread through me. No problem in our house. No need to nag our schoolkids to rise and shine. But this child is handing me a variation on the theme. Could it be that his Friday the thirteenth birth was an omen, or the tooth he was born with, a rare enough occurrence to earn him a large, front-page photo in the local weekly, the Vermillion, South Dakota, *Plain Talk?* Seven months later, he was back in the news. Bouncing in his swing, the town's famous baby had knocked out and swallowed his tooth.

Or perhaps we burdened our third son psychologically by giving him his father's name, implying that he ought to be studious, earn a Ph.D. before age thirty, and live up to expectations usually conferred upon the firstborn. Strictly speaking, our son's name is "Ned Anthony," while his father's baptismal name is "Nathaniel Nicholas." Kept home by her duties toward ten other children, Ned's mother sent her ten-day-old sixth son off to church to be baptized "Ned." He was brought home as "Nathaniel." The officiating priest felt conscience-bound to replace her choice with a bona fide saint's name. Surprisingly, given her respect for all things priestly, his mother went on calling him "Ned." But all of this conjecture boils down to this: a six-year-old with an aversion for school.

Hunger is the culprit, I decide, and cut the crust from one of the six loaves of bread I've just taken from the oven. He slathers butter on it, then squeezes honey from a gooey plastic bear. I slice three more pieces. Between bites, Dan, Mike, and Elizabeth ply their doubting brother with the benefits of school: fun on the bus, friends, recess, hot dogs for lunch. Ned Anthony listens, shrugs, and replies with cheery conviction, "I'm just not gonna go all day every day, that's all."

Apparently, he imagines boarding the school bus whimsically, when the weather's too nasty to be outdoors, when something interesting is going on in first grade, when he hankers for a hot dog, when the spirit moves him. Cooped up at a desk trying to earn the teacher's praise with neat papers and straight letters might be what the world expects of a six-year-old, but the hazel-eyed boy before me seems to be heeding Mark Twain's advice: Don't let school get in the way of your education.

Until now, his classroom has been the vast Wyoming outdoors. We celebrated his first birthday a few weeks after moving from South Dakota to our small ranch in the foothills of the Big Horn Mountains. He took his first step under the backyard willow tree; at age two, he became the family rodeo clown, plunked out of harm's way into a five-gallon milk can while his older siblings, mounted on brooms, rampaged around him. He's the kid in the photograph album with the bandaged hand, the one pouring water over his little sister's head as they share a bedtime bath, the one wearing face paint and an Indian headdress, the one out on the farthest limb.

His lessons explored how to skip rocks through fresh cow manure for maximum splash, how to catch an escaped piglet by the tail, how to transform an old baby buggy into a go-cart and the empty box of a grain truck into an overnight camp. Perched on the branch of a tree, he can assess for himself the worth of his work, while an A on a report card is a symbol made meaningful only by comparison and a teacher's interpretation.

But Mark Twain isn't running the public school system. Attendance is not optional. The law says my son must be tamed to sit still in a classroom; he must learn to read and write and do arithmetic. Like so many child-rearing issues, it's a situation to play by ear, but I anticipate plenty of discordant notes. This fourth child may trail his older siblings around, but he goes only so far with me.

"I doy-ing *out,*" he replied as a two-year-old when I announced nap time. Even if it hadn't been twenty below zero, the inevitable meltdown at four p.m. kept me on course. I read him *The Tale of Peter Rabbit,* selected for its moral, then tucked him in, along with the doll he cared for so tenderly. "Sing the lullaby you sang to her yesterday," I suggested. He scowled and squeezed her neck. "I doying *out,*" he reminded me. I closed the door against his muttered mantra. Fifteen minutes later, I inched it open to check on him. No little boy anywhere. No doll. No bedding either. Had he gone out, after all? I checked the windows. I looked under the bed. Behind it. Under the dresser.

I opened the closet door. There he was, naked and clutching his doll, sound asleep atop a mound of pillows and blankets, shirt, jeans, socks, underwear, and shoes flung about like the effects of a defiant, exhausting striptease.

But the conscientious objector in my kitchen is fully clothed, calm, and licking honey from his lips as if sampling the sweet taste of freedom. No doubt, he sees himself frolicking in the yard at home while his siblings stagnate behind school doors. The rebel in me sympathizes with his wish to follow his bliss. The genes donated by his dad demand fresh air and breathing room.

"Don't confront it," advises my in-house psychologist that evening when I report our son's resolve. Ned's oblique approach reflects his rural childhood as much as anything he gleaned from Erikson or Piaget. My practical education began only five years ago, when we took up this bucolic life. Alone all day with small children, ten cows, and a town upbringing, I had everything to learn. My first teacher was a savvy milk cow named Grace, who came with the place. By using her horn to lift the chain and unlatch the gate, Grace could let herself into the yard, where the grass really was greener. The day I spied her brazenly mowing and fertilizing our lawn, I hurried out, swung the gate wider, and invited her to exit. She chewed her cud and studied me. I marched up to her and delivered walking orders. "Leave. Now." She swished her tail. I circled behind her and shoved verbally. She ambled deeper into the verdant lawn. I was the only person on the premises over five. Until Ned came home, the yard was full of Grace.

Herding cattle through gates may be Ranching 101, but even skilled cowhands find it a formidable job alone. With a feisty animal, it takes two people, one situated near the gate to shoo the critter along, alternately closing in and backing away, encouraging rather than confronting, and the other strategically situated as a parameter, resolute and forbidding. Timing and intuition are key.

At dinner, Ned and I circle our son, assuming through our conversation that he's going to school. No need to probe his psyche or explore his feelings. We know what's lurking there.

"After school tomorrow," says Ned to his namesake, "be sure to water that calf in the barn."

A pair of hazel eyes lift to study his dad's face.

"Mr. DeJarnett called today and asked me to chaperone the first-grade field trip to the llama farm next week," I report casually as I ladle stew into bowls. "But . . ." I glance down at my swollen belly, seven months pregnant with our seventh child, then at the two little girls sitting on either side of me, Monica, two, and Alane, four.

"Have you ever seen a llama?" Ned's looking at Mike but talking to Ned Anthony.

Mike nods. "Llamas are like cows and camels. They have two toes."

Monica stares at me, then slides off her chair and fingers my sandaled foot.

"No, honey, " I laugh, comprehending. "Not 'Mama.' *Lah-ma*."

Ned's poised at the gate; I'm planted in the yard. Our son is watching for an opening. But the next morning, he's dressed for school and eating oatmeal with the others at the table. When they leave, he picks up his notebook and trudges the quarter mile up the road with them. From the living room window, I see him pause, look back, then lope to catch up. At the cattle guard between our road and the main one, they halt in unison and peer down. Dan jumps across. The others spring away in alarm. Mike and Elizabeth linger a moment, then dash across, but Ned Anthony turns toward home. I hold my breath. He spins around, charges forward, and leaps. The yellow bus pulls up, and they all get on.

The two young daughters at my side wave wildly, then realize their plight.

"I want to go, too," pouts Alane.

Monica puckers up. "Me, too."

"But I'm making bread this morning," I tell them. "And I need some helpers." An improvisational comment has decided my day.

MY MOTHER SPENT most of her waking hours bustling in the kitchen, slicing, peeling, stirring, pausing now and then over her prayer book, but she never involved my sister or me in food preparation. We set the table and dried dishes. Cooking and baking were her work. Now and then, she surprised us with homemade bread, high, coarse-textured loaves waiting on the kitchen table when we came home from school. But every Saturday throughout my childhood, she made pies. First, she gathered her equipment—bowl, pastry cutter, rolling pin—then she cut shortening into flour, added water "as if it were gold," flattened a fat ball of dough into a submissive round, deftly rolled it out and dropped it triumphantly into the tin, then zipped a paring knife around the pan and trimmed the crust to a neat edge. As a woman, I will make crust exactly as she did, but cooking will never be my primary art form.

Ned's mother produced twelve necessary loaves of bread every other day. Their daily dessert was homemade bread drenched with honey from bees kept on the family farm. When food supplies dwindled, she added leftover bread to fresh milk and served it as soup. One afternoon, over coffee at her kitchen table, she described to me the hard work of kneading big batches of dough toward the end of pregnancy, a frequent condition for her, given the thirteen children she bore to term. I listened politely, not realizing that soon enough I'd find this out for myself.

Now, as Monica dumps flour into an enormous bowl and Alane scours the cupboards for the two small pans that will hold loaves shaped by her hands, I stir and pant with the effort. We were still newlyweds when Ned, in a nearby chair, looked up from the abnormal-psychology textbook he was poring over. "You know what I miss? Homemade bread."

Eager bride, I flipped through *Betty Crocker,* my sole recipe book, until I found a section called "Yeast Breads." The short list of ingredients implied a simple task. Ned promised advice, so I skipped over details about dough resting and rising and rising again. This was a culinary endeavor, after all, not an Easter service. Kneading befuddled me first. Ned intervened, digging his fingers into the dough, folding and turning it the way he'd seen his mother do. At nine p.m., I covered the mixture with a dish towel and set it to rise on top of the small stove that heated our apartment. At ten p.m., when I lifted the towel, the unrisen dough lay still as a tomb. I covered it again and hoped for a miracle. At eleven, Ned demonstrated how to shape the loaves, remarking as he rounded up dough that it seemed different from his mother's. I alerted for a spat. So comparison would be our marital bone of contention. But the budding psychologist quickly recouped. "This dough feels a lot better. Sturdier. Or something." At one a.m., I opened the oven to two dismal loaves, heavy and, indeed, sturdy. Ned cheerfully sawed off a chunk and camouflaged it with honey. I vowed to master the art of making bread.

My first effort went awry, I know now, because I tried to hasten the rising time by setting the dough on a too-warm surface that killed the yeast action. The secret to bread making is patience. The ingredients are few, but

essential; the process simple, but exacting. The main requirement is presence—not anxious hovering, but strategic
availability—knowing when to set the dough aside to rest
and when to tend to it. The reward begins when you slide
those rounded loaves into the oven, where, mysteriously,
they rise and brown and scent the house with promise.

Bread with honey, the sticky staple of Ned's childhood,
became our tradition, too. Often, as we were leaving the
Midwest after a family visit, Ned's mother would tuck a
few gallon buckets of honey amid assorted children in
the recesses of the Travelall. And so it was that an aura of
intrigue developed around Murdo, South Dakota. This was
the town where time mysteriously shifted from standard to
mountain and the place where a bucket of honey, un-
observed and of its own accord, turned over onto the
suitcases.

Another day, when industrious four-year-old Ned
Anthony toted a gallon can of the stuff into the living room
and spilled it on a braided rug, I swore on the spot that I
would rid our house of honey and the homemade bread it
depended upon. Alas, I'd grown accustomed to the trace of
yeast wafting in the air. And to the therapy inherent in beating and kneading and punching down dough, and to the
thrill of successfully executing an expanded repertoire—
Swedish Limpa, potato-cinnamon bread, whole wheat,
Russian black bread, rye. And above all, to the pleasure of
lifting those lovely loaves from the oven and offering them
to my hungry children.

AT THREE-THIRTY, I'm back at the window when the
bus stops. The kids loiter at the cattle guard, then mean-
der down the road. Ned Anthony detours to the barn,
climbs the fence, and disappears inside. A few minutes
later, he's outside again, racing Elizabeth to the front step.

She lands first. The front door slams. I slice four pieces of bread.

"There was a skunk in the cattle guard this morning." Ned Anthony announces the obvious highlight of his day.

"Stupid Danny woke it up," says Elizabeth. "And then we were scared to cross."

"I hope it's there again tomorrow," says Ned Anthony. He looks at Elizabeth. "And I hope you get sprayed." He takes a bite his jaw works hard to accommodate.

She sticks out her tongue. "And I hope you fall in."

His eyes fire back what his full mouth won't allow.

One day at a time, he went to school, at first motivated by the possibility of a skunk to hurdle along the way, next by the opportunity to see a llama, and then by the possibility of getting to know real live kids whose last name wasn't "Tranel," boys with no aggravating big sister, kids eager to play kickball and leapfrog with him at recess. On the playground, climbing monkey bars and inhaling fresh air, he stored up the nutrients necessary to survive indoors. And gradually, he discovered that spending time inside with paper and pencils was not as oppressive as he had imagined. Even though his body had to sit still, his mind could make exhilarating leaps. But summer was his season.

Odd, then, that the day after school was out, the game he chose to play was school. On the lawn in the midday sun, writing studiously in the three old school desks their dad rescued from obscurity, were Dan, Mike, and Elizabeth. Odder still was Ned Anthony in the role of teacher, ensconced in a lawn chair, glasses on his nose, a large book on his lap. But oddest of all was the apparel he chose for this work: an old prom formal of mine, a pale green strapless affair with a stayed bodice that stood the ruffled bosom up around his chin. An hour later, he was in shorts and cowboy boots, wobbling down the road on a bike as Mike ran along behind shouting out tips on maintaining balance. And still later, the two brothers were wheelbarrowing equipment from one play site to another where they began converting the picnic table into a Kool-Aid stand. He felt no need to fasten an anxious eye on Ned and me, as Dan was prone to do, attending to our every worried sigh. But neither did he possess his oldest brother's patience with younger siblings. He went off with Mike, who said, "Let's play," and detoured them to Dan, who said, "Let's work."

This was the aspect of country life I treasured for my children, this unselfconscious play, so different from my growing up, when I was constantly reminded to think about what the neighbors might be thinking. Away from peer demands and the cultural compulsion to schedule every waking moment in a child's day, prepubescent children can bask in the freedom of androgyny. Little girls drive dump trucks and tractors through the dirt; little boys play dress-up and croon lullabies to their teddy bears.

One evening after a storm rumbled through and left a rainbow arcing on the horizon, I said aloud a line from Wordsworth that I remembered from high school, "My heart leaps up when I behold a rainbow in the sky." Our children rushed outside to look for the pot of gold. Ned, who knew the poem by heart, finished it:

> *So was it when my life began;*
> *So is it now I am a man;*
> *So be it when I shall grow old,*
> *Or let me die!*
> *The Child is father of the Man;*
> *And I could wish my days to be*
> *Bound each to each by natural piety.*

It was a poem he loved and often quoted when he talked to parent groups about child rearing. I detected a tremor in his voice as he said the line, "the Child is father of the Man" and wondered if it was connected somehow to his childhood without a father.

The word *piety* evokes images of eyes rolled upward and hands clasped in prayer, but natural piety is altogether different. Natural piety is serious, but never solemn, to borrow Russell Baker's distinction between these terms. It refers to what is innate, uncontrived, instinctive: love for the things of nature, reverence for the faithful morning sun, the drama of a full moon, the mystery we sense beneath our physical world, the insights and intuitions and irrepressible acts of children. Solemn acts are self-important and calculated for effect.

As fourth child, Ned Anthony played seriously while his older siblings educated him. Wide-eyed and malleable, he followed them around, observing causes and effects, noticing incongruities, at times outwitting them with mischief, learning to play fair and to be resourceful, taking mental pictures and developing perspective while in the midst of things.

Perceptive and attuned and sitting next to Dan in the front pew at Mass one Sunday, three-year-old Ned Anthony tugged on his brother's arm, pointed to the priest at the altar, and asked in a rebounding whisper, "How come God wears cowboy boots?" What caught his eye was the disparity, the odd union of solemn, celestial garments with serious, earthly footwear. This unruly need to question inconsistency was an act of natural piety. So was his reluctance to surrender his days to the unrelenting demands of school; and the affection he held for a lean, half-coyote, half-Greyhound dog named Queenie, for whom he built a house, a labor of pure boyish love accomplished with a hacksaw because he had no other tool. So was his uncanny ability to locate a sibling's Achilles' heel and mark it with a nickname. And, yes, natural piety was in the instinct that prompted him as a nine-year-old to slice into a golf ball. The exploding guts grazed his eyes with tiny fragments. We rushed him to the hospital emergency room, where a doctor washed away the effects of his curiosity. But there was no getting rid of his determination to explore his surroundings and to assert himself against boundaries and assumptions.

Testing boundaries is an essential part of play. *How high can I go?* a child wonders. *What will happen when I land?* He leaps. He falls. The resulting bruises and bumps teach him about limits: the limits of ability, of gravity, of sofas and tables and anxious parents. He learns about himself and his choices. Sometimes he gets up and keeps going. Other times, he cries out for comfort. But to play with concentration, he has to be able to trust. He must be free to test his instincts and intuitions. And he needs someone to console him when he lands hard or his dreams explode.

Play isn't frivolous. Its lessons prepare us for adult commitment. Usually, in our idealistic twenties, we make a leap of faith into an imagined future. Immediately, we run into limits—the restrictions of time and energy and ability, of our backgrounds and situation. Soon enough, we're counting down the days to a thirtieth or fortieth or fiftieth birthday and discovering our dreams and reality don't merge. We may find ourselves so far out on a particular limb that scrambling back to safety means leaving behind a career, a partner, a home, a perspective.

But as we leap and fall and begin again, we look back and see a plot. An unhappy ending started us off in a happier direction. A sudden hard fall taught us how to land.

Failure forms us; it binds our days "each to each." We begin to understand who we are and what we're for.

NED ANTHONY DID GO to school, although not always enthusiastically and not always all day every day, I learned years later when he confessed to more than one spring afternoon spent playing along the banks of the Tongue River. There were other days in his years from fifth through eighth grades at St. Labre Indian School when he dallied in the hay meadow, pondering ways to avoid the testy boys poised on the playground with their dukes up. And there were years when teachers failed him, not through a grade on his report card, but through their own inability to teach their subject matter skillfully or to distinguish discipline from punishment, or simply to respect the vulnerability of young people. The coach, for example, who selected him for first string on the high school basketball team and then capriciously refused to play him—or maybe it was out of spite, provoked because we questioned scheduling practice on Thanksgiving Day.

Agile and eager, Ned Anthony chafed against the coach's game. But gradually, he took up the challenge: week after week, he sat on the bench, quietly determined to stick it out. Waiting for the starting buzzer of the last game of the season, the fans, fed up with what they'd observed, began to chant: "We want Ned. We want Ned. We want Ned." The coach played deaf; the chant grew louder. Finally, the coach nodded toward the bench. When the boy who'd been sidelined all season slipped out of his warm-up jacket and ran onto the court, the crowd leapt up and cheered.

A few hours after Ned Anthony's high school commencement ceremony, Mount St. Helens erupted in Washington State, killing fifty people and spewing ash over the entire Northwest, including our ranch north of Broadview, eight hundred miles east, where graduates and parents were gathered for a celebratory pig roast. Without the tragic dimension, the event might have been construed as Mark Twain mischief, proof of the energy pent up beneath the lid of school. Suddenly, kids—the bright, the anxious, the lackadaisical, energetic, sensitive kids contained for years in classrooms geared to a nonexistent norm in a system emphasizing method over content—were discharged to make their own way.

As we delivered child after child to dorm after dorm, I began to hear the anguish beneath the raucous surface of college life. Like bawling calves on shipping day, young people are herded into dorms where they stand knee-deep in a glut of unnecessary goods hauled from home. Guidelines and parents gone, they're turned loose to cope with the vagaries of college bravado: around-the-clock noise, casual sleeping over, hall parties focused on booze, dissipation apparently the required introductory course. In high school, students can blame sober choices on hypervigilant Stone Age parents or athletic contracts. In college, they risk being shunned as a geek, a wet blanket, someone who can't unwind and have fun.

As an uneasy freshman at Gonzaga University in Spokane, the recalcitrant first-grader relied on strategies learned as a fourth child: observing, considering, evaluating, discerning. Where did upperclassmen stumble and fall? Did the dazzle of the night before compensate for the gloom of the morning after? How did other kids deal with the awkwardness of meeting girls and making friends and finding their niche? And who was that freshman whooping it up at last night's party, dancing like a wild man, clearly having more fun than those lolling about with drinks in their hands, yet also clearly sober?

What ultimately convinced him to practice temperance, this son told me years later, was his desire to assert his individuality. He knew nothing then about the three great-grandfathers, all pious, God-fearing men, who drank away their family farms. The happy fault of his birth order, that mix of stubbornness and reticence and sensitivity, had grown into a keen wish to be different from the crowd. Later on, when we did discover alcoholism as the addiction thriving on our family tree, younger siblings in the throes of the college drinking dilemma could turn to him. And he could say honestly that fun is better when you can remember it.

College classes revised Ned Anthony's understanding of school. The Jesuits interpreted education in the Latin sense of the word, *educere,* meaning "to lead out" (although for too many years, only boys were considered worthy to be led anywhere). Instead of the squelching that he considered synonymous with the classroom, he was being challenged by the great questions and systems of thought. Students met Plato and Aristotle and Aquinas in required philosophy classes and professors in the hall.

"Come in here and we'll set up an appointment to talk," said Father Frank Costello, beckoning to Ned Anthony from the doorway of the political science department.

"Where do you imagine yourself in five years? Ten years?" he asked as they sat together in his office the next day. "What are you good at? Where do you struggle?" Did he dare tell this priest that he imagined himself outdoors doing work he could touch and see and smell? That he struggled with the dissonance between his dreams and the path held out by our culture as the way to success?

Another evening, as Ned Anthony hurried across campus to meet friends for a basketball game, along came

Father Costello to waylay him with a question. "On your way to the debate?"

"Well, actually," stammered the political science major, "actually, I'm going to the game." At Father's skeptical glance, he added, "I might not have a chance to see John Stockton play again."

"Or to watch a debate of this caliber," came the discomfiting reply. *Just remember,* he was saying, *the choices you make create the shape of your life.*

"How do you think your time here will affect your life?" asked Father Costello as graduation approached. "Do you ever envision yourself as the father of a sixteen-year-old daughter? Do you think your education has equipped you to answer her questions?"

These same matters, in a different guise, were often under discussion in our family room among the many college friends who spent holidays at our Broadview ranch with Ned Anthony. On this particular day after Thanksgiving, five of them were lounging in front of the fireplace after an afternoon of sledding at ten below zero.

"So what do you think you'll do after we graduate?" asks a voice I recognize as Tom Michaels's, whose fascination with Wild West activities kept him coming back to the ranch year after year through college.

"Anybody going to *gradual* school?" chimes in Ned Anthony, employing his brother Mike's word for the creeping weariness he experienced in that theoretical realm.

"Not me. I've already got loans up to my ears."

"Maybe I'll go to Europe. Get a Eurail. Bum around for a year."

"If I were you, Tranel, I'd stay right here," said Tom. "Ride and rope all day. Hunt rabbits after dark."

"This place is too small. You can't make a living on a couple thousand acres of dry land."

"We could pool our resources. Buy us a really big place."

"Dream on, Tombo."

"I'm planning to."

In the beginning, Tom was a fascinating guest at our Thanksgiving table, a Sacramento native, his family's fourth child, too, who grew up swimming and surfing. He dangled tantalizing descriptions of "California chicks" in bikinis before fourteen-year-old Paul. He went sledding with Adrienne and Ben, joined Alane and Monica for Jane Fonda workouts, rode and roped with Ned Anthony, walked the ridges with my husband on the lookout for eagles, and over coffee, tried to convince me that Will James's *Smoky, the Cowhorse* was of greater literary merit than Henry James's *Portrait of a Lady*.

Rumors of snakes hiding in the hay and mice scritching in the walls motivated him to plop down a discarded mattress and bunk in the barn. He dressed for the role of Montana cowboy in Wranglers, scuffed-up boots, and a ten-gallon hat that he'd hung on a post and shot full of holes. Two times on a horse and he had the rhythm; at sunrise, he saddled up and rode across the silent fields.

After graduation, Tom joined Ned Anthony at our ranch for one last fling of freedom before facing the somber task of finding work. By day, they cowboyed. Over dinner, Tom, a business major, discussed seriously with Ned Anthony and Pa T, the name he called my husband, the business angle of ranching.

"WHAT DOES IT TAKE to make a ranch viable, Pa T?" Tom asks, and helps himself to corn on the cob. He grins at Paul, who's skirmished successfully for the place next to him and in the process, disturbed the usual seating order. "You grew this corn, dude?"

Paul glows.

"Paul's our gardener," says Ned, and then takes up Tom's question. He describes the impact of corporate farming that has made large, lean operations and smart management the key to survival. "Hard work, too. And good luck." Blizzards during calving season, droughts three summers in a row, roller-coaster prices, these are the inconstancies he names.

"Jeez. How do people cope?" Tom nudges Jennie. "Pass me those rolls, will you? Ma T, I could smell bread baking from the north pasture."

"Tombo!" Monica glares across the table. "I'm the one who made the rolls."

Tom flashes his dimples. "Really? Wow! So are you gonna marry me?"

"I'm taller than you."

"I didn't hear 'please,'" says Jennie, holding on to the bread basket.

"Please marry me," begs Tom. She surrenders the basket. He plops a roll onto his plate and looks his question at Ned Anthony.

"A lot of them *don't*," he replies. He names places that have been sold, some of them proud third-generation spreads, others dreary parcels somebody's been trying to run the way his granddad did. "He's the guy who's glad to get rid of it and move to town. Then there's the one who sells out and stays on. He's seventy-five years old and living in a trailer out in the middle of nowhere because ranching is all he knows."

"Hmm." Tom frowns. "But what if you decide to go for it anyway? What would you need?"

"To make a living?" Ned Anthony shrugs. "About fifty sections. Twelve to fifteen hundred cows."

"And an outside job," I interject with a laugh but hear

the sting of truth. Ned and I have never completely cleared the hurdles set up by our dreams and differences. Hints of these difficulties surfaced in the third summer of our marriage, when he hired on with a combine crew harvesting wheat in the rolling hills north of Pullman. He was working on his doctorate degree in psychology at Washington State University, and the twenty dollars he earned each day, combined with his teaching assistantship, would be our livelihood during his last year of course work. For six weeks between summer school and fall semester, his day began at four a.m. with breakfast served on-site, a hearty meal designed to keep the crew going until noon, when they were refueled to last until dusk. Sunrise to sunset, seven days each week, Ned operated a tractor-pulled combine. Days, weeks passed when our two young sons, Dan and Mike, didn't see their dad. One day we arranged to meet midday, midfield. Riding on the combine with him, they could observe harvest, the frenetic endeavor that pits a year's work against the whims of weather—a hailstorm, cloudburst, or sudden wind that could devastate a crop.

Out there, as machines grazed the abundant amber fields, my husband's obvious contentment unsettled me. A year from now, he would be a psychologist confined indoors, dealing in abstractions. What would become of the Illinois farm boy so blissfully engaged in tangible work? And if the farm boy had his way, what would become of me and the future I imagined as the wife of a professional, living in the country, Ned as the country gentleman and I as the mistress of our genteel life?

But Grace intervened. Before I'd even begun to put that first country house in order, milk began arriving in our kitchen faster than Betty Crocker and I could keep up with it. Two gallons daily, released from the astonishing teats of the cow we bought with the place. Anyone who's grown up drinking homogenized milk from clean cartons will forgive my dismay at the prospect of drinking that warm, foamy fluid brought from the barn. Gingerly, I lifted the manure-splattered bucket and strained the milk into a pasteurizer. Dutifully, I processed it; frugally, I made custard and pudding and sour cream cake and every milk-based concoction I could come up with; from the cream, I hand-churned butter, an uncertain project that seemed to depend upon the moon and stars and my good humor. Besides, successfully separating the curds from the whey only meant milk to contend with in another form: buttermilk for biscuits, pancakes, Irish soda bread. Furtively, I drank store-bought skim and sent an SOS to neighbors to come and partake of our overflowing Grace.

AFTER DARK, Ned Anthony and Tom sat on the steps of the bunkhouse to contemplate the questions that came out with the stars. The successful mission of the space shuttle *Columbia* promised the sky as the limit and a college degree as the necessary ticket, but for young people graduating in 1984, being grounded by reality seemed a likelier scenario. The country was emerging from a recession; Reagan's priorities were money-driven, organized around military buildup and technological development, not people. Corporate executives chafed against restriction, and the idealistic young chafed against raw ambition, perhaps intuiting cowardice beneath the corporate compulsion to merge.

What would become of two innocent young men whose hearts insisted on going out? Could they hope to find honorable work that would use their gifts, offer meaning and direction, provide enough financial security to live responsibly within a community? Or would the world order them back inside, telling them to sit down and be quiet and listen to the lectures delivered by the culture?

Insure, assure, be sure. Invest in stocks and bonds, not unpredictable human hearts. And when you leap, make sure you're not the guy who falls.

Night after night, Tom and Ned Anthony pondered a universe bright with stars but refusing to illuminate a path for them. Out for a walk one evening, I saw the two silhouettes against the night sky and intended to stop and talk. But I noticed a light glimmering in the barn where Tom bunked and detoured inside to turn it off. A dusty bulb dangling on a cord cast playful shadows across the hay. As I watched, I heard my father's tired footsteps following his children from room to room, night after night, turning off lights and muttering the same question: *Do you think you own the power company?* We did, of course. When you're young, energy *is* yours. Your body moves light. And power has no price.

My dad walked about town paying bills on time, buying inexpensive cuts of meat at the corner grocery store, selling to neighbors the fat gooseberries from the bushes in his garden. He worked hard, held a job throughout the Depression years, guarded spending, and refused debt. And before anyone considered the environment, he considered the electric bill. His frugality, combined with my vision for our country life—a pastoral setting for raising children—roused traits in me that became Ned's blessing and curse: restraint and questioning. *A tractor? Why? What would you do with a rake? Aren't sixty-three acres enough?* Ned's imagination strained against fence lines; he was dreaming of land in sections, cattle in herds, a working ranch in the West.

It was when I was on my way to the grocery store with a two-foot-long list and a clutch of coupons in my hand and met him coming down the road with a saddle that I bristled. I was sure my thrift was funding his frivolity. Never mind that he'd traded the saddle for hay with no out-of-pocket cash. All of this getting and spending went against my grain and my dad's example, especially when what was gotten stayed outdoors. Forget the new leather sofa, says the country boy, we need another cow. But that same boy gets the gate and assumes a flat tire is his job, and those were qualities I appreciated.

"He's not exactly a kid's horse," I sniped as Ned led his proud purchase, Prophet, a half-ton of quivering muscle and power, past the row of admiring eyes. Later, when I looked out the window and saw him astride that handsome buckskin stallion with three-year-old Ned Anthony riding in front of him, secure in his dad's embrace, I amended my judgment. Briefly.

Ned's amendment was Smoky, a sweet-looking pony complete with cart, but the epitome of Shetland stubbornness. Imploring her to move kept our frustrated kids loaded in the cart for an entire summer. But five-year-old Elizabeth upset the calm and the cart by climbing on bareback and trotting Smoky past three disgruntled brothers. They tore after her, pelting insults.

"Baca is a beauty," Ned said of the bay quarter horse mare he brought home next. She was also a bargain, like the fifty half gallons of ice cream he'd bought the week before. "A dollar apiece," he told me as he crammed packages into the freezer. "And it's summer. It'll be gone in a month."

While the kids ate ice cream, Baca carried and gave birth to Poco, a charming buckskin colt; the next spring, she birthed another, and the following year, one more. Ned bought and bartered saddles and riding gear. He hustled deals on sleds and skates and bikes and skis and toboggans. Then, for no particular reason I could see, he bought a dump truck, inept and loose-jointed, like the one running amuck in *The Happy Man and His Dump Truck,* a story our children loved. A good-for-nothing truck, not even useful for hauling trash to the ranch dump, a weekly chore Ned did with a tractor and wagon so the kids could ride along. But even the dump truck justified itself, like every other bargain he'd fallen for, by serving as our moving van later on.

Ned's Christmas gifts to me were similarly effusive. I had nowhere to go in that long, off-white wool coat with its silver fox collar, but I liked imagining myself en route. And I reluctantly admired his exuberance.

To be fair to myself, coupon clipping was my way of contributing to our financial well-being. Hadn't my dad taught me that a penny saved is a penny earned? I shopped for winter coats after Christmas; I made drapes and patched blue jeans; I studied grocery ads. I used up all that milk.

To be fair to Ned, he was expansive in his approach to work, too. As expenses went up, he worked longer and harder and more purposefully, and I glimpsed something stirring beyond good deals. True, the grand piano he bought twenty years ago was secondhand, but when Alane arrived home from college at two a.m. and pounced on the keyboard and woke the whole house to Bach, the joy was brand-new. Now, during the holidays, when Ned asks Ben or Adrienne or Jennie to play and he sings along, compensating for tone deafness with enthusiasm, I see the child who is father of this man.

To be fair to us, when we pulled together, Ned and I were a balanced team. He lunged; I braced. The play between possibility and limit enlivened our hearts and work. When we were open to each other's influence, we spurred each other to growth. When we were under the influence of our separate fears, we spurred each other.

For a while, in the spirit of the "dysfunctional" times when a putative 96 percent of the population suffered from the disease called "codependency," we strove to become impervious to each other's ways. For another while, we called our troubles a "romance addiction." We weren't home schooling our kids or gathering rose hips to spin into wool, but our heads were full of images from Laura Ingalls Wilder. Gradually, we began to suspect that any illness afflicting most people might very well be the human condition, that *felix culpa* that impels us to go on together as courageously and compassionately as we can, given our precarious existence here.

What we were up against was the task of commitment: learning to accept the flesh-and-blood reality of an "other" who saw things differently, someone we professed to love but who also disappointed and hurt and confounded us. Regardless of what the world says and we might hope, intimacy is not a fling in the bedroom. Rather, it's getting up after a lousy night's sleep and trying to be decent to each other; it's the all-day, everyday effort to maintain goodwill and respect while working things out. And it's accepting that some of those things may never be resolved.

I reached up and switched off the light and groped my way through the dark barn; my pulse picked up at the sight of a rope coiled snakelike in the shadows near the door. But when I went out into the starlit night, my son and Tom were gone.

Tom traded his Wranglers and boots for a suit and tie and went to work in the financial department of a San Francisco bread company. Scheduled and salaried, he was counting the months until his first vacation, when he would return to real life as a Montana cowboy.

1985: THE YEAR of the terrible drought, when pastures never did green up, and April brought searing sun, and grasshoppers finished off the petunias and then assaulted the lawns and after that chewed paint off houses, and a neighbor sighed and told me over our post office boxes one morning that even her "soul felt brown." Tom arrived beaming, untroubled by the dismal condition of the land, eager to spend his vacation digging post holes in that unyielding ground and fencing in the blistering sun. At night he and Ned Anthony sat on the barn steps and talked back to the stars.

Two weeks later, on July 13, as Tom left our ranch for the long drive home, he announced a plan to swim in every body of water from Montana to California. The phone call came late that afternoon. An hour out of Billings, Tom dove from a bridge into the Yellowstone River.

Our son's birthday became the anniversary of Tom's accident. And it would be years before Ned Anthony celebrated that day again. His dearest college friend was paralyzed and doomed to a life in a wheelchair. What was there to celebrate?

"There's a purpose. Things will work out. There's meaning in all of this," we tell ourselves in these moments. "Providence," we begin, but our thoughts trail off into questions. Where is Goethe then, to say nothing of God?

FOR THE NEXT few years, Ned Anthony alternately wrestled calves and his own future. He moved to Seattle for two years, where he worked as production manager at Pacific Coast Feather Company. He returned to the ranch for a while; he earned a master's degree in education and finished a practicum at the University of Iowa. He was in the process of applying for admission to Ph.D. programs when the boy inside demanded another hearing. *Do you think you'll be happy spending your life indoors? Can you imagine yourself shuffling through papers and numbers and abstractions the rest of your life?*

And then letters began arriving from his elderly grand-mother. Have you considered becoming a priest? she wanted to know. Young people risked their innocence, she believed, if they squandered too much time in a state of single irresponsibility. She promised to pray for his religious vocation, as she did for every grandchild who tarried single into their mid-twenties. It was a daunting proposal: two of her eight sons were priests; four of her five daughters were nuns.

Still, she'd put her finger on a contemporary di-lemma—the hesitancy to commit that suggests young people have lost trust in themselves and the world. But lin-gering in the security of indecision is risky, too. Too much looking before they leap can dissipate momentum and par-alyze the young with fear. Through leaping and falling, they learn the lessons that help them find their way and their work. And discover the delight that comes when their gifts fit the life they've chosen.

Perhaps a more pervasive concern is the failure of our culture to hold up to our young people something worth striving for, something worth committing themselves to. The social ills we lament aren't entirely the fault of the fam-ily. The culture defines the values that shape the family. And when those values aren't worth working for, what are young people supposed to do?

Just as corporations and developers began buying up farms and Californians began lusting after Montana land and ranchers sold it to them and moved to town, Ned leased thirty sections north of Roundup, Montana, and began building fences and buying cows. Now Ned Anthony had an opportunity to expand a family avocation into his vocation. Ned had his working ranch. And I had a dilemma: how to reconcile the satisfaction of seeing my husband and son merge their dreams with the unsettling effect this had on the present. We were extended even farther; the ranch where we lived was becoming a stopping place on the way to the real one, seventy miles away.

ON THIS JULY afternoon in 2001, Ned and I join Tom and his older brother, Jim, for a picnic at their campsite in the ponderosa pines. Every summer since his accident, Tom and Jim have flown from Hawaii where they live and work to Montana where they vacation. The exception was 1995, when Tom came in late May to be best man at Ned Anthony's wedding.

What is he thinking? I wondered that day as I looked at Tom seated in his wheelchair near the altar, his gaze steadied on the bridal couple. Sunshine glinted across the stained-glass windows of the country chapel; a tractor moved along a horizonless wheat field, like a ship sailing into the sunset. My mind drifted on its own sea of images and feelings, the crest and fall of hopes and dreams, the magnificent obsessions Ned and I set out with as naive twenty-three-year-olds plunging into the future with no life jackets, no prenuptial agreements, no backup plan.

What were we thinking when we bought that sixty-three-acre ranch in the foothills of the Wyoming Big Horns and moved four children into a two-bedroom house? Or when we brought a child into the world every other year during an era raging with social tumult? We were thinking plenty of room outside for children to play, I would have answered then, a mountain view, irrigated land almost as green as the Mississippi bluffs where we grew up. We were thinking we could raise our children on our own turf and terms, that we were young and resourceful and could handle whatever came our way, that we could expand our house and hearts to accommodate children. We must have been thinking hope, too, if hope is a thought.

What was my son thinking that day as he stood gripping the hand of his bride, Dana, his eyes glistening with a confusion of joy and awe? And what was she thinking as he slid a wedding band next to the diamond he'd given her the previous July on his birthday? Is it possible that they weren't thinking at all? Is it possible that thinking is secondary to faith in the leaps of youth?

Every year, several friends meet Tom and Jim in Montana. This summer a couple of college buddies and a friend from childhood have come; they're here now picnicking with us on Tom's land. "Tom's land" was once ours, the ranch north of Broadview where he rode and roped and bunked with the mice in the barn. After we moved to town, we sold the house and adjacent land to a retired California couple. Tom bought the parcel to the north where the eagles soar.

"Our land" is that original working ranch north of Roundup, expanded to two hundred sections where Ned Anthony manages a three-thousand-cow operation. He pulls up now in a pickup. His five-year-old son, Nathanial, jumps out and skips toward the group feasting on grilled sirloins.

While we eat and talk, we glance south toward the house hidden by the trees. Nathanial is eyeing Tom; he stands back and ponders the wheelchair; he studies the fork fastened to the cuff strapped to Tom's left arm; he watches as Tom lifts that arm and feeds himself a bite of steak. There are questions building inside this boy that I hope my son is prepared to answer.

"Hey, dude." Tom sends Nathanial a dimpled smile. "See that eagle up there?"

Nathanial tilts his head and squints skyward.

"What do you think he can see?" Tom asks.

"Mm." Nathanial frowns in thought. "Prob'ly the whole world."

"That's why I'm coming back as an eagle in my next life," says my husband. It's a fantasy I've heard a hundred times.

"Oh, *Gram*pa," says Nathanial, amused at this elderly musing.

"He even has his nest picked out," I tell Tom. "In the rims across from our house."

Tom laughs. "Pa T, I'm with you. Let's go over there and see if we can find a nest for me."

Jim lifts his brother onto the front seat of their Jeep Cherokee and secures him. Their friends squeeze in back. Nathanial scrambles into his dad's pickup. Ned and I opt to walk a shortcut through the pines. I watch as the vehicles pull away and follow the trail tires have worn in the grass. They reach a closed gate. Ned Anthony gets out, fiddles with the latch for a minute, then swings open the gate and signals the others through.

While the Blossoms Still Cling

ALANE

I awake to May's first light, shaken by this dream: I am walking up a steep, shadowy path and come upon my daughter, Alane, veiled and kneeling on the ground. Pink and blue bundles surround her. She lifts one and offers it to me. As I lean to take it, I'm struck by brooding serpent eyes. Swaddled like a baby is a snake—rather, a mere torso of a snake, a fragment, as if she's taunting me with something unfinished, or broken, like a promise.

I lie pondering both the dream and the bedroom wall laden with reminders of my fruitful marriage bed: ten portraits of babies and ten high school graduation photographs, and between the two groups, a photograph of the perpetrators, Ned and me. These are the faces I scan as I fall asleep and when I wake. Each assemblage of ten is arranged in three rows: four photos in the top row, two in the middle, four in the bottom. Comprising each middle row are Alane and Monica, fifth and sixth in our family, born two years apart in May in the midst of the unbounded sixties, the "little girls," we called them, a pair, embedded and central. They grew up with family activity at its peak. They watched older siblings grow big hair and shave their heads, sit out the game on the bench and score the winning point, explain with straight-faced logic why the family car was ticketed at a teen kegger, fall in love and out of sorts, skip school and graduate as valedictorian; they learned that high school led to college and a trip to the airport and, if they were lucky, some loot left behind on the bedroom floor.

These two daughters were the heart of the family, the bridge between our youthful ignorance and the older, wiser parents we wished ourselves to be. They were the dividing line, too, between the older siblings and the younger ones who were underfoot and into their things. The division elevated Alane to the position of oldest of the younger kids, with its confusing combination of restriction and responsibility. *Why do the four oldest kids get to go to the concert at the Astrodome?* she wondered on our family trip to Houston. *Why can't I . . .* fill in the blank. But if we skimmed her off the top, Monica would insist on her rights, too, and we'd have an insurrection on our hands.

The quirk of birth order put to advantage Alane's co-operative disposition. Sensitive and loyal, she was the child who picked up my mothering slack. She made intricate gingerbread houses, improvised doll clothes, washed jam from fingers, played the piano to the tune of younger siblings' demands, read and rocked and helped and cared. Her maternal tendencies somehow seemed connected to the fact that her birthday always hovered around Mother's Day, her due date. The year she was seven, she gave me a box of Cracker Jacks and a homemade card with this message: "I hope you have a happy Mother's Day. I had a happy birthday. Mother's Day makes me feel just like a Mother. I love you very much. Love, Alane Tranel."

But now she's taunting my dreams with swaddled snakes. In waking life, she's thirty, married five years and expressing no interest in feeling just like a mother.

I tell myself she's a carefree sixties kid "doing her thing" as a psychologist in the Psychiatry Division at the University of Iowa Hospitals, that the world has more to gain from her research on schizophrenia than from another child, that she and her husband are creative in ways beyond biology. I tell myself that she'll have her fling at freedom and discover it's another word for nothing left to lose.

It's not that I expect her to affirm my life by imitating it. A different thought nags me: I'm to blame. I've made her barren by my demands. By burdening my daughter with premature responsibility, I've robbed her of desire and spoiled for her the sweetness of mothering.

Ah, desire, the culprit lurking beneath so much human suffering. But isn't it also the stuff dreams are made of, what Augustine meant when he said, "Our hearts are restless until they rest in thee," the patient hope that allows the apple to ripen to fullness on the branch and the child to blossom beneath her mother's gaze, the yearning that causes us to imagine possibilities and strive to achieve them?

"WHAT YOU SEND FORTH into the lives of others comes back into your own," my mother threatened throughout my childhood. I say threatened, not promised, because she didn't apply those words to my good behavior, which, by the law of averages, surely occurred occasionally. Out it came, though, whenever I sassed her or fought with my sister, or ignored the whistle she blew to call me home from the neighborhood. No doubt she said it the day I bit the hand of the dentist trying to pry open my clenched jaws. But when I was five and avenged some childhood slight by smuggling a paring knife into the living room and carving the buttons from a brand-new overstuffed chair, I heard only silence, that terrible calm between the deed and its discovery.

I was my mother's trial and delight, the cherished infant she paraded up and down the street in an extravagant new buggy purchased by my frugal father for me, his last child. I was the young girl who, according to my mother, required a spanking every week or so just to "clear the air."

In the book of babyhood memories she kept for me, my mother wrote: "At sixteen months, she walks and talks and climbs like a two-year-old. She can say, 'I want down. I want a bite. Bad baby.' And a number of other words." Bad baby! Bad? For wanting down? For wanting a bite? Or for saying so?

I was too young to know that offering the fruit, not asking for a bite, was the silent feminine task.

"SHAME ON YOU," says the fortyish, bearded man I met an hour ago in a poetry workshop at the University of Iowa. I'm in Iowa City for the 1995 Summer Writing Festival. It's taken me four decades to travel the ninety miles from Dubuque, my hometown on the oak-burdened bluffs of the Mississippi, to the literary mecca of Iowa City, where, once upon a time, I imagined studying journalism and rubbing shoulders with writers at the university's Writers' Workshop. But the small city in the midst of Midwest cornfields was a den of liberalism and debauchery, verboten to a naive seventeen-year-old Catholic girl who was bound to lose her religion and virginity in the same night. Now, safely past seduction and my prime, I'm here striving to *become* a virgin in the original understanding of the word, the emphasis not on chastity but on self-possession, whether or not a woman trusts herself and can connect to others without silencing her own voice. But the compelling reason is that our daughter Adrienne will be a senior in high school this fall. In a blink, I'll be at the airport gate waving good-bye to our last child.

But now I risk ostracism. "And how many children do *you* have?" an ebullient woman has just asked me in front of all twelve people in our workshop. I hesitate. Admitting the truth is tantamount to strolling into a Sierra Club convention and proclaiming myself a clear-cutter. "Five daughters," I say at last. When she digests that, I add, "And five sons." Before anyone can ask if I'm Catholic or Mormon, I mention my home in Montana, where there are only three people per square mile. Usually, the Wild West theme takes the conversation down another trail.

But this group won't be detoured. Eyes widen as they fathom the number ten. "Did you *want* a large family?" someone asks in a tone implying masochism, ignorance, religious fanaticism. "Or was it some kind of *spiritual* quest?" This incredulity suggests that a trip through hell with Virgil may have been Dante's way to salvation, but modernity offered alternatives: mountain retreats, yoga, birth control.

Other comments are more sensed than said. The flicker of an eyebrow that accuses me of selfish disregard for the welfare of our planet. A sudden silence that implies I've polluted the Earth with progeny, been a pawn to the patriarchal system, lived vicariously. And then the *Shame on you*.

"Why *did* you have ten children?" an elderly poet asks straightforwardly over dinner that evening. His résumé includes several volumes of acclaimed poetry, prestigious awards, tenure at this respected university, and one daughter.

Why must I explain myself to his poised pen? Others aren't asked to defend their chosen mode of creative work. Instead, they proudly trace its origin. "Every night for an hour, my mother sat on my bed and read to me," a writer tells his audience. "I remember the sound of her voice as I lay beneath the blankets listening to *Great Expectations*." Others say they have no peace unless they produce words or lines or colors. They publish chapbooks and schedule art shows.

I have no memory of my mother reading to me. Instead, there were those grim accounts of lonely men, mothers dying young, the lost babies behind the perpetual grief in her sister Bertha's eyes. "There's safety in numbers," was a slogan she wove through our lives. As a teen, I took it as a warning not to go off alone with a boy. Now I wonder if it was a conclusion arrived at through loss, an insurance policy against devastation.

"A lust for life," I tell this poet now, referring to the childbearing-as-antidote-to-death theory that Jung has persuaded me is part of my unconscious intent.

"What about the life of your mind, your creative interests?" he counters. "If you lusted for life, I should think you would have no children." Obviously, he doesn't limit life to a physical seed planted in the dark recesses of a female body. Nor does he intend to let me off the hook with psychoanalytic jargon.

I confess to my interrogator that the demands of mothering have put my interests on hold for a few years. "So long, in fact," I say with a laugh, trying to make light of it, "that I'm no longer sure what it was I wanted to do when I finally had time to do it."

"Aha!" he pounces.

I've laid tile and hung wallpaper and hand-churned cream to butter and made prom dresses and curtains and coats and peace and bread; I've packed up every spoon and plate and sock and book in the house and moved more than a dozen times; I've bitten off more than I could chew and kept on chewing; I've been absorbed, frustrated, fed up and happy, but I can't explain myself to this man.

WHAT COMES TO ME the next morning when I wake in the humid underworld of my daughter's Iowa City home is the sweet scent of apples. Upstairs in her sunny kitchen, Alane industriously peels and slices and simmers the wind-falls we picked up yesterday at an orchard north of town. They were blown too soon from the branch by a recent storm and bruised in the fall, and there's no waiting for the right mood or moment to salvage them into sauce. Wind-falls won't keep.

Out there in yesterday's wet abundance, I couldn't decide what held more promise, the apple-laden trees, or the radiant blue eyes of the white-haired couple who own the orchard. Chug, the ruddy-cheeked husband, de-scribed it as a "hobby gone out of control." He belongs to the follow-your-bliss-and-the-money-will-follow school of thought, although the money was taking a long time to catch up, said his wife. It was a wistful project that appeared to have less to do with the bottom line than doing work they could pronounce good. And now their orchard boasted two hundred varieties of apples, and couples were scheduling autumn weddings beneath the ripened fruit.

Chug's satisfaction seemed tied to the metaphor of apples. Long before cane sugar became cheap and common in the United States, he told us, apples were the main source for the experience of sweetness, a taste universally appreciated. Sweetness came to symbolize what was choice and satisfying. People desired it; possessing it brought fulfillment; apples offered it. And so did Chug.

"Mom, I can see that glint in your eye," Alane said. "You're thinking there's a poem in this, I bet."

I was thinking that breast milk is sweet. And that a nursing newborn can see as far as its mother's face. And that perhaps this is where desire begins, in the nourishing promise of a mother's gaze upon her child. But I was edgy about this subject with her, so instead I smiled and said, "There's a poem in everything. But it's like bliss and money: sometimes the lines come a long time after the idea.

"Wait," I called to Alane as she began scooping apples into a bucket. "I want to take your picture." She paused under a branch and smiled at me through the focus and click. "Good," I said, and then again, "Good." I meant her pose and smile and the light in her eyes, the reality of her, and of Chug, too, and all the desires consummated in this sweet fruit.

On the way home, Alane and I tried to account for the apple's bad reputation—Eve with her tempting fruit, Snow White's envious stepmother and her poisoned apple. Alane said she'd read that the apple in the Garden was an erroneous assumption that went back to the Middle Ages. It would have been too hot for apples in that part of the world. "If Eve offered Adam anything, it was probably a pomegranate."

That evening in the kitchen, Alane's husband, Chris, who was trying his hand at grafting apple trees, told us that the taboo connected to apples might be due to the small amount of cyanide in the seeds. "Apples don't 'come true' from seed," he went on. Every seed grows into a completely new variety, often neither attractive nor good to eat. "So if you want edible apples, you have to plant trees grafted from proven, known rootstock."

"It sounds a little like the family tree," I said. "In-laws are the rootstock. So you'd better get to know them. . . ." I let my words trail off, wishing they would vanish altogether. Chris and Alane had been married almost a year before he met the formidable tree that is her family.

When I glanced at Alane, I saw hidden deep in her eyes a remnant of the expression in the photograph she sent to us after their wedding six years ago: she and Chris in bridal dress smiling beneath a leafy branch. Inside her smile lingered feelings too complicated to untangle: her happiness, certainly (her love for Chris, the hopes they held together, the beauty of that June day in Iowa), but also sadness and a teary incomprehension of her family's absence. Why had the people who claimed to love her chosen not to participate in the joy of her wedding day?

MY INSTINCT this morning is to go up to the kitchen and help, but Alane shoos me away, reminding me that the child I'm here to care for is my inner one, the neglected waif who wants to be a writer. I retreat downstairs and reach for my notebook and pen and scribble a few words, but my attention wanders in maternal spans and comes to rest on shadowy shapes in the corner. "Chris's pottery," Alane explained the other day when she brought me here, opening up the futon, apologizing for its lumpen character, wishing me an enjoyable stay, then gesturing toward the piled vases, platters, and bowls. "That's his passion. But then there's anthropology, gardening, photography, and his work as a counselor." I lift a teapot now and turn it around, noticing the uneven run of glaze, the accidents of the kiln that create the distinction and the beauty.

"I LOVE the Catholic Church," Alane had written to me in early spring of 1989, "and that's why I'm so disappointed when we let archaic rules control us. I know there are ideal ways of doing things, but we're not always ideal and things don't always go the way we want."

The issue started out this way: Chris had been married before, a childless marriage that had been over for several years, but a hindrance to a sacramental marriage in the Catholic Church. Alane took their quandary to a priest who laid out church regulations: locate Chris's first wife; conduct interviews; obtain records; find proof of some flaw that would render that first union invalid in the eyes of the Roman Catholic Church—a psychological or spiritual impediment, impotency, a criminal past that would clear the way for a Catholic ceremony. Alane, honoring her own and our beliefs, tried to comply.

We exchanged letters and telephone calls. "If I can't have a 'sacramental marriage' it won't be the end of the world," she wrote. "I'd like to do it in the church but I'm going to do it either way. I'm not angry (yet!) but I don't have a lot of patience for these kinds of things—is man made for the law, or the law made for man?"

Her patience gradually thinned to the determined core she'd revealed as a child in her high chair. Twice she'd held her breath until she fainted. Fury, explained Spock when I ran frantically to my reference shelf, self-preserving passion, seen more often in "a baby who's unusually happy at other times." *So far, no further,* she was saying. *So much, no more.* Inside the amiable child lived a resolute spirit.

That spirit surfaced at strategic moments. After one semester of graduate school at the University of Wyoming, she came home for Christmas and announced that she did not intend to go back. Decision made. No discussion. She was twenty-two. She trusted her own judgment but not her

ability to cope with the onslaught of opinions she anticipated from her family.

Ultimately, she relied on her perceptions regarding her
marriage, too, answering her own question about the law
by refusing to endure the inquisition. She abandoned the
prospect of a Catholic wedding. She loved Chris and would
marry him in June in a nondenominational chapel on the
university campus. Her letters began to emphasize the
simple nature of the anticipated ceremony. She hoped
we could make it. The traditional, typically anxious meeting between beloved and parents was never arranged. This
indifference confused me. She seemed hesitant, even reluctant, to involve us, as if our presence might be discon-
certing.

The worried discussions Ned and I held about our
daughter—was she uncertain about her marriage? resentful
toward us? acting out of fear?—created an oasis of unity
during a time of friction. I had finally screwed up the
courage to buy a house in town, a move I'd begun psychologically a decade before, but one that complicated Ned's
ranching pursuits and put us at anxious odds. Now we
agreed: Alane was striving for independence. It was like
leaving graduate school—she feared family entanglement
would bring distress to a decision she'd considered, believed
to be right, and intended to carry out. And so, we would set
her free.

When Alane married Chris Smith in that campus
chapel on June 21, 1989, the only family members present
were Monica, the maid of honor, and Dan, who lived in
Iowa City. We remained in Montana, feigning confidence.
But I was anguishing and unsure, denying every instinct in
my soul.

I'm anguishing this morning, too, while upstairs Alane
is humming happily in her kitchen, as if she's forgotten or

forgiven, as if she no longer grieves or wonders why? why? and why? while down below, I'm hostage to apple-scented memories and at a loss for words.

IN AUTUMN, MY mother's clothing carried the scent of apples, the Jonathans and Winesaps and Gravensteins that she kept in bushel baskets in her closet because it was the darkest, coolest place in our house, a small, unlit space under the eaves where her dresses hung, shadowy garments she slipped into and out of surreptitiously. As apples sweetened in the dark, my mother practiced the Victorian modesty preached to her while my father waited. In the morning he waited at the kitchen table and read from his prayer book as a pot of coffee brewed on the stove, and upstairs my mother dressed for the seven o'clock Mass. This was the way they began each day together. At night he waited in their double bed beneath the crucifix on the wall while, sequestered, she removed her housedress and cotton slip, unhooked the corset with stays, unfastened garters and stockings, and put on a flannel nightgown, then pinned to its collar a small cotton bag containing medals blessed by the priest, images of St. Jude, St. Anthony, the Blessed Virgin Mary, holy reminders of man's dark wait.

"WAIT," I CALL to my daughter Alane, who is scampering across the yard. "Stand over there, under the apple tree. Yes, yes, right there, under the branch with all the blossoms. Look, you match the flowers." She jiggles to a stop and looks down at her new playsuit, up at the branch, down again. Her right hand clutches birthday treasures: a bright card, a mesh bag full of plastic sandbox toys. Her left hand fiddles with the hem of her new playsuit. She tilts her head and sends me a shy blue-eyed smile. I catch it with the camera's click.

Today is her fifth birthday, May 13, 1969. A week ago, her playsuit was a length of cotton on a bolt, tiny cream-colored flowers and green leaves sprinkled over a peach-colored background. While buds opened on tender branches, I snipped and stitched and seamed, and, at ten p.m. last night, after baths and milk and cookies and prayers and poems and stories and drinks of water and trips to the bathroom and drinks of juice this time and my muttered prayers for patience as I maneuvered the bedroom door to the precise angle prescribed by the pajama-clad dictator inside the room, I sought the solace of needle and thread and finished hand-sewing the hem.

And now there they are: the apple tree, the homemade playsuit, and my five-year-old daughter, all abloom. I boost her up to pick a blossom. When I tuck it into her hair, the musky fragrance recalls my mother's hair, and, in that moment, my mother's sitting once more at the kitchen table and I'm standing behind her coifing the thick waves she took such pride in even as gray silvered into snowy white.

A few days after the photograph, mountain snows blanket every branch and bud with white.

"WAIT FOR ME," I tell Alane in mid-June as she dances up and down at the door. Dressed in the playsuit she's worn faithfully since her birthday, she's as restless as a willow in a windstorm, eager to climb into the car and drive the ten miles to Sheridan for the annual town birthday celebration for children turning five. Three-year-old Monica begs to go along. I ply her with the promise of a treat, then repeat child-care instructions to Ned, whose amiable head nodding, meant to reassure me, escalates my anxiety over leaving behind my nursing baby, eight-month-old Paul. Ned's child-care methods differ from mine, reflecting our temperaments and—unwittingly—Mayan Indian wisdom, too:

a mother should hold the baby close so he knows the world is his; a father should take the child to the highest hill and show him how broad his world can be.

Ned is a fervent follower of the highest-hill philosophy, but sometimes he simply sends several children up there to look around for themselves while he busies himself in the foothills. He's watching them, he tells me when I protest. This laissez-faire approach seems more male than female, at least this particular female with her bothersome imagination.

After four or five children, though, it's difficult to keep track of who's where when and why, which complicates anticipating what might happen to whom and how. Gradually, I'm giving it up. Or maybe Ned's optimism—he hasn't a drop of Irish blood—is rubbing off on me. "Try it," he says to both daughters and sons. "Go for it. You'd be good at that. Sure, climb that mountain. I'll be right here at the bottom if you need me!"

Even as I chafe against it, I appreciate this quality in my husband. Every snowfall summons him outdoors to construct snowmen with the kids. "Make 'em big," he calls as they scatter to roll snow. "Hustle. That's the way. Keep going." He drives up with the tractor and mounts the mammoth balls into a sixteen-foot snowman, a frosty Francis Bacon soaring over nature. But Alane and Monica subdue the snowman beneath an old-fashioned shawl and babushka, lest he forget the female hands that formed him or tomorrow's sun that could finish him off.

In spring, Ned rounds up children for backyard baseball, a game with one simple rule: every pitch is a strike. The results are simple, too: every kid learns to swing.

My dad provided care and constancy, but he was too weary to hike to hilltops or toss outlandish possibilities my way and yell, "Swing!" My outdoor activities were tame and often solitary. In summer, I took dolls on picnics and the city bus across town to the public swimming pool. In winter, I trudged with my sled to a farmer's hilly field and stayed until my fingers ached from cold. Other days I rode the bus to the city ice rink, where I pinched my feet into a pair of misfit skates and wobbled round and round until dusk. Eventually, loneliness and discomfort sent me into the kitchen for warmth and light and mothering.

When Alane scrambles into her usual backseat spot in the car, I invite her up front. She frowns and hesitates. "Yes, I mean it," I repeat. "Up here with me." She bounds over the seat and plops down to ponder me. I pat her pink knee. "Ready to go?"

She chews on her lower lip and eyes me as if recalling warnings not to ride with strangers. She wiggles closer to the door.

"What's wrong?" I ask.

Her solemn eyes follow my fingers turning the ignition key.

"We'll have fun," I assure her. "All the other kids will be five years old, just like you. And there'll be a clown with balloons. And cake and ice cream and . . ."

"It's just that . . ." She glances into my eyes, then down, her dark lashes fringing her cheeks.

"Just what?"

Cautiously, she turns her blue eyes toward me. "It's just that . . . I've never been alone with you before."

My hand stops with the half-turned key. Can this be? In the five years since her birth, can it possibly be true that she's never spent time alone with me? I scour the days just past. Friday, Thursday, Wednesday, back to the stolen hours of sewing, when she was the only child in my thoughts. As I fit the collar to her playsuit, pinned in the zipper, measured the hem, I recalled the November of my pregnancy, when the nation reeled with news of our murdered president. Through my private months of waiting, the public mourned, and then it was May, the quintessential day of her birth, nearby church bells ringing evening Angelus, the sound of God becoming man, melodious and faint, drifting across a lawn laden with lilacs, the startled cry when she came from my body, the marvelous grace of a fifth healthy child, the joy of taking her home to four eager siblings and settling her on the dining room table to slowly unwrap her before their fascinated eyes. Afterward, we staged an impromptu holding ceremony, when each of them took a rapt turn sitting next to me on the sofa to cradle her in their arms.

Inside the cover of Alane's Memory Book, I pasted a poem from a magazine page, "Song for a Fifth Child." "Mother, oh mother, come shake out your cloth!/Empty the dustpan, poison the moth . . . Where is the mother whose house is so shocking?/She's up in the nursery, blissfully rocking." But it was the last verse that expressed the lesson my fifth child brought: "Oh, cleaning and scrubbing will wait 'til tomorrow,/But children grow up, as I've learned to my sorrow./So quiet down, cobwebs. Dust, go to sleep./I'm rocking my baby. Babies don't keep."

How, then, can the words my daughter just said be true? *I've never been alone with you before.*

"I have an idea," I say. "Today let's pretend that you're the only child in our family."

Her eyes widen. "At the birthday party? You mean you're not gonna tell people that I'm Number Five and I'm five years old?" This is the clever remark I've been making for the past month, but now I hear only a callous echo: *Number Five.*

"Today you can be Number One. The one and only," I tell her.

She looks out the window and seems to consider this idea, then asks, "But what would happen to Monica? Would I have to sleep in that big bed all by myself?"

"You'd still have Susie." Susie is her bedraggled doll whose stiff sprouts of hair suggest either an aggressive hairdresser or a recent shock. Her staring, chronically open right eye makes her the perfect guardian for the two little girls she sleeps between.

"But if I didn't have any brothers and sisters, who would I play dress-up with? And hide-and-seek?" She turns suddenly toward me and gasps. "What about my birthday cake?"

"What about it?"

"I couldn't tell the kids at the party about it." I'd baked a large sheet cake, cut it into pieces to form the letters of her name, frosted them, and inserted a candle in each one. A-L-A-N-E, proclaimed the chocolate cake. The converging fives pleased her: she was the fifth child with five letters in her name and five candles on her birthday cake. Now she's silent for a minute, then wrinkles up her nose and shakes her head. "I don't like to pretend stuff that's not true."

Playing dress-up was one thing, pretense another. No sophistry for this child.

BUT FOR a few hours, she truly *is* my only child. As she collects a yellow balloon from a red-nosed clown, I admire the delicate hue of her eyes and imagine. Instead of being crowded into the chair with three or four others, she nestles alone in my lap. While we rock, I croon a lullaby meant just for her. Surely this sweet-glancing girl would secure an indulgent yes to everything. *Of course, darling. Certainly.* There would be nothing handed down or homemade for this child. Instead, everything brand-new and brand named.

Every morning I would brush her luxuriant blond hair, then dress her up and send her out to be the apple of the neighborhood eye. And oh, the toys! Dolls with both eyes wide open. At the end of the day, I'd sit at her bedside and read stories until I heard her rhythmic breathing. Gently, then, I'd cover her and stand trembling at my risk: in losing her, I would lose everything. But here my imagining breaks down. Loss can't be divided by five, only multiplied.

Through the afternoon of clowns and birthday cake and cart rides, her words haunt me: *I've never been alone with you before.* Beneath them, I hear yearning and, beneath the yearning, a plummeting sense of some careless trait in me I'd rather not acknowledge.

But I have proof of the promise: a photograph of my rosy-cheeked daughter smiling beneath the blossoms of her fifth birthday, a remnant of flowered fabric from her play-suit, and the lingering nickname that began as my song for my fifth child.

"Little Baby Ruffle-Bottom pulling on her toes, she'll upset herself and somersault and fall right on her nose," I chanted to her when she was a plump eight-month-old baby dressed in ruffled leotards that she insistently tugged off, toppling herself in the process. The other children playfully repeated it until it evolved into a nickname. "Bommer" is the name her siblings still affectionately employ.

One of the ways I expressed love was through sewing, something I began as a means to an end the summer after our marriage when our student budget had little leeway for the maternity clothes I needed by then. Sewing, I discovered, satisfied my desire to look at the spent day and see some accomplishment and yet be present to my children. Anything that required focus—a telephone conversation, reading, simply thinking something through—quickly incited children to riot, but whenever I was anchored to a sewing machine, they played nearby in a contented make-believe world of trains and blocks and hospitals for one-eyed dolls.

And so it was that I created the outfits Monica still refers to as their "Big Sneeze" suits. They were inspired by a childhood story in which a man habitually sneezes so violently that everything within range flies asunder. Hats and noses and ears and clothes shoot upward and land askew, hair on the wrong head, an ear where a nose should be, one person's sleeve on another person's arm. I applied the idea to outfits for my middle daughters, using the same pattern for each, but intermingling two different fabrics. The right sleeve of Monica's top matched Alane's bodice, for example, and the yoke of Alane's bodice was like the left sleeve of Monica's top, and so on. Each outfit was similar but unique, like these two sisters who shared the same genes and bed and many traits, but were very different girls.

THE FIFTH CHILD is lucky, I thought, as I watched Alane's temperament unfold. Cheerful, but vulnerable to a stern glance or chilly word, she needed only a nudge in the right direction. We took her in stride. Benign neglect, I called it, consoling myself when mundane chores cheated me of time and energy for her. Sensitive to the demands on Ned and me, she made few requests. The Christmas she was seven, she set out the toys she'd received the previous year and advised Santa in a note that she needed nothing more. But the yearning spirit inside the sacrificial child had the last word: "P.S. Santa, if you have something special in mind, it's okay to leave it." That same year she promised to practice faithfully if she could take piano lessons. And she did.

She was the child called in from play, summoned home

from roaming thoughts and meandering fantasies: *Will you diaper the baby? Make a pudding? Take your little sister for a walk?* And she came. Always, she came. And veiled any resentment from my eyes. Until the summer she was fourteen and in the throes of that baffling, sometimes downright grim phase when the most charming child turns into a self-centered monster growling by day and prowling by night. After suffering through two or three of these creatures, you grow accustomed to scowls and sulking. And if you have younger children, a three-year-old, for example, who wants you and you alone to tuck him into bed and listen to his prayers, your self-esteem endures. Alane's sullen silence seemed right on schedule. I failed to understand that she was mute with confusion, her pulsing body overwhelmed by the shadow of my pregnant one. "I don't know why Mom needs to have another baby," she whispered one night to Monica in the other bunk bed. Years later, I learned that my pregnancy had fallen like frost on her budding sexuality, cheating her of time and tender motherly attention as my focus turned inward on my tenth child.

Before I had time to put the photographs recording all this into an album, or even to process it in my own heart, she was eighteen and on her way to the University of Notre Dame.

IT WAS the classic fall scene: parents and college-bound child at the airport gate, bulging luggage, reminders to phone and write, jokes about sending food and money, hugs and kisses, tears swallowed with cavalier remarks about fall break coming soon. In that interlude would come plaintive, amnesic phone calls in which the home and family she claimed to miss would bear no resemblance to the one she was now so eager to leave. We talked of trivia and a hundred unimportant things. And then she detected my tears.

"I thought you were jaded," she teased.

Jaded? Older, yes. A bit more tired. But jaded? So this was the memory she was taking with her: a spent, depleted mother sending her fifth child off to college, the child she was never alone with simply waved away, like a moth from the flame.

I returned from the airport to a house suddenly huge and empty. Four-year-old Adrienne took my hand and said, "Don't cry, Mom," but her words only brought more tears. Soon her small hand would be waving good-bye from the runway.

FOR THE SECOND summer in a row, I'm lodged in the subterranean bedroom of Alane's Iowa City house. I'm ready to take a break from the workshop routine—mornings spent writing, afternoons critiquing, and evenings attending readings at Prairie Lights Bookstore, where an encounter with a famous writer is entirely possible, if not in the poetry section, then certainly in the fiction aisle. It was there where Alane and I heard Jane Hamilton read from her novel *A Map of the World*. During the question-and-answer session, the novelist mentioned that her mother, Ruth Hamilton, had longed to be a writer and, in fact, had written the popular poem "Song for a Fifth Child." Alane touched my arm and sent me a sidelong smile. I put my hand on hers.

After a sultry week of clinging clothes, mushy crackers, soft newspapers, and air so wet I wanted to wring it out and hang it up to dry, yesterday's caterwauling wind churned clouds into thunder and lightning, and a storm marched in like a furious parent determined to settle the argument once and for all. The Saturday air is pleasant and promising good behavior.

Alane and I drive northeast to the gentle hills unrolling

south of my hometown, Dubuque. As a child, I would lie before summer's open window and search the horizon for the cross rising above the oak bluffs surrounding Mount Olivet Cemetery. I knew the cemetery by heart then from Sunday visits with my mother and dad, who planted flowers and prayers on the graves of relatives. The tall tombstones meant someone important lay below, like Bishop Linehan, whose stately stone provoked in me a desire to climb to the top, where I stood triumphant and defiant, sensing that hope belonged to the here and now, not the afterlife. But, always, my mother would spy me and scold, "Come down; that's no way to treat the dead." And down I'd jump and run to the grave, where she stood hovering over someone whose life was done while mine was all ahead.

This glacial garden is green, grass, bushes, trees, unrelieved green until your eye longs for its complement. And now I see it, the splash of red that is my daughter's maternity dress.

"Mom?" Alane calls from a few graves away. Is this a dream or a memory? Shall I answer yes or no? Am I the child in a blue straw hat hopscotching from one tombstone to the next while chanting the names of the people eternally at rest: Grace, Henry, Catherine, Elizabeth, James, Thomas, Mary Ann.

Or am I the daughter standing beside the coffin in the funeral home, trying to explain death to myself as well as to the two young daughters clinging to my side. And what shall I tell my mother's unsuspecting enemy now approaching—Anna, her German neighbor, grayer and slower, but still recognizable. "Look at her," I hear my mother grumble as she points to the east window. "She has her wash on the line, and it's not even seven o'clock."

"You've lost a good mother," Anna says simply, then glances down. "And are these pretty little girls yours?" Shall

I answer, *Yes, Alane is eight.* I touch her blond hair. *And Monica is six.* She buries her face in my skirt. Or is the answer no? No, not mine, because the moth's moment in the light is my moment, too. All around us darkness beckons and my daughters must enter it alone.

Or am I the woman being summoned now across the graves? "Mom? Here they are." Alane signals to me with her right hand. "Holmberg. Charles John and Anne Marie." Her left hand rests on the swollen belly under the gathers of her dress. Her eyes shine like a five-year-old's on the way to a party. Her thick French braid suggests a maiden frolicking through *A Midsummer Night's Dream.* But she's thirty-two, five months pregnant with her first child, and here in this cemetery with me.

Anticipating a child has roused her curiosity about uncles and aunts and cousins who've vanished into the earth where we now stand. The family tree is no longer a diagram in a book, but a living organism.

"I remember being with you at the funeral home," Alane says softly now, as we stand, one woman full of life, the other hoping to reclaim a life she didn't lead, at the edge of two rectangular depressions in the grass. "Wasn't your mother's dress dark green?"

Dark green, the color of a leaf lying in the shade, chosen from her shadowy closet to wear to Mount Olivet to lie down next to my father, waiting two long years. In spite of the closed face and set mouth of my mother's body in the casket that day, I saw the smile that lit her face. Instead of stilled fingers entangled in a rosary, I saw her busy hands slicing apples for a pie, cutting shortening into flour, deftly rolling out a crust. Before the casket was closed, I kissed her, but when my lips touched that stony cheek, I regretted it. I wanted to remember her warmth, the light in her eyes that gave away the love behind the scolding, the hopes she held for me if only I would keep the ribbon in my hair and say yes instead of no and stand quietly at the graveside instead of climbing tombstones.

Gradually, Alane and I locate family graves and recall the stories of uncles and aunts and husbands and wives, weddings and funerals, births and baptisms. She talks about Adrienne's baptism in the tiny country church early on Christmas Eve. "Did I ever tell you how upset I was the summer before she was born?" she asks.

"Monica did. A few years ago."

"Hector Protector." She laughs, referring to the nursery-rhyme title that describes Monica's tendency to insist not only on her own rights but also on Alane's. "But I'm glad she was."

"Your protector?"

"No, that Adrienne was born. Even though it seemed like a bad idea at the time."

"Amen," I say. I'm on the verge of telling her about that first prenatal visit when my doctor handed me a pamphlet on Down syndrome. The statistics on babies born to women over forty had haunted me all summer. But I know the vulnerability pregnancy brings and say instead that her new dress reminds me of one she wore in high school.

She tells me she had more nerve than talent as a seventeen-year-old when she played the organ at Notre Dame's Sacred Heart Church for Mike and Jane's wedding in 1981. This leads to talk of other family weddings—Elizabeth's in St. Patrick's Cathedral in Billings, Monica's outdoor wedding at the ranch, Ned Anthony's in a little country church last year—and then a silence that slowly fills with memories of Alane's phone call to me after she returned to Iowa from Ned Anthony's wedding. How hard it was, she'd said, to play the piano for that ceremony, to watch the entire family provide the love and support she'd longed for.

Beneath her tearful voice over the telephone, I'd heard the anguish of a child bewildered by arbitrary family roles, unfathomable decisions. *Why do they get to, and I don't? Why were you there for them and not for me?* A child who didn't ask Santa for too much, or for anything at all, but was willing to accept whatever he had in mind. A young woman who assumed her marriage outside the church to a divorced older man was the source of our anxiety that spring, and then retreated into her middle-child ways, subduing her own wishes rather than making emotional demands on those she loved. This was the trait that made all the difference even as I failed to appreciate it.

I remember telling her that day that we wanted to set her free, that we sensed her need to separate from the family. I remember using the word *detachment,* and how hollow and dry and meaningless it sounded. I remember crying, as I asked myself the questions she was asking me. Crying because I had no answer for either of us. Crying because there are some moments you can't relive, and some choices you do regret.

And I remember what I didn't tell her, that a few days before her wedding, Dan called and pleaded with me to change my mind. *How can you and Dad just not show up for your daughter's wedding?* How I had wavered before that reasonable question and the distress with which he asked it. I passed the dilemma on to Ned when he came home. We've been through this, he said. We've talked it over endlessly and analyzed it and made a decision. My waffling had trained him to hold fast; wallowing in indecision was torture for a man of action. If I had said, "I'm going," he would have, too; I know that now. But in the spring of

1989, that was a risk not in my repertoire. I'd grown up hearing there was safety in numbers. Sticking your head above the group was for heroes and saints willing to get that head lopped off. *My* urging, *my* discontent, *my* needs were behind the impending move from our Broadview ranch that year. And *my* head was sticking out too far for comfort.

I yearn to make sense of this to Alane now, but when I try to speak, I feel myself sinking deeper into this dark terrain. Unnerved, I laugh and change the subject. I tell her that her dad and I, still practicing our we'll-work-it-out philosophy, haven't selected a burial site. "I'm considering cremation," I say. "My ashes could be divided into ten so all of you could just carry me around. Perpetual motion instead of eternal rest. On the other hand, a final resting place might be more sociable. People could visit."

"Maybe love is like a resting place," she says, then tells me this is a line from the song she and Chris chose for their wedding. Her comment catches me off guard. So do her eyes, lustrous with tears.

"Alane, I don't know . . ." I begin, but I can't explain what I don't understand. All I have is conjecture, a little more distance and time. "I wish . . ." Nothing more comes, so I take her into my arms and we stand over my mother and dad, lying side by side, and between us forgiveness moves and so does the child within her.

A sudden snake slithers through the grass, switching around the tombstone and disappearing into green. "Just a garter snake," she says, turning to watch it.

"I'm not afraid of snakes anymore," I say. "Living with rattlers has toughened me up. Pay attention when you're on their turf. That's the key."

"'Watch for snakes.' That's what you said every time we went out to play. But once in a while, you'd forget, and then I'd feel scared, like maybe your warning was what kept us safe."

"ARE YOU the Mrs. Tranel who used to live on top of the hill in Ashland and had all those children?" asks the woman behind me in line at the boarding gate a few days later. I'm in Denver, connecting to the flight that will take me home to Billings. She's recognized the name on my luggage and explains that she used to live on a ranch on the Tongue River and remembers seeing our family at Sunday Mass at St. Labre.

Shall I answer yes? But that was twenty years ago. My children are grown. In another month, when Adrienne leaves for college, they'll all be gone. And I'm traveling alone, on my way back to a house in town, by way of an apple orchard and an Iowa cemetery. So is the answer no? But I *did* live on that hilltop. And my children did come from my flesh and desire and willingness. But *no,* after all. I'm not the same woman. As for my children—they were never really mine.

THE FOLLOWING SPRING, Alane telephones to ponder with me the dream she had the previous night. In it, Chris and their baby son, Kazimier, are sitting together on a sled at the top of a snowy slope. Alane gives the sled a hard push that sends them down the hill. In the distance, father and son dissolve into one great white serpent that plunges into the fertile soil of a farmer's field and disappears. Alane wanders alone, grieving and filled with fear, until suddenly the grave opens and delivers two white snakes. She takes them into her arms and gives them her milk.

"What do you suppose it means?" she asks.

Immediately, I see pink and blue bundles and the remnants of snakes swaddled as babies that she once offered to me in a dream. I see the statue of Mary with her foot upon the snake. And the images of great mythological goddesses with snakes entwined in their hair or standing breasts bared, arms outstretched with a snake in each hand, reminders of the power once held by the female deity. Patriarchal religions stripped away that power and cast the snake as the evil element in the Garden. Snake dreams are common, I've heard, whenever women begin to discover their own authority.

I've sometimes counted on my children to fill my life with experiences and meaning. I've been unsure of my feelings, afraid to take responsibility for choice making. I've lingered at the crossroads of life, knowing that to choose one way meant to give up another, but there was quiet Hestia kneeling on my midnight path, the virgin goddess of the hearth in the guise of my daughter, offering me reminders of my power. Hestia is the spirit urging women to pay attention to what matters to them, to choose rather than to acquiesce halfheartedly, to maintain inner quiet in the midst of everyday noise. She is the voice reminding the harried world that love is like a resting place.

She is the child asserting herself in the high chair, the five-year-old shyly but surely declaring what she sees, the fourteen-year-old retreating inward for clarity, the student leaving graduate school because she knows this is neither the time nor the place for her. She is the young woman who counts the cost, then chooses the path of her heart and learns along the way that sometimes it's more painful *not* to acknowledge desires, that reaching out with feelings to those who matter in our lives is a risk worth taking.

"I WATCHED the Grammy Awards for pop music last week while I was nursing Gisela," Alane writes to me a few weeks after the birth of their second child, a daughter, in 1999.

"One woman was wearing thigh-high boots, a short black miniskirt, and push-up bra and singing, 'I feel like a woman.' I thought, well, so do I. To reproduce and nurture a child, that's where our power is."

A few weeks later, her note shows a hastier hand. "It's going to be twice as hard to go back to work this time. Although I'm beginning to need adult contact. Having fantasies about a chance to read something other than Dr. Seuss."

Ultimately, it seems to me, if a woman is to possess her full power and not merely remnants of it, she will need to convince the world of what she knows: that love and work are not separate issues. Love is work. It tests character, exposes the core of our personality, confronts us with hurdles. In a patriarchal culture, it helps to have a father who will take his daughter to the hilltop and show her how wide her world can be.

ALANE HAS PLANTED her daughter's placenta along with a rosebush in her Iowa backyard. In winter, she plops down in new snow and makes angels with her young son; in summer, she splashes with her children in their tiny plastic pool, as if she's the oldest of the little kids with the perfect excuse to play. She treasures this time with her children, she tells me in letters; she wanted more of that with me. She writes that sometimes she feels sad about what we both missed.

My consolation comes when I see her unwrapped heart, open to longing, willing to care, not only for her family but also for herself, asserting her need for professional work, treating herself to a chamber concert on a Mother's Day afternoon, practicing new pieces on the piano after her children are in bed. Becoming a mother hasn't magically healed the hurt of "benign neglect" or anxious decisions, but it has shown her the fierce nature of parental love and the pangs parents suffer over not doing enough.

I recall the summer afternoon I dropped into her office to visit. She introduced me to a coworker who looked back and forth between us, smiling with delight. "I love seeing mothers and daughters together," she said. "The similarities in your gestures, smiles, tone of voice. But the differences intrigue me most. What separate women you are."

"Mother-daughter Big Sneeze suits," Alane said, smiling at me.

This is what I experience now when I look at Alane's two-year-old daughter, Gisela, whose blue eyes laugh like her mother's. She has the same female curves as Alane did as a child, the same sweet expression that compels you to pick her up, but when you do, she struggles and demands, "I want down." When Alane and I become absorbed in conversation and Gisela feels ignored, she commands us to "stop talking." In her crib is a quilt made for her by Alane's sister Elizabeth. I imagine Gisela grown up, spreading it out to show a friend, saying, "My aunt Liz made this when I was born. See this little piece of fabric—the peach-colored piece with the tiny flowers? It's a remnant from a playsuit my mother wore when she was a little girl. She told me her mother made it for her for her fifth birthday."

The remnant I will keep for myself is this: The Mother's Day note I received from Alane this year, when her May 13 birthday and Mother's Day *did* converge. "Happy Mother's Day!" she wrote. "I love the connection with my birthday—I'm your present. You're my present. Aren't we both blessed among women?"

Yes.

Backward Against the Stream
·
MONICA

"Mom, will you be home next Tuesday?" my daughter Monica asks casually, as if she weren't two thousand miles away, emotionally as well as geographically. She's calling from Camden, New Jersey, where she's just finished her second year of law school at Rutgers.

I hesitate. The silence between us fills with the residue of recent years, grievances both real and imagined, my sins of omission and commission, her prickly twenty-something independence superimposed on a middle child's fierce sense of justice.

She announces her plan to stop in Montana on her way around the world.

"Around the world?" I try to match her breezy tone while containing the deluge of questions on the tip of my tongue. Surely, she doesn't intend to drop out of law school

with only one year left. The fragile truce we've been nego-
tiating the last few years won't withstand candor. And candor has always been my strongest link with this spirited
daughter.

"Mom? Are you there?"

"That sounds exciting." The lie falls flat. "That you're
coming home, I mean."

"Coming *through*," she says. "To see everyone before
my trip."

"Through," I repeat. *Through*. Yes, with children, it's
always through. "It'll be great to see you," I say, and mean
it, even though I suspect the daughter I'm anticipating may
not be the person who arrives at my door.

"Actually, *we're* coming," she amends brightly. "Mike
and I." They're driving to the coast to take a ferry to Alaska.
They've heard there's excellent money to be made working
on fishing boats.

I swallow hard at the thought of a guy in tow. My
antediluvian thinking connects cross-country trips to love
and marriage. My daughter and this guy, Mike—whose
name is all I know about him—are planning to rent a car
and steer their uncommitted relationship through some of
the very same states where her father and I honeymooned
on our way to graduate school in Washington State. If
our older children indulged in such sprees, they shrewdly
kept it to themselves, an approach alien to Monica's ingen-
uous soul.

"So I suppose we'll need directions to your new house
in *town*." She's disappointed in our capitulation to town living, even though, until now, last year's move from the ranch
has had no effect on her life.

"We still spend weekends in the country," I assure her.
"And holidays." I hear myself apologizing for an anguished
decision I know was right. One after another, our children

were graduating and going off to college. Our youngest two were nearing adolescence. The complexities of a forty-mile commute to Billings to work and school—sudden snowstorms, complicated schedules, long days that brought home teenagers grouchy with hunger and fatigue—were no longer offset by toddlers playing in the yard. And the expanded ranch operation meant Ned spent frequent Saturdays on the place north of Roundup. More often than not I, the born-and-bred town kid, was the sole family member at home on the Broadview ranch.

Full-time mothering and rural living made hard work of pursuing interests I'd set aside and yearned to rekindle. Each spurt of frustration sent me off to town to explore solutions: apartments, rental houses, homes for sale. But always I came home humbled, reluctant to undo the way of life we'd worked so long to establish. One night after a storm swept through, Ben and I stood on the wet east deck, breathing the sweet aftermath of rain, watching stars splash in an ebony sky, listening. A coyote howled in the distant rims; a coyote chorus replied. Ben and I joined in. "We couldn't do this in town," he said. How, then, could we ever move? How could we leave behind this sky? A year ago, we compromised. Just as we'd done at Big Horn when we were unable to break clean and move on, we bought a house in town and kept our country place.

"Just so you don't sell the ranch," Monica cautions. "I might want to get married there someday."

So that's it. She's coming home to introduce her future spouse. Their trek across the continent is not altogether without commitment, a rationale I find more palatable.

She short-circuits my supposition. "Don't worry. I have absolutely no plans for marriage. But I want to show Mike where I grew up. Are any of the horses still out there? Maybe we can ride."

"Thumper," I say. "And Jack. And Tom."

"Really? Oh, I'm glad." She laughs with girlish joy. For a second after she hangs up, I think she really might be coming home.

OF THE PLACES we've lived since Monica was born—the Wyoming foothills of the capricious Big Horn Mountains, the vulnerable prairie town of Miles City, the untamed, pine-covered shale hills girdling Ashland, Montana—the ranch on the edge of the Bull Mountains is closest to her heart. She was a spunky ten-year-old in 1976 when we bought the twenty-four-hundred-acre wheat and cattle ranch north of Billings. Although small by western standards, the unbounded fields inspired in us a mysterious mix of significance and insignificance. So did the stars competing in the deep night sky, each one striving to shine brighter than the rest. Monica quickly discovered the highest spot on the ranch, the top of the grain bin, and regularly climbed there for celestial guidance.

As I settle the receiver into place, I wonder if she's remembering, too: summer swims when a sudden rain filled the ditch; stacking hay with brothers and sisters beneath the ardent August sun; those radiant winter days when gleaming ice enticed them to skate for miles on the Musselshell River. I see her astride a horse galloping full-speed across an unfettered field. I hear her pounding on our bedroom door in the middle of that summer night when the bats escaped the eaves. *Dad! There's a bat in my room!* For weeks, at dusk, we grabbed racquets and played frantic tennis as stray bats swooped through the house. I recall the car wreck that left Monica's seventh-grade classmate dead and sent her with paper and pencil to the grain bin roof to form her confusion into a poem.

Warmed by memory and anticipation, the problems of

those years dissolve like snow on a south slope. But I know the north slope, too, where misunderstandings, hurt feelings, and rivalries can linger in the unforgiving shade.

ON SUNDAY, Ned and I drive to the country. The truth is, it's been three weeks since we've weekended there. The tedious trip across the treeless alkali flats north of Billings gives us time to talk. He says it would be a "damn shame" if Monica quit law school now; he thinks she'd make an excellent attorney.

I agree. If a quick mind and a passion for fair play are requirements, she's qualified. She was the child who kept her eye on the three maraschino cherries in the can of fruit cocktail and made sure they were divided evenly. "This half is bigger. No, now that one is." She was the one always asking, "Why does she get more juice than me?" and "Why do the boys get to go outside before breakfast and the girls don't?" The boys in question failed to see milking the dairy cow at dawn as privilege or opening a snow-plugged road at twenty below as prerogative.

"He could be a psychopath on his way to jail," I grumble to Ned, meaning Mike Whoever-he-is.

"That's cheerful."

"Or a sweet-talker leading her down a dead-end road."

"She doesn't lead easily. He'll find that out in short order."

"Maybe we should have given her more rein. Or at least a room of her own."

"And her own TV and telephone and car. And more money and attention."

"Well, what do *you* think this trip around the world is all about?" I'm asking for his sincere insights as a psychologist now.

He exhales an unprofessional, fatherly sigh. "It's a fad.

Young people spend five or ten years roaming around the world looking for themselves before they settle down. Afghanistan, Timbuktu. You name it."

"Alaska."

He shrugs. "Yeah. Or Antarctica. Or Istanbul. But maybe it's for the best. Who knows what they want when they're twenty-two? Did we?"

"Twenty-four. Monica's twenty-four."

"Two, four, twenty-four. No matter. She's always managed to find a way to challenge the system."

"Swimming against the stream. That's what my mother called it." I recite the proverb. "Most any old fish can swim with the tide and drift along and dream, but it takes a real, live, strong one to swim against the stream."

"So that's why she's rowing backward on that river," says Ned.

"*That river* is the Schuylkill. And I recommend calling it by name when she's here. She told me rowing reminded her of being on the ranch. That she loves the early-morning quiet on the water. By the way, all rowers face backward when they're going forward."

"Huh! How do they know if they're coming or going?"

We pass the Broadview post office, and then the school, the one-story brick building where each morning for thirteen years, I dropped off grade-school children in varying numbers until we'd dwindled to an average American family, a boy and a girl.

"She challenged *that* system," Ned says, thumbing left.

Indeed. Running down the sidewalk after school. *I hate lining up and walking behind that poky teacher.* Incomplete math homework. *Why do we have to write down stuff if we can work it out in our heads?* Singing too loud in chorus. *I like to sing.* Singing too loud on the school bus. *I like to sing, and I think I sound good.* Singing in the hall. *I was happy.* Being too rowdy at recess. *Bobby is a sissy and a tattletale.* Lack of cooperation. *I don't see why I should tell some weird woman from Billings if I wear a bra or not.* (During a "growth and development" session at school, the public health nurse asked, "How many of you don't wear a bra but think you need one?" At the show of hands, she said, "If you tell your parents the other girls are wearing a bra and you want one, too, I can't imagine they wouldn't get one for you.") In seventh grade, Monica upset the status quo by signing up for Shop instead of Home Ec, a first in a community where wives routinely help husbands feed and fence and brand but gender lines were drawn around school power saws. Monica won her case and spent the semester constructing a shadow box and a precedent. The following year, two boys signed up for Home Ec.

She swam upstream, and we paddled behind when she absolved us from compulsory attendance at every single grade-school basketball game. Parents could be a pain, she said, implying that kids, unwatched, were free to play, not perform. But parental involvement—perfect attendance at games, unquestioning support of school athletic programs, taking the whole thing seriously—is the lifeblood of coaching careers. Early in the season, coaches rally parents to tell them what they've already told their kids: Love means being in the bleachers; college scholarships go to the athletically gifted. Imagining delinquent children and outlandish tuition bills, conscientious moms and dads turn kids' play into a solemn event. Even if we'd succumbed to this sales pitch, Ned and I couldn't have carried it off. We had other children with other needs—an infant to nurse, a preschooler with an earache, a high school junior needing counsel.

Still, we went to our children's games as often as possible. And saw things that troubled us. Knee braces on too

many young basketball players. Red-faced fathers screaming at referees. Kids clamoring to play but for some unfathomable reason sitting it out on the bench. While our kids
earned letters, we earned a reputation as dissidents. Our
kids were tall and strong and eager, but we kept missing the
point. We believed athletics and physical activity were critical. What better way for young bodies and spirits to recreate
and thus be *re-created?* Done to excess, however, sports
turned into one more source of stress. When teams traveled
long distances on school nights or in bad weather, we questioned priorities; when Friday afternoon pep rallies sup-
planted English or science classes, we considered the cost;
we worried that adults might be teaching children to rely
on an audience instead of on their own hearts for direction.

Ironically, by the time our youngest child graduated
from high school we'd attended more athletic events than
the most allegiant parents of smaller families. Football, volleyball, basketball, tennis, track—cross-country, distance,
hurdles, discus, javelin—and rowing, the sport Monica
took up in college after she injured her knee in pickup basketball. As we watched sports programs grow into greedy
monsters devouring more and more youthful time and energy, we developed convictions against using the school system as their keeper. Allocating more resources to perfecting
kids' hoop skills than to instructing them in life skills
seemed a shortsighted venture. Games were the social glue
holding communities together, but kids were paying the
price.

But sometimes as I watched Monica, an enthusiastic
athlete who literally and figuratively threw herself into the
game, I wondered if, despite her disclaimer, she equated
our imperfect attendance and attitude with a lack of love
for her.

Nor could I dismiss the role of the family football fanatic—my mother. I tell Ned now that I think my mother instigated the career plan Monica announced when she was eight years old. *When I grow up, I'm gonna be a Notre Dame football player.*

He darts a furtive glance my way. He's accustomed to my leaps in logic, but as he points out now, my mother died when Monica was seven.

I remind him of our first trip to the Midwest, when my mother took the infant Monica into her arms and flashed down her golden smile, all those front-tooth crowns sparkling like victory medals. As infant grew into girl, our yearly trips to my mother's Midwestern kitchen washed over Monica the same scents and sounds and spunk that impressed my childhood. I lapse into memories of my mother's defiant soprano: "Cheer, cheer for old Notre Dame. Wake up the echoes cheering her name." For my mother, whose Irish psyche was bruised by history, Notre Dame football was an entrée into mainstream America, a way of winning the ethnic war.

Saturday after Saturday, she spread her artillery on the kitchen table—bowls, rolling pin, pie tins, flour, sugar, plump Iowa raspberries—then fixed her ear to the voice rasping from the tiny radio on top of the old refrigerator: "The stadium's jammed here today, folks. Fans are rarin' to go as Notre Dame's undefeated Fighting Irish meet the undefeated Army Cadets."

She would bless herself, sling an apron around her neck, and tie it firmly at the waist. While the Irish made touchdowns, she would make pies. Throughout my childhood, the tribal battle raged on. When a pale, soft-spoken English couple bought the empty lot next to ours and planted their property stake deep in our Irish territory, my mother went into action. After dark, she darted out and carried it back to the boundary where it belonged. "English land-grabbers," she muttered the next time she saw a suspicious mound of fresh dirt. Sure enough, when night settled, out she went again for another ten-yard dash.

"Monica caught the spirit of the Fighting Irish," I say aloud. "But she didn't want to go to Notre Dame."

"Your mother should have arranged for a football scholarship."

"Too many siblings went there." I mean Dan and Mike and Alane. And Jennie had just finished her sophomore year there.

"And it wasn't far enough away," Ned adds.

Monica chose Georgetown. But we considered Washington, D.C., a huge, crime-ridden city utterly incompatible with our daughter's country naiveté, her love of solitude and outdoor activity. To say nothing of the tuition costs, a significant factor when two children are enrolled in private universities. When Gonzaga University in Spokane offered her a hefty scholarship in the honors program, we urged her to accept. She'd been imagining herself as a maverick at an East Coast school, and when we sent her off in the wrong direction to a college a brother had graduated from, a fault line formed between us.

"In our family," Monica will tell me years later when we talk about this decision, "even going away, separating physically, isn't enough." She saw the struggle to stand out as peculiar to her, when, in fact, sibling rivalry reflects the basic human condition: the tendency to compare, the wish to make the biggest contribution, the desire to matter more than anyone or anything else, the unspoken longing to be a hero.

How *does* a sixth child gain distinction in a family of ten? She can't even claim fame as *the* middle kid, because technically the fifth child is in the middle, too. The maraschino cherry problem shows up at every turn—making sure you get counted in. But parental love doesn't come from a sixteen-ounce can. It can't be divided and doled out in equal portions. Parents learn that when a second child is born. But children are hard-wired for justice. They believe in "show, don't tell."

Why then, do we mumble "Love you" at the end of every telephone call, "Love you" from offices and cars and supermarket aisles? Partly as a remedy for the mute affections of earlier eras, no doubt, but there's an anxious tone, too, as if hidden on the shelf amid the sugarcoated cereals is a social worker telling us to make sure our child feels loved. Or perhaps it's a subliminal nod to the reality that our lives are tenuous and our children precious and that no one may be at the other end of tomorrow's line.

RIDGES AND COULEES break up the dryland plateau that sprawls north of the Yellowstone River rims; pine trees emerge on low hills in the distance. We drive past the sunlit sandstone ledges that we recognize now as a rattlesnake den. Its discovery one summer triggered a range of proposals from impetuous high school boys: pour gas inside and burn 'em up; lure them out and shoot them. The compromise we settled on was presented, predictably, by our son Mike, the budding environmentalist. Now and then it might be necessary to kill a rattler straying onto our turf, he conceded, but we had no right to invade their den.

Just beyond the snake den is our turn, the mile-long gravel road leading to the Spanish-style house tucked into a northern slope. Slowly, we pass the corrals with their faded red fences.

"Fences need paint again," says Ned. "Haven't been touched since Alane painted them."

I count back. "When she was fourteen. The summer she was so quiet."

"How do you remember that stuff?"

"I was pregnant with Adrienne." He accepts this logic. My method of keeping track—by pregnancies and births and moods—is different from his but one he more and more often relies upon.

We take the short, steep hill where the rising moon once surprised me, so enormous and near I imagined driving through it.

Ned cites the spots that always drifted in; I point out the tire tracks leading through the ponderosa pines to the sledding hill where our kids flocked like sheep bundled in mismatched wool, unpaired mittens, clashing caps and coats, a resplendent parade of pragmatic rural fashion. Sadness waves through me as I realize that the places my children knew intimately—the Sledding Hill, the Dump Road, the Johnny West Coulee, the Christmas Tree Ridge, the sites they recall over holiday tables—are mere acquaintances of mine. When they went out, I stayed indoors to savor the solitude.

The courtyard door creaks open into the sunny space where petunias once grew. Ned says he'll make a round outdoors. I walk through the silent rooms. The dining room looks vast, the large table and twelve chairs are forlorn without the crowd, the conversations, the inevitable crash of a glass, the fuss over spilled milk, the birthday cakes and candles, the baby in a high chair smearing beets on her face. Flies—big, shiny black ones—buzz against the windows and thump against the glass door to the north deck. Two shades of brown merge on the deck rail. We never could match the color from summer to summer. I imagine stained knees and hands. I hear the child Monica ask, "Do I have to paint each slat? There are fifty-four."

Although we've moved the piano to town, its melodies haunt the living room. "Summer to Remember," Monica's resolute duet with Jennie. Schmaltzy stuff. Prophetic, too, shimmering with enthusiasm and wrong notes. I pause at the north window and look toward the Snowy Mountains, their timeworn, gentle peaks a dramatic contrast to the jagged, young Crazies to the west. Flies buzz in this room, too, up and down the glass. A dry wind stirs the pines, recalling the summer afternoon Monica raced into the kitchen, urging—*Hurry! Right now!*—out to the deck to watch the Holy Spirit coming through. "The wind!" she announced. "It's blowing really hard. Just like in the story we read this morning in vacation Bible school. And we're all gonna be sore with fear." I laughed and intoned in a Poe-like cadence, "'Tis the wind and nothing more." I reminded her that this hot wind came through regularly on summer afternoons, that soon a roll of thunder would tantalize the dry land with the promise of rain. "But it's all bluster," I said. "It means nothing." Excitement drained from her eyes as if I'd just doubted the existence of Santa Claus. I didn't know she was on the lookout for the Holy Spirit's action in her life, that irrefutable proof of her connection to grace, the magical potion that wins friends and influences classmates. She imagined herself reporting her dramatic sighting at tomorrow morning's Bible school, but my mundane interpretation ruined everything.

Like the wind teasing the arid ground with the chance of rain, Monica's telephone call taunts me with possibilities. The anticipated delight of her visit brings a nagging sense that I haven't done enough for this child, that I missed the brooding, sensitive nature beneath her bravado, that too often I mistook exuberance for rashness. I was prosaic when poetry would have served better, cautious when enthusiasm was called for, preoccupied when she needed someone to listen, and occupied continually.

But beyond all of this is the memory of Alane's wedding, and a decision Monica neither understands nor forgives. She'd put her allegiance squarely with her sister and taken Alane's hurt to her heart.

A few days after serving as Alane's maid of honor, Monica, despite excruciating back pain, competed in the U.S. Rowing National Championships at Indianapolis. That evening, she collapsed with a ruptured disc. A week later, she called to tell us that she'd had surgery and was doing fine. The disc healed quickly enough, but the fault line in our relationship bulged ominously.

LOVE LETS OTHERS be perfectly themselves; love doesn't try to twist another to fit his own image. Love is patient. Kind. Unconditional. Love never has to say "I'm sorry." But the north slope is real. And clinging to it is a chilling reality: human love *is* conditional; everything *does* depend. On sun and shade. On her touch. His tone of voice. A mother's aching feet. A father's tired heart. A first-grade teacher's glance. The words we hear and those that are said. What we do and what we wish we'd done. If I had allowed my heart and gut into the decisions of my head, if grandparents lived nearby, if we had more money, more courage, more help, fewer wants, if I'd paid more attention, if I'd transmitted serenity to Monica in utero instead of frenzied activity—painting rooms, tiling floors, striving to enlarge our too-small house at Big Horn before her birth—if we hadn't taught our children to march to their own drummer and then worried when we didn't recognize the beat, if I had bloomed where I was planted instead of restlessly seeking some ideal place, if being human wasn't a condition, yes, then I could have loved patiently, kindly, unconditionally. And there would be nothing to be sorry for.

BUT THESE FLIES, where have these flies come from? I hate their buzz, the sound of static. The house is taking on an empty odor. No bread bakes in the oven. No chocolate chip cookies cool on racks on the counters. No apple-scented hair spray drifts from the bathroom.

The back door slams. "Everything's fine outside," Ned calls as he comes through the rooms. "The horses are over in the north pasture. They have plenty of grass. Water, too."

"What are these flies doing here?" I demand indignantly, as if he'd invited them in. "And why are they killing themselves against the windows?"

"Bluebottles," he says. "Just trying to get outdoors where they belong. Can't blame them. It's stuffy in here."

"We should sell this place," I say, suddenly angry with the splatters and buzzing and stagnant air. "Why are we holding on to it? After Christmas . . ." I go off to the kitchen in search of a dustpan, then return to whisk up dead flies. Ned opens windows to let in the scent of pines and let out dazed flies while I inventory kitchen supplies and put fresh towels in the bathrooms.

How can you bear to live in that mess? I hear myself scold as I stand in the hall and look into bedrooms eerie with order. Rooms that expanded to accommodate drums and black lights, electric trains and bedtime buddies are now emptied of life. What was it someone told me—that the cervix is impervious to burning, tearing, cutting, that only contraction causes pain?

There's nothing more for us to do here today. We drive back up the gravel road, past the tire swing dangling lifeless from its rope. Beneath it, the grasses have grown thick and tall. Their colors are subtle with the season. Burnished yellows, greens fading to gray. The sun whirls and dances a last few frenzied measures before settling down beneath the golden blanket thrown across the fields.

"Maybe next spring would be a better time to put it on the market," I say, as we reach the highway and turn toward town.

Ned nods but says nothing. He's heard this wavering before. We're silent the rest of the way home. Or should I say "back to our house in town"? I no longer know where home is for us. Some say it's where your memories are. Or the place where you feel safe. Or where you grew up. What is the determining memory that pronounces one place home and not another? And where will our children go when they long to go back home, the way Ned and I return to the Iowa-Illinois bluffs along the Mississippi? In our restless search for the ideal place, we've left them with nowhere to call home.

AT ELEVEN O'CLOCK Monday evening, Monica calls to report that they're stranded in Rapid City. "The Volvo broke down," she says jubilantly, as if car trouble on bleak roads is part of their itinerary. "But we're covered by Triple A."

I tell her we can't wait to see her, that Adrienne has made chocolate chip cookies especially for her, that Ben has made a path through his room. She says they might want to stay at the ranch. If they stay at all. My heart thuds, but I manage a neutral-sounding, "Oh?" and then a cautious fact. "Adrienne is hoping you'll room with her."

She laughs. "Adrienne!" Her youngest sibling's name, nothing more, but I hear affection, amusement, and a tinge of something I can't pinpoint.

. . .

EARLY TUESDAY AFTERNOON, they arrive. My daughter, tan and fit, her dark, curly hair falling to her shoulders, and her traveling companion, Mike, who looks about her age, innocent enough, but not part of my mental bargain. I evaluate his muscular build, the shock of unruly brown hair that he flicks off his forehead with a shake of his head.

She gives me a vigorous hug. "Wow!" I say, and grasp her arms.

"From rowing." She flexes her biceps and smiles her wide, disarming smile. Tears threaten. I hug her again. "It's good to have you home."

"It's good to be in Montana," she says, as if letting me know that she defines home as mountains and prairies, not a house inhabited by her family. In fact, her current home appears to be the overstuffed gym bag sprawling by the front door.

She strides through the living room to the window and stands looking out at the small yard enclosed by a high wooden fence. Her fingertips dance up and down the glass like flies buzzing against a country pane. "No mountains," she says.

"But a park next to our backyard." I point to the grassy span between our yard and the elementary school. Scattered across the baseball diamond are skinny-legged boys in Little League uniforms. A sudden deep voice shouts to a small figure on the batter's mound. "That's the way, Timmy." Then, "No! Jesus! Don't do that. What's wrong with you?"

We sit in the sunroom and drink tea like polite, repressed characters from a Jane Austen novel. I volunteer photograph albums from Monica's childhood; she flips carelessly through years of work and worry, decisions, disappointments, joys. She squeals and points to a picture. A curly-haired little girl balances barefoot on the lowest slat of a board fence. Her back is turned; her diaper hovers near her ankles. Across the fence stands a lamb looking up expectantly.

I laugh. "Fluffy. Do you remember how you climbed up there every day to talk to him? 'Huffy,' you called him."

"But Huffy dropped dead. The night before the boys were going to take him to the fair. I thought it was because I told him not to go."

"Look." I catch another page and point. "You, playing school." A quintessential October day, the front yard of a rambling yellow house, five-year-old Monica hunched over, writing at an old school desk fastened to a second desk by wooden runners. How had those painted desks with their hinged seats and gaping, useless ink wells merited a trip in the moving van from Wyoming to Montana?

"I loved those desks," Monica says, as if I'd asked the question aloud. "Especially after you made me quit kindergarten."

"You make me sound like an ogre." I explain that taking her to kindergarten meant packing up two-year-old Paul, and unsettling Jennie from her cradle. "Besides, I thought it was better for you to be home." Home-grown children seemed to me a bit like homemade bread. Distinctiveness came from the variables—temperature, measurements, the hands that kneaded the dough.

She frowns. "The day after you took me out, the kindergarten kids had a picnic. And the day after that, Mrs. . . . what was her name, my teacher? . . . she dropped dead, and I thought it was because I dropped out."

"It was an aneurysm." I catch her gaze. "I had no idea you were feeling so responsible as a five-year-old."

She shrugs and laughs, but it sounds thin. "Well, how *could* you? I mean, you were always so busy."

I want to delve into this, but her finger has moved on to another picture. In it, seven children in first communion dress join hands to circle the altar of St. Labre Mission Church. Next to Monica, the circle breaks. "I had that huge wart on my little finger," she says. "It looked like a cauliflower. And no one would hold my hand. You kept telling me it would go away by itself, remember?"

"I was wrong. But that was my first experience with a wart."

"Mom's first wart. At least I was first at *some*thing."

Why can't I get it right with her? I should be better by now at sloughing off retrospective slights, overlooking the twentysomething penchant for shining a fluorescent light on parental failings.

Mike, weary of stories out of context, mumbles something about checking the tires on the rental car, and goes off. Monica roams about the house.

"This, I want you to know"—I gesture at the door of my study—"is my first bona fide room of my own."

"And these are your books? And your computer?"

I nod. "Another first." I show her the ex–laundry room, equipped now with easel, brushes, and paints. "I banished the washer and dryer to the basement," I explain. "Out of sight, out of mind."

She turns down the corners of her mouth in dismay.

"Appliances," I reassure her. "Not children." But when I sigh, she puts an arm around my shoulder.

"I'm glad for you, Mom," she says gently, as if caught in a moment of remorse, but it vanishes with her next words. "You really are a city girl at heart, aren't you?" Her tone implies a character defect and our move to this house a surrender to the easy life.

Upstairs, she surveys the two rooms at the end of the

hall, each with a queen-size bed. A half-worked puzzle is spread on Ben's desk; Fievel, star of *An American Tail,* stares at us from Adrienne's pillow.

"*They* have their own rooms, too! And their own beds! My little brother and sister, spoiled town kids. Where are they, anyway?"

"Ben's at football practice."

"In June?"

"The coach calls it 'open gym.' Football practice can't start *officially* until mid-August. But the kids lift weights all summer. The coach isn't supposed to coach. So he just sort of hangs out and hints. A great role model for how to cheat the system, wouldn't you say?" I roll my eyes and give away my unresolved questions.

"Oh, Mom, mellow out. Lifting's good for Ben."

"Not necessarily. There are issues of bone growth and—"

"Don't be such a grinch. Even Socrates thought sports were good for people."

"In tandem with fine arts," I say, surprising this college philosophy major with my bit of knowledge. "Can you imagine Socrates coaching Little League? Trying to talk with rabid dads about the Greek ideal?" I part the blinds. "There's Adrienne now." We watch her eleven-year-old sister coast into the driveway on her red-and-white bike. Her ponytail swings as she leaps off and races toward the house.

Monica meets her at the door, lifts her up, and whirls her around. Adrienne, wide-eyed, asks, "Do you realize how much I *weigh?*"

"Ninety pounds." She lifts her again. "And seven ounces."

"How did you know?" Admiration lights up Adrienne's face.

The two sisters shoot hoops in the driveway. From the kitchen, I see a wild ball land on the garage roof.

"Go after it, Adrienne," Monica urges.

Adrienne screws up her face and shakes her head. "I can't. It's too far up."

"Sure you can. Just climb up there."

Adrienne looks up, toward Monica, then up again. As if summoned, Mike pulls up in the Volvo. He boosts Adrienne onto the roof. She crawls the few feet to the ball and shoves it down.

Monica claps and cheers. "Way to go! I told you you could do it."

Adrienne glows. What a piece of work a big sister is!

Monica challenges her to a race to the park. As I watch them leap the small irrigation ditch behind our house, then vie for swings, I think of Jennie's comment one evening after she and several siblings biked the Cooke City Highway. "Why do we turn everything into a race? I started out to have fun, but all the way up, I found myself looking around to see who was catching up."

I prepare lettuce for the chicken sumi salad and set the table for dinner. When Ned arrives, he joins his daughters for a croquet match on our lawn. At seven, Ben stumbles in, mute with hunger, a rangy fifteen-year-old continually surprised by the size of his own feet. After dinner, when his speech returns, he tells us the coach wants him to keep lifting weights and get himself up to about two-forty so he can "do some real damage." Ned's eyes meet mine. We tolerated the tradition of inscribing a skull and crossbones on the helmets of high school kids who made a "good stick." We let pass the written critique a coach once sent out at season's end, praising high school kids for playing "hurt and injured." But this?

Monica hears our silent comment, looks at Ben, and

sends me a warning glance. "Adrienne beat me in every race," she says, feigning distress as she puts her arm around her little sister. Adrienne wiggles closer.

"Does running hurt your knee?" I gesture to Monica's left knee, scarred by two surgeries.

"Not really." She unhinges Adrienne and stands. "We have to get going." She says they need to leave this evening. Now, in fact, or they might not make it to the coast in time to catch the ferry.

No time for the ranch, then. No riding. No chance to talk. No bunking with her little sister. And no questions. Simply let her go. The child desperate to be counted in is now a young woman asking to be counted out.

I embrace her again and again, then turn and fake a broad-minded hug for him, this wet-behind-the-ears interloper audaciously assuring me that their venture is a good and necessary thing. Responsibility swells his chest as he tells me that by the end of summer, they'll have enough saved to pay for their around-the-world adventure.

When Monica gets into the car, I lean over and kiss her. Touch her hair. Her cheek. She spies my tears and laughs. "Oh, Mom. It's not like I'm going away forever." I wave good-bye and watch the jam-packed Volvo with its Triple A sticker disappear around the corner. *Damn this uninsured mothering life.*

THAT NIGHT, as I do every night, I sit on the edge of Adrienne's bed and listen to the concerns of her day. "Why did Monica leave so soon?" she asks. "Is she ever coming back?"

"Of course," I promise with more confidence than I feel.

"What was Monica like when she was little?"

"Rambunctious. Into everything. We called her 'Baby

No-No' because that seemed to be what I was constantly telling her." I explain that we chose her real name because she was born on the feast day of Saint Monica, who was the mother of Augustine. Saying this, I wonder if that tenacious woman who pruned her son with her prayers might have some pruning advice for me.

I tell Adrienne about the feisty eight-year-old who declared that she was neither girl nor boy, but "tomboy," free to fence shirtless in the sun rather than pod peas in the shade. And that in sixth grade Monica's favorite subject was mythology and she made a clay cup patterned after Socrates' hemlock chalice. I tell her about the grain bin roof. And the sandstone rock Monica and Alane called their Carving Rock. There, they etched their names and the dates of their first menstrual periods—one day apart. I'd prepared Alane, but Monica had taken me by surprise. I tell her about the afternoon Jennie and Monica rode horses and impulsively stripped off their clothes to trot, Lady Godiva fashion, through the sunlight. But a sudden audience appeared on the horizon, a group of cows, wide-eyed and drifting closer. They scrambled for shirts.

Adrienne giggles. "Tell me more."

"The day Monica packed for college, she wore a red hat."

"That's *all?*" She's seeing Lady Godiva folding clothes into a suitcase.

I laugh. "No, jeans and a shirt. *And* a red hat."

"Why?"

"She said red made her feel brave."

Adrienne's eyes glisten with tears. "I wish she was my sister. Now, I mean." She brightens. "Could I get a red hat?"

"That one's still here," I say, and kiss her good night.

. . .

FOUR LONG, SILENT months later, Monica telephones. She's in Seattle. Alone. In fact, she's been there for over a month, staying in a Jesuit retreat house.

She's fine, she assures me, fine. Happy, in fact. She's had time to think. And pray. And talk with a Jesuit priest in his late sixties, Jack Morris, who's become her friend and spiritual adviser. He's taught her an amazing thing: When you're lost, you're found. "Did you know that, Mom?" *When you're lost, you're found.* She asks if she might spend the holidays with us at the ranch before she goes back to law school in January.

DURING THE LONG, dark days before Christmas, before everyone else arrives, Monica and I linger over tea, this time not as polite, wary strangers, or as a mother fretting over her child's wrongheadedness, or a daughter mining the past for slights, but simply as two women learning to be friends. We go for walks and make Christmas breads. She plays the piano and sings carols, indomitable and off-key. Something's changed that we don't put into words, but it grows brighter and steadier, like the candles we light every night on the Advent wreath, one the first Sunday, two the second, three, and finally four, and then it's time to go to the ranch for the holidays. This year, I don't squander time protecting my quiet indoors, but flock with the other mismatched sheep to the sledding hill. Only once do I stay inside. In the middle of a Scrabble game, while my opponents go out to the east deck to howl back at coyotes, I steal consonants. Ned plays Monopoly and checkers and chess with anyone who'll accept his rules. Every evening, Ben puts on Yurii and goes outside to churn homemade ice cream that we eat later, shivering by the fire. We stay up too late and get up too late and talk too long over coffee in the kitchen. We argue dishwashing details via Post-it notes stuck on cupboard doors:

LOAD YOUR OWN DISHES, PLEASE. THANK YOU, THE MANAGEMENT

What if the dishwasher is running? the Crew

What if I'm topographically disoriented and I can't tell if the glasses go in the bottom or the top racks? Sincerely, Dishoriented

What if there isn't any more dishwasher soap? the Crew

What if I only eat from paper plates? the Tree Killer

What if I fell down and broke both wrists while skating, and loading/unloading the dishwasher is a physical impossibility? Quasi Modo

Order takeout and skip the whole dish thing. Ann Landers

And then it's time to dismantle the Christmas tree, a task we dread. When the tree is gone and the window bared to January, we all will return to our routines. But on this afternoon in 1991, the task is even more poignant. Ned and I have decided to sell the ranch.

My helpers are Monica and Jennie. They dawdle and debate. Should they save the tinsel or throw it out with the tree? Who gets to eat the last candy cane? A few ornaments crash-land. The rest I pack away.

As afternoon dwindles to darkness, I sit down on the sofa. Monica asks me to read *The Shiniest Star,* a favorite Christmas story from their childhood, here in this room, one more time. She sits down next to me. Jennie falls quiet and walks toward the kitchen.

"Jennie, come back! We need you, too. Mom, you sit in the middle. And put your arms around us like you did when we were little."

Squeezed between two tall, adult daughters, I gather the loose pages of the worn-out book and begin. The hero of the story is a shy angel named Touslehead who constantly compares himself to two other little angels whose stars glow brighter than his. Even so, he keeps on polishing his star, even the back, which doesn't show. One night, he looks down through the darkness and sees men on camels looking up, shouting, "Look! It's the star that God has promised, star of guidance, star of love." In that moment, he realizes that *he* is the bright star of Christmas. Slowly he leads the Wise Men to Bethlehem.

Slowly we drag the tree, stripped of the season's shimmering symbols, to the nearby coulee, the burial ground for over a decade of trees. And everyone goes their separate ways.

I return from the airport after seeing Monica off and find two notes in her handwriting on the kitchen counter. The first is the familiar T. S. Eliot quote about arriving where we started and knowing that place for the first time.

I unfold the second.

Mom: This time has been more than I could have hoped for. . . . I take with me the most special relationship I have with another woman. I have friends and sisters but I have only one mom and I am so blessed to have you as a friend also. I know you're not perfect and I know that forgiveness is a process. But I feel that we've both begun a great process and I pray that it continues.

A few weeks later, Monica calls to tell me about last night's dream. In it, each of her sisters was wearing a necklace with a star. Everyone except her. What does the dream mean? she wonders. Do her sisters possess some quality she lacks?

I tell her maybe Touslehead prompted the dream, that the two of them have a lot in common. But when I hang up, my motherly conscience examines the past and flinches. Has her holiday epiphany dimmed so soon? A remedy comes to mind. For her birthday in May, I'll give her the missing star. I search the stores, but find nothing. Not one necklace with a star. I enclose a practical check inside her birthday card, but whenever I walk down a store aisle, I watch for stars.

June brings the final stage of moving from the ranch. Cleaning out closets, packing up. What does one do with the collection of stuff? Halloween costumes, fuzzy lion suits, gaudy clown outfits; packets of letters and first-grade report cards. I unfold a lavender dress with pink ribbons and lace, the dress I made for Monica's eighth-grade graduation. I come upon a collection of her first-grade artwork— a series of women remarkably like those of Willem de Kooning, each bearing the dismaying label "Mom." I find parkas, scarves, mittens without partners. A mothering habit, I suspect, this guarding against the cold of empty closets. I want to forget the move, to stay here in this house where we've lived longer than anywhere else, where my fingers track light switches in the dark and my ears understand every sigh and creak the house utters. I'm on my hands and knees reaching for a box when I notice something shine in the carpet. I pinch the glimmer between my fingertips. A small gold earring sparkles in my hand. A star.

I'm not someone who looks in closets for signs and

wonders. I'm too skeptical to call psychics on 800 numbers or pay attention to astrological forecasts. But I confess to a moment of wonder at that star, that tiny glimpse of light during the darkness of change and uncertainty.

I send it to Monica, of course, along with the tale of its strange appearance. I add this P.S.: "It was lost, but now it's found."

A few weeks later, she calls. "Guess what, Mom. I've lost the earring. I can't find it anywhere." What shall I do now with this dilemma?

A FEW EVENINGS later, as Ned and I sit in our town backyard and bemoan the lackluster city stars, I locate one that seems to outshine the rest and send an SOS to Saint Anthony and my mother. On Earth, he was among her repertoire of heavenly intercessors, which also included Saint Ann, mother of Mary, an expert with maternal advice, and Saint Jude, patron saint of the impossible, the category where she put me early on. Saint Anthony is the patron saint of lost objects, finder of everything from misplaced glasses to lost souls. The secret is to ask, then search no more. The answer comes as a fleeting thought: *Look in the refrigerator* (where once I found my reading glasses); or resignation: *Forget it, you can live without that blue scarf;* or happenstance: *The city star falling before our eyes at this moment!* Seeing it, I realize that today is my mother's birthday. Surely then, this is the flash of her smile, her pledge of heavenly help. What was lost will be found.

FIVE YEARS LATER, on my mother's birthday, I think of the lost star. Perhaps this is the moment she and Saint Anthony have been waiting for, this Olympic moment in Atlanta,

1996, when the sister without a star is going for the gold. Monica is rowing with the U.S. Women's Eight, the team that won the '95 World Championships in Finland and is favored to take the Olympic gold. These powerful competitors are graduates of Harvard, Dartmouth, Wisconsin, Rutgers, Berkeley—knowledge seekers who would have made Socrates proud.

Except for Ben, who's studying in Europe, our entire family is here—the pregnant, the destitute students, the in-laws, the conscientious objectors. Everyone has come to cheer for the family middle kid in the middle of the boat. So has Fred Michini, the Philadelphia man Monica married that rare, warm first day of May 1993, a few weeks after she passed the Pennsylvania bar exam. In the outdoor wedding chapel pruned by her brothers from thistles and yucca, with the Snowy Mountains as backdrop, Father Jack Morris, Seattle Jesuit, witnessed their vows. A few months later the ranch sold.

Our presence in Atlanta is irony at best. At worst, hypocrisy. Ned and I, preachers of the golden mean and complicators of coaches' lives, are geared up in team T-shirts and hats with the Olympic logo: *Imagine a world without limits.* Mugs, shirts, backpacks, and posters issue the same challenge.

But my imagining is stalled on the opening night ceremony, when the Olympic torch, glowing with human-kind's dreams, was delivered into the hands of Muhammad Ali, an athlete tragically broken by his sport.

Limits spring up everywhere. The drama of the torch-lighting ceremony is overshadowed by a fact of history—the ritual was inaugurated by the Nazis for the 1936 Berlin Olympics, their way of connecting themselves to Aryan culture. The tales of tarnished stars tell of human limitation:

the athlete who injects someone else's urine into his bladder so he can pee drug-free; the Andro-pumped superstar who gambles years of his life for a moment of glory; the greedy officials seduced by money and fame; the doping regimens calculated for endurance, strength, alertness.

Limits, according to the Greeks, enable experience to become wisdom. Limits give birth to imagination. They provide meaning and form. Without them, our fantasies would be at sea without a port. The limits of loneliness urge us toward love; rules trigger rebellion and its by-product, responsibility; the limits of our life span engender dreams of immortality and the desire to do something timeless and meaningful and heroic. Today's culture tells us to admire the transient, the shooting star that careens through the dark and burns itself out for a moment of recognition. But when the superficial sheen of a star is confused with the glow of inner life and character that marks a true hero, we lose our models for spiritual growth.

Nevertheless, I imagine Monica's team crossing the finish line a boat-length ahead of the others, eight women striding across the stage to accept the gold medal, my mother's smile beaming on her triumphant granddaughter.

But the U.S. Women's Eight, photographed and interviewed daily on their way to that shining moment, comes in fourth. No gold. No silver. No bronze. What had happened? Did the deluge of attention distract and destroy them? Was it the moon? A menstrual cycle? One person who didn't pull her weight? That night, I lie awake listening to the music of insects in the Georgia dark. I see Monica's face, stunned by defeat, contrite before people who love her, as if she fears she's let us down, as if that's her greatest loss. A worse fear forms in me: Perhaps our doubting minds pulled against our daughter as she rowed. But wasn't Monica an expert at going against the stream?

. . .

I SUSPECT my mother and Saint Anthony have schemed this second chance. For here, in the frenzy and magic of the Summer Olympics, 2000, we've converged again: three of Monica's brothers—Mike from Alaska, Ben from New York City, Paul from Montana—and her sister, Adrienne, from Madrid—and Ned and I, too, chastened and grateful to be warming our winter blood in the spring sun of Sydney, Australia.

This time we won't ask dumb questions about coxswains and sculls and sweeps. Jammed in deregulated proximity during our fifteen-hour flight across the Atlantic, we studied up on the sport. We learned that rowing, done well, looks elegant and effortless but, in fact, demands virtually everything a human being can bring to an athletic competition—aerobic ability, technical talent, exceptional mental discipline, balance, ability to utilize oxygen efficiently, and (here, my feathers ruffled) pain tolerance and the ability to continue to work when the body is demanding that you stop. Oars must enter the water at a precise angle and moment. The rowing motion should have no discernible beginning or end, but be fluid and continuous.

This time we won't debate the boundaries of imagination. Imagining a world without limits may be simply an exercise in human hope. Imagination is more important than knowledge, said Einstein. What we can imagine, we can do.

This time the daughter who's been in the middle of a big, imperfect family won't be in the middle of the boat. She's chosen to go it alone, to single scull, a tough event she doesn't expect to win. This time her goal is not the gold, but to prove her strength alone. She hopes to qualify for the finals, to be among the six boats racing for a medal that predictions have given to the woman from Belarus. It's a preposterous plan. Playing your own game and knowing you won't win sounds as absurd as love without desire. As futile as polishing the back of a star. It's a decision that means our image won't be reflected in her medal.

Inevitably, each of us reaches a point when some sacrifice must be made for an ideal. The most important question then becomes: Why am I doing what I'm doing? Is it true for me? Or is it an apparent good that requires a betrayal of some part of me? To answer honestly, I have to be alert. If I'm sitting backward in a boat, I have to watch for markers that tell me my course is straight. I can't focus on the cheering crowd or measure my progress by other boats. I must row, row hard, and not look back at the finish line with its medals and applause. I must trust where I'm going because I know where I've been.

On the early-morning water, when Monica is alone in that small boat at the starting line, my heart hammers with hers, ready to leap at the sound of the gun. I wish I had a bright red hat. I plead with my mother and Saint Anthony, with any and every celestial power who'll grant my daughter clean catches, consistent speed, endurance, a strong pull. Monica places third and qualifies for the semifinals. In that race, she comes in sixth. She's missed the finals. By a matter of seconds, she's fallen short of her goal. I dread facing her disappointment again.

She surprises us. She's neither defeated nor apologetic. "I did my best," she says. "I rowed as fast as I could." She seems resigned, even satisfied, as if she'd come to terms with something that may never be resolved.

IN RETROSPECT, that solitary venture took the whole crew: Saint Anthony, my mother, Touslehead trailing his star, Ned and me dragging our heels, and Monica sitting backward in a boat, slicing oars for countless hours through the mine tailings of Milltown Pond, a Superfund site out-side Missoula where she lived then. But it was Monica *alone* who glimpsed the truth sparkling like a tiny star in that toxic water: our greatest fear is not the darkness, but our own light; our deepest dread is not our limitations, but our possibilities. Shall I go the way of the hero or the star?

Beneath the Snow, Spring

·

PAUL

*T*he road is closed. A heavy orange gate barricades the highway. In front of it stands a stern-faced sheriff holding up a forbidding palm. Absolutely no one can travel north. Spring has arrived in Wyoming, and we're in the midst of it. The prairie is blank and white. Snow swirls and sweeps and stacks. It stops us. Stops everyone. Lineage, destination, desperation, nothing can alter the case the weather has made. Pickups, four-wheel drives, huge rigs idle on the highway's snowy shoulder. Truckers, businessmen, skiers, families like us stare forlornly from the cage of their vehicles.

No. There are no families like us. Six children, ages two to ten, are packed in the back of our four-year-old green Travelall. The license plate says ARDELLA, which is the name of the woman married to the man who sold us the car last month. Now we call the car "Ardella."

We're stuck in Kaycee, a spot on Highway 25, the only north-south interstate that dares to divide this untamed Wyoming prairie. We live near Big Horn, a small community south of Sheridan in the foothills of the mountains. On good roads, we're two hours from home.

We *must* get home. Now. Soon. Today, May 1, 1968. We've been in this car since Phoenix. Alane, who'll be four in two weeks, was carsick this morning, and she's threatening a repeat. Her face is white, her eyes huge and expectant. Nine-year-old Mike, the brother she's sitting next to, shrinks back in disgust and terror. I'm ready with a gallon ice-cream bucket that I keep hidden. Seeing it could set her off.

Restless two-year-old Monica has finally fallen into a tranquil, sleeping heap on the middle seat. But alas, a riot threatens in the "way back," the farthest reaches of this enormous vehicle. The reach it exceeds is my husband's, who tends to dispense discipline pragmatically to the child closest to him.

Someone sat on someone else's coloring book. The first someone yanked it out and, in the process, tore a work of art in two. The present task is to determine liability: *It's your fault. No, it's your fault. You yanked it. You were sitting on it. You should have asked. I told you to get off. You didn't say please. It's nobody's fault,* says Dan, ten. *It's both of your faults,* says seven-year-old Elizabeth.

"Come up here and sit between your mother and me." Ned grasps the nearest arm and summons the body attached from the free-style throng to the sedate front seat. The others facilitate five-year-old Ned Anthony's climb over the seat. His shoe whacks Elizabeth's ear. She's of the eye-for-an-eye school and whacks him back. "There, see how it feels." He lands headfirst in the ice-cream bucket.

The truth is, we're all sick—sick of one another. Sick of

this vacation. Sick of this car. We need space. We need a piece of quiet, the gift Ned invariably requests when some occasion inspires a child to consider adult wants.

We've just come from a week of sunshine and swimming and togetherness in a posh Phoenix resort. This was a professional trip for my husband, an adventure for the children. And for me? I'm not sure. I've never been able to diagnose the character trait that lured me on those outings. Sometimes I think of it as bravery; other times, generosity, even self-sacrifice; now and then the word *foolhardy* rears its head. Sometimes it seems I've spent my entire married life in a car, starting with our two-thousand-mile honeymoon trip from Iowa to Washington State, then all the back-and-forths of graduate school, the annual treks home to see our parents, and, in between, jaunts like this one that turn professional conferences into family opportunities.

When we arrived at the genteel Arizona resort the previous week, my spirits sank. The hotel complex was arranged around a courtyard with a large swimming pool. A bevy of glistening professional sunbathers stretched out on chaise longues. At nearby tables, elegant women wearing casual chic sipped frosty drinks from tall glasses while they perused magazines: *Vogue, Mademoiselle, Glamour.* Clusters of suave men with salon haircuts and mirrored sunglasses hung around them. Lazy conversation buzzed like sunstruck bees. An occasional laugh stung the air.

I'm two and a half months pregnant. My swimsuit is five years old. My tummy pooches out. A purple varicose vein twists a tortuous path from inside my right thigh to outside my knee, then across my calf to my ankle, where it ends in a tangled blue root. Nature, it seems, has tattooed my limb with a family tree to remind me that I'm my mother's daughter, trained to put forward my best foot—or

leg, as the case may be. As the youngest daughter of struggling, first-generation Irish parents, my mother set out to
redeem the image of that ethnic group. She squelched any
rowdy tendencies that surfaced in my brother, my sister, or
me. *Hush! Do you want the neighbors to hear you?* She kept
Emily Post's *Book of Modern Etiquette* handy for quick con-
sultation. She insisted that we sit up straight at the table,
keep two feet on the floor and one hand in our laps. She
monitored grammar like a cave hydrologist might measure
drops leaking from a crevice, as if careless verbs eroded
character. Here in the unfiltered light of the Arizona sun, I
was doomed to disgrace.

One glance at the shimmering blue water sent our children into a dance of delight. They're dryland kids whose
water recreation has been confined to the shallow irrigation
ditch trickling along the west edge of our lawn. They've
captured huge turtles, built rickety bridges, sailed makeshift
boats, waded in knee-deep water and ankle-deep mud, but
they've never learned to swim well. Their skills depend
upon enthusiasm and sporadic summer classes.

They shot off to ransack Ardella for their swimsuits.

I scanned the poolside crowd for the telltale mahogany
physique of a lifeguard but saw only warning signs: SWIM
AT YOUR OWN RISK; CHILDREN UNDER TWELVE MUST BE SU-
PERVISED. I stood wringing my hands, praying for a cloud to
drift into the unbroken sky, for the heavens to rumble open
and drop a lifeguard onto the scene. I assessed my lifesaving
capabilities. I could probably pull a small child out of water
three feet deep.

A ragged gang of boisterous children returned, dragging tattered gym bags, jangling toys, and mismatched luggage over the flagstone poolside, bumping back and forth
past the slim and the suave and the sophisticated. One

vagabond stopped, scooped his hands into the pool, and flung out enough water to enrage his sister and dampen the careful coif of the woman sauntering by.

Relaxed brows furrowed. Languid bodies tensed. Thoughts of ruined vacations gathered like a thundercloud. I looked around for the mother of this group and found all eyes on me.

Ned Anthony apprehended me and held up his bandaged right hand to demonstrate how he intended to elevate it over the water. His palm had been stitched together the previous week after he tore it open climbing a barbed-wire fence. He promised not to get his wound wet. He vowed he would simply "splash around" a little.

As for me, I was sentenced to sit here alone in my sagging swimsuit in the midst of all this panache. While Ned attended meetings, I would be stripped of dignity as I struggled to enforce law and order.

They splattered away the afternoon, swimming their own versions of freestyle, stirring up enough commotion to beach several other swimmers. Ned Anthony's bandage swelled to a club. The older kids made chairs of their interlocked arms, boosted him on board, counted to three, and tossed him upward. He came up laughing and asking for more. I abandoned my image, recklessly shedding the tent-like denim shirt that served as my hideout, and settled in close by, scanning and counting and feigning serenity. One, two, three, four, five, six. Other vacationers were drifting farther and farther away; I was becoming a setting for *The Lord of the Flies*.

Alane disappeared momentarily from my radar screen. My heart flipped and raced, but she soon surfaced, sputtering and wiping her eyes.

"She tried to drown-ded me," she wailed.

"Big baby," scolded Elizabeth. "I told you to hold your nose when you dunked your head."

The next day, Elizabeth got her due. Her swim top stayed underwater when she came up, an event that raised the decibel level by several screams and plunged her (and me, for different reasons) into humiliation. We were hitting our stride. My misgivings gave way to belligerent confidence. To hell with impressions. I liked being here in the spring sun with my eager band of swimmers.

Day number three promised me some off-duty time. Ned's meetings would end by noon, and he would take over as lifeguard. I intended to sneak off to an art gallery, where I was assured there were no marine scenes, no watercolors, nothing evoking wetness, only clay sculptures and oil landscapes of mountains and prairies.

I added a book to my morning poolside routine—Thomas Merton's *No Man Is an Island.*

The word *island* had seduced me into bringing this monk along. I imagined glorious hours of solitude in the sun, alternately meditating on my missed vocation as a cloistered nun and cavorting spiritually with a man who was searching, not for answers, but for faith. But at the moment, the *Vogue* magazine cast off on a nearby table looked infinitely more practical than his first chapter, titled "Love Can Be Kept Only by Being Given Away."

A happiness that is sought for ourselves alone can never be found: for a happiness that is diminished by being shared is not big enough to make us happy. . . . True happiness is found in unselfish love, a love which increases in proportion as it is shared.

This news destined me for ecstasy. If only I could learn to share. So far, mothering had taught me to squirrel away what I didn't want diminished: M&M's, quiet moments, tentative thoughts. Enough of this sharing talk. I looked up and counted—one, two, three, four, five, six—and flipped through the pages until I spied the word *individual*.

> *First of all, although men have a common destiny, each individual also has to work out his own personal salvation for himself in fear and trembling.*

Fear and trembling? I was thinking sun and lethargy. Merton was the wrong choice for this outing. Instead of lying here hedonistically, I'm being urged to find meaning in my existence. And there was no shifting the responsibility to somebody else. I had to make this discovery myself, "from within."

This monk was unsettling me. How was I supposed to make lonely discoveries from within when I hadn't had my insides to myself for these past eleven years? My uterus and stomach and liver and bones were in a constant state of flux, shifting around to make room for someone else. As for the meaning of my existence, that seemed to revolve around getting up in the middle of too many nights, not willingly, to praise God in Vigils and Lauds, but begrudgingly, to visit the sick, feed the hungry, give drink to the thirsty, who presently were sating themselves on pool water.

One, two, three, four, five. Five? Someone was missing. Who? There was Dan flailing in an awkward backstroke. And Mike memorizing the scene for future torment. There was Ned Anthony's waterlogged wrap waving above the water. A triumphant Monica, shouting for everyone to look at her, rode on Elizabeth's shoulders. Alane! My almost-four-year-old daughter was missing again. Was she the victim of another dunking lesson? I watched for her to surface. She didn't.

"Mom! I have to go potty!" Monica yelled from her perch.

"Not now. Can you wait?"

"No!"

Elizabeth nervously unloaded her and hauled her ashore.

What had become of Alane? She was here a moment ago. My heart clutched and made a drum of my chest. My eyes raked the water and the flagstone around it. "Alane!" I called to the others. "Where is she? *Where is Alane?*" Silent terror. A moment of immobility. Then frenzy. Two people broke away from the social set and walked along the pool's edge. I grabbed my shirt—my mother had whispered from the wings—and worked it on as I ran the circumference calling my daughter's name. What had happened to her? There was no sign of her in the pool. So she hadn't drowned. Kidnapped, then. Someone had lured her away.

I ordered everyone out of the water, put Dan in charge, and alerted Ned. He rushed from his meeting and we raced around the grounds, searching behind bushes, weaving through cars in the parking lot. A dusty black Oldsmobile screeched away. A bearded man was driving; bouncing up and down in the backseat was a child. Our daughter. I was sure of it. Screaming for help as she was whisked off by a pervert. I ran to our hotel room to call the police. At the door, I reached into my shirt pocket for the key. It was gone. I jiggled the door handle. It was unlocked. I pushed it open.

"Mom?"

Fear switched to anger. I trailed the voice to the bathroom. There was my missing daughter, straddling the toilet and smiling at me with blue-eyed innocence. "Hi, Mom."

I was trembling. "Where have you been? How did you get in here?"

"With the key. From your shirt."

"You unlocked the door?"

She nodded. "It was easy."

"Don't ever, *ever,* EVER go off again without telling me."

"I knew the way."

"But I need to know where you're going."

"Why?"

"Because I'm your mother. Mothers need to know where their little girls are. After this, tell me before you go anywhere. Do you understand?"

"Even if I know the way?"

"Even if you know the way." I slid my hands under her arms to help her off the toilet.

"I can get down by myself." She jumped off the seat and pulled up her swimsuit. "Ready, Mom?" She reached a hand toward me as if I were the one who'd been lost.

Part of me wanted to chastise her with tales of kidnapped children, horror stories that would keep her close to home. Another part of me was amazed at the assurance that sent her off alone. All the way back to the pool, I argued with myself about how to teach her appropriate caution without generating fear. Confidence is something I want for my children.

WHAT I WANT most now, though, is to be out of this blizzard, out of this car.

"If you hurry right over to the motel, you might still be able to get a room," the sheriff tells us. He's a stiff brown Carhartt bundle with a bulbous red nose. When he gestures, his whole arm moves as if he had no elbow joint.

"One room left," the balding desk clerk at La Siesta declares without looking up. The skin on his skull is white and shiny. Black-rimmed half glasses sit on the bridge of his nose.

"There are eight of us," says Ned.

This lifts the clerk's head. He peers over his glasses through the window toward the grimy car.

"You got some kind of team with you? Nobody's going anywhere in this weather. You the coach?"

"I'm the dad. Those are my kids out there."

He screws up his eyes and looks again. He shrugs. "Room's got two beds. Two double beds."

"We can add cots," I say.

"Cots?" He turns his ear toward me as if I'm speaking a foreign tongue.

"Rollaways. Extra beds." I gesture rectangular shapes.

He stretches his lips into turned-down corners and shakes his head. "Nope. There ain't no extra anything here tonight. Just two double beds."

I look at Ned with dismay.

"I'll unload and lock up Ardella," he says.

The clerk jerks to attention and corners a suspicious glance our way. "You got something with you besides kids? Somebody who needs locking up?"

Ardella is easier to explain than most of the choices we've made.

THE MAN HASN'T exaggerated. La Siesta is nothing but a configuration of trailers, wrapped together with dun-colored metal siding. Our room would qualify for an experiment in sensory deprivation. No TV, no radio, no telephone. No extra anything. A gray linoleum floor. Beige, undecorated walls. A small window with dusty venetian blinds. And two lumpen beds with tired brown chenille spreads.

For lack of anything else to do, we eat dinner at four-thirty. The only restaurant is the Hole-in-the-Wall Bar and Café, just around the corner. It's dense with smoke and travelers. Some have cheerfully surrendered to being stuck. Others grumble in disbelief. "Of all the damn places."

The unexpected business boom has overwhelmed the waitress, whose pace was set years ago. She ambles to the easy rhythm of a few morning coffee drinkers, an occasional traveler, the handful of ranchers who stop at noon for homemade beef barley soup. This onslaught of stranded people is making her grouchy. She takes one look at us and rolls her eyes. She looks across the packed room of packed tables. She counts us.

"Shirley!" she bellows into the kitchen. "I need some help out here."

A fat, red-haired, sixtyish woman appears in jeans, a pink sleeveless blouse, and a stained white apron. She wipes scarlet-nailed hands on her apron and counts us with an accusing finger. With a nod of her head, she beckons us to the corner, shoves two small chrome tables together, and wryly observes the children as they scramble for chairs. She shakes her red head and yells to the waitress, "I got 'em all setting down now, Pearl. You take it from here." She disappears into the kitchen.

Pearl plods toward us through a morass of legs and boots. She announces the menu with grim detachment. Corn chowder. Chili. Hash browns. Chicken-fried steak. Take it or leave it, her sullen eyes say to the wrinkled-up noses of children grown fussy on resort cuisine.

"They all want chili," says Ned. Six heads turn toward him. "But Dad . . ." Dad doesn't flinch. He learned long ago that some situations demand a dictator's hand.

I'm wondering if I dare deviate without setting off an insurrection. I hate chili, and I suspect the infant inside me does, too. "Would you by any chance have oatmeal?" I ask Pearl, knowing that won't rouse any envy.

"For supper? You want oatmeal for supper?" Pearl's candor is daunting.

"I have a bit of a . . ." I say, and gesture vaguely toward my stomach.

She arches an eyebrow as if she's assessing my obvious fecundity and leaping to the right conclusion. She bites her lower lip and nods. "Yeah, I can probably scrape up a bowl of oatmeal. Can't guarantee how it's gonna taste, though."

She heads for the kitchen like a determined missionary.

"All those kids yours?" a jocular man in a down vest and red baseball cap inquires from the next table. "Or is that some kind of school?"

"Ours." My public policy is to keep it simple.

"Anybody ever tell you what causes that?" He chuckles at his own astuteness.

We, of course, do know what causes it. People have told us. Several hundred times. We also know the effect. All across America, waitresses panic. We've been counted in restaurants from Washington to Illinois to Texas. At service stations, fellow travelers gape when we open the car doors and turn the kids loose. The quick-thinking among them close their mouths and stake a claim on the bathroom.

With the man is a white-haired woman with a chiseled, expressionless face that no longer finds him funny. If she were wearing the habit of a Presentation nun, she could double for Stoneface, the principal of my parish high school, St. Columbkille. Stoneface—we called her Sister Fabian to her face—marched us around school according to rules as rigid as her countenance. We wasted inordinate amounts of energy defying her. Lipstick was verboten, so we wore it. Nylons were required with our uniforms, so we skipped them. When the day was over, she marched us out of school to the tune of John Philip Sousa. As we passed her, she gave our lips and legs the once-over. Before every prom, she rounded up the girls and laid down the law on decency. No strapless gowns. No gowns with spaghetti straps. No dresses with revealing necklines. No sleeveless outfits. No seductive clothing that might lead boys astray. Chastity was a female responsibility. We slipped lacy little jackets over our strapless gowns as we went into the school dance. When we came out, we slipped them off again and went about the business of temptation.

Undoubtedly, Saint Columbkille, the school's patron saint, and the Blessed Virgin, every girl's intercessor, saved us from ourselves. His statue towered on the left side of the church, directly to the right of hers. Together, they totaled a sum much greater than its parts. He was an Irish saint, which meant to me that he'd gone to Ireland, like Saint Patrick, to baptize infidels and chase out snakes. Dressed in a coarse, dark, ankle-length robe, he held up his right hand in a patriarchal gesture of both blessing and caution. Mary, cloaked from chin to toe in an opaque white gown and capacious blue mantle, offered open arms and hands, while she gazed serenely downward toward the snake coiled beneath her virgin feet. Here was our challenge as young women: to heed the patriarchal admonition, to be receptive but chaste. Sex belonged within the bonds of marriage, which had as its primary purpose, according to Catholic teaching, *the begetting and rearing of children in the love and fear of God.* The secondary purpose was the mutual support of husband and wife. But we were flesh and blood, not plaster and paint. We had lusty notions that spilled between categories.

Ned and I are prime examples, sitting here in the Hole-in-the-Wall Bar and Café, surrounded by the effects of our concupiscence, none of them conceived out of obedience to church law, each the product of pure desire.

All this puzzling over saints and snakes must be showing in my eyes. My oldest son is looking at me with a worried expression.

"Mom, does your face hurt?" he wants to know.

"No-o-o." I put fingertips to my cheekbones.

"It's killing me." Dan relishes his joke. So do his brothers and sisters. They take turns repeating it. The hilarity gains momentum. They're cracking each other up and making plenty of noise in the process.

The sigh of relief I hear as we leave the café is not imagined. We've finished off Pearl's patience right along with the chili.

For lack of anything else to do, we go to bed at seven-thirty. Maybe a miracle will melt the drifts during the night and let us out early. We discover that lying cross-wise, five children fit in a double bed. Lying on their sides, immobile, two adults and one child also can fit in a double bed.

But to fit is not to sleep. We begin what turns out to be a long, dark night of rolling and punching and fretting. Loud whispers: *My stomach did not either growl. Get over! I hate you. Quit hogging the bed. Mom, she called me a hog. Ouch! You did that on purpose. Whew! Who farted? Beans, beans, the magical fruit, the more you eat . . . Shut up, I'm trying to sleep. You shut up.*

"What time is it?" I whisper across Monica to Ned.

"Eight-thirty."

"Oh, my God, is that all?"

"Mom, are you saying your bedtime prayers?" pipes up a voice from the mob on the other bed.

I suppose I do sound a little like Job, out of patience

with an insecure, bored God who livens up his immutable existence by designing devious tests of love.

Monica flops her leg across my chest and whines. "I don't see why I hafta sleep with you and they get to sleep together."

"There will be many things in life you won't understand," her dad intones.

When the blockade is lifted the next afternoon, we rush north like prisoners freed from a civil war.

Home at last. Home, where I know that beneath the snow spring is gestating. Along the front-yard fence, daffodils quicken and soon will push through the drifts like a flash of hope.

MY PREGNANCIES have been healthy, my labors uncomplicated. These factors have influenced my attitude toward childbearing. So, inevitably, has my Catholic upbringing. The church bolstered its ban on artificial birth control with idealistic portrayals of family life. We were creatures of a place and time, inhaling attitudes like air. Many couples, not just Catholics, "increased and multiplied" to the extent of four or five children.

But now it is 1968. The whole country seems to be reeling on a fault line. Traditions we were taught to cherish tremble on the brink. Just as our family becomes terrifyingly dependent upon social institutions—schools and churches and other families—those institutions begin to crumble. University students dynamite buildings and strong-arm deans. Martin Luther King Jr. is assassinated. Thoughtful people drop out to do their own thing. Paul Ehrlich drops his *Population Bomb*. Two children. No more. Each day, I feel more vulnerable. Fortunately, I have a grace period before it becomes obvious that I'm not socially responsible. Before I begin to "show."

. . .

A WEEK AFTER our Kaycee adventure, my membranes rupture. I'm eleven weeks pregnant. My doctor hospitalizes me and prescribes bed rest and hormonal treatment to "quiet" the uterus. A gravindex test comes back positive; the fetus is alive. The doctor explains that if I don't go into labor, the membranes will heal and the pregnancy continue. But statistics are against that. The usual course is labor and loss of the baby. I lie in the hospital bed and watch evening's canted light hesitate on the windowsill. In spite of varicose veins and crowded beds and posh people at poolsides, in spite of common sense and Paul Ehrlich, I want this seventh child.

A week later, tests reaffirm the baby is alive. I leave the hospital but must receive a weekly hormone shot to help sustain the pregnancy. On my first day home, I phone an appliance store in Sheridan and order a clothes dryer. Whatever has motivated me to do without—a learned abnegation, a skewed sense of thrift, a perverse need to do things the hard way—no longer holds. Hauling heavy baskets of wet laundry from the basement to the backyard day after day would be rash. The child growing within helps me see what I haven't seen before.

THE FORMLESS SEASON of Wyoming's spring continues. The sky refuses spring. Ominous gunmetal clouds cling to the peaks of the Big Horn Mountains. From the early-morning window of our living room, I can see our mare, Baca, standing alert on the rise south of the barn. Her mane flares wild in the unrelenting wind. She whinnies and shifts and nudges something on spring's chilly ground. I see it then, the dark shadow of her foal. She has dropped it into the pasture's only pool of melted snow. At noon, she still stands over the unmoving body. Dusk rises but her vigil of grief and hope goes on. I place my hand against my grow-ing belly and feel the shape of her confusion. In the dark waters of my womb, my child moves.

NED COMES to our bedroom door one early June morning to tell me the news he's just heard on the radio. Bobby Kennedy has been shot. My first thought is his wife, their children, the child she carries. Politicians are replaceable. Fathers are not. The fault line rumbles and widens. I'm more and more grateful for this refuge we call home. Here we feel safe from the chaos overwhelming the world.

On July 26, my mother's seventy-seventh birthday, my brother, John, calls from Louisville, Kentucky. His wife, at forty, has just delivered their fifth child, a girl, six weeks early. They have named her Patti. But something is wrong. Within twenty-four hours of her birth, she undergoes heart surgery. For weeks, her life depends on monitors and machines and fate. In the course of this, doctors confirm the fear my brother hasn't been able to say aloud. Patti has Down syndrome. "Why?" my brother asks. "What's the purpose in this?" I have no answer.

Because my due date is October 30, I've been joking about expecting a Halloween spook. But my sense of hu-mor falters with the news of my brother's child. My precar-ious pregnancy confronts me with the utter vulnerability of childbearing. Life, like a spring snowstorm in Wyoming, has stopped me in my tracks.

In order to prevent the possibility of my pregnancy going overdue, my doctor discontinues the hormone injec-tions on October 1. At noon on the eleventh, as I peruse recipe books and resent having to get dinner for visiting rel-atives—three men, oblivious to their bad timing—my labor begins, three weeks before my due date. I am rescued from cooking but frightened that this early delivery bodes ill. The labor is harder, I think, for the worrying.

At six p.m., a scrawny, beautiful, six-pound boy wails his way into the world. Our seventh child, Paul Nicholas Tranel. The moment the doctor lays him on my abdomen, he quiets. The moment he is taken away, he howls. Later, when he is returned to me as a cleaned-up bundle, he opens his eyes and stares with a kind of preternatural wisdom. Slowly, I unwrap him, count his fingers and toes, and turn him over to stroke the downy skin of his back, barely the width of my palm. My spirit soars with gratitude as I realize his perfect form. I breathe the sweet peculiar smell of newborns. Everything is clearer and sharper; I am permeated by some strange, profound, unknowable truth, a grace granted the first hours after childbirth. My heart seems to grow and grow until it bursts through my chest and sits outside my body, utterly exposed.

"NOW YOU TAKE CARE of yourself," my mother warns when I call to tell her our baby is safely here. She still thinks of me as her willful youngest child, out to test the limits of endurance, my own this time, not hers. Whatever she imagined for me when she sent me off to weekly piano lessons or said "look it up" when I asked the meaning of a word, or defended my prom décolletage to sharp-eyed Sister Fabian, I doubt it included mothering a brood of children in the West. "Why, there's nothing out here," she said incredulously after a train ride to visit us. Maybe that's the logic. I'm her domestically incompetent daughter, the one assigned to dust the upstairs because it didn't show, while my sister, thorough and conscientious, dusted the main-floor rooms that visitors would see. Maybe living in Wyoming is like being sent upstairs to dust.

"My goodness, he's a hungry boy," says the nurse that evening as she comes into my hospital room with Paul, squawking and sucking his fist. "And your seventh child! How do you manage? I can barely handle my *two*."

The lab technician who draws my blood at five a.m. the next morning says quietly, "So you're the woman with seven kids. We called it quits after one." I can't read his expression in the darkened room, so I say only, "The first one is the hardest."

The truth is, seven children aren't seven times one. By the time a fourth or fifth child is born, you've accumulated an abundance of equipment and a few important skills. You have a crib, high chair, booster seat, youth bed, potty chair, stroller, and cast-off clothes from friends in five states. Between Christmas and birthdays, Lincoln Logs and Legos multiply like rabbits. Quantity promotes efficiency and economy. A trip through the grocery store takes longer and costs more but not seven times so. In fact, you're downright lucky, as your kids tell you, because you have so much help carrying those barge-size boxes of Wheaties and Tide from the car to the kitchen.

And you've gained perspective. The silver soup ladle that disappeared last summer will turn up next year, buried in a corner of the sandbox. Walking a block with a toddler is not an hour wasted but one spent with a Zen master who points out pebbles and bugs and every little live thing. When your steely-eyed two-year-old heads toward the table lamp, you remind yourself she isn't out to destroy the furniture or your sanity, she's testing her ability to think and act independently; you do your best to help with the lesson and keep the lamp intact.

Experience compensates for lagging energy. So do your kids. Every spoon, sock, and controversy is no longer your sole responsibility. Children between eight and twelve years old are willing and able helpers. And more engaging mod-els for younger brothers and sisters than parents, even though we like to think we're the crucial component in our three-year-old's life. I've watched our older kids, Tom Sawyer–style, charm the younger ones into helping with chores. They haul water to calves, weed the garden, chase cows out of the yard and pigs into their pen. The younger ones exercise their own form of guile to get big brothers and sisters to do their bidding. And sometimes, they simply provide older brothers and sisters with an excuse to play again.

In February, as I change four-month-old Paul's diaper, I notice two small blistery red spots on his thigh. Now all seven children have chicken pox. The other six lie in vary-ing stages of fever and itch on the family room carpet, lined up Kaycee-style. I consider calling the lab technician at the hospital to amend my words. Sometimes seven are fourteen times one. By day, I maneuver through the tangle of arms and legs to dispense calamine lotion and sympathy. By night, I rail at God in the Job-like way I learned overnight-ing in that Wyoming motel room. I complain about the labyrinthine ways of providential love. I ask for energy and patience. And because I believe we live by grace as much as by our own cunning, I summon a generous supply of that. Ultimately, what keeps me dabbing pink lotion on red blisters and reading stories and thermometers is not a felt infusion of some mystical substance, but a plodding con-fusion of duty and love. Maybe grace arrives on foot, not wings.

THE TELEPHONE CALL comes on a Sunday morning in late July. I'm still in bed. Paul, nine months old, nuzzles into my breast and greedily gulps his morning's first milk. I finger the fuzz on the back of his head and marvel at nature's way, at how simple things are between my baby and me, this child who landed on Earth just nine months before man first landed on the moon.

My brother, John, is calling to tell me our mother has had a stroke. She returned home with Dad from Mass, put a pot of coffee on the stove, and went upstairs to change from her Sunday dress into a housedress. As Dad set the table for breakfast, he heard a thud on the kitchen ceiling. He found her lying limp on the bathroom floor, unable to talk. "Scared the hell out of him," my brother says. "He yelled for Anna, next door." It was she who called the ambulance. Anna, the industrious German woman who consistently beat my mother in their unspoken race to hang out Monday's laundry. "They took Mom to Mercy Hospital." John's voice catches. "I'm leaving for Dubuque right away. You never know"—he swallows—"about these things."

I see my mother, still wearing her Sunday dress, crumpled between the toilet and the tub with its old-fashioned legs. "I'll meet you there this evening," I tell John. As I hang up, I remember that tomorrow is July 26, the first birthday of his daughter Patti.

Tomorrow is our mother's birthday, too. She will be seventy-eight. I have mailed her card, but I had intended to take her gift with me when our family drove to Iowa in mid-August. I knew she'd be delighted with whatever I chose for her, but I also knew she'd consider Paul the best gift. Her eyes would light up and she'd tell me all those months of worry were worth it. She'd coo and cluck until Paul rewarded her with a smile. I'd been counting the weeks until I could show him off to her.

But everything has changed. Paul and I are flying to Iowa alone. I'm thirty-five years old, and this is the first time I've flown on a jet. I'm a wife and the mother of seven children, and I'm not ready to let my mother go.

She feels otherwise. She said so during last year's visit when we sat at the dining room table with its crystal bowl full of wax apples, oranges, and bananas, tempting artificiality I had come to hate. Her fingers fretted with the lace tablecloth as we talked. She said dying didn't frighten her. She was the tenth in a family of thirteen children. She'd lost brothers and sisters and parents and nieces and nephews. She accepted the fact of death. What she did worry about was ending up in the wrong funeral home. She wanted to look her best at the viewing. She hated the way a certain place did up women's hair.

Doing up hair has been a sore spot with me since childhood. Every Saturday evening, just before bedtime, my mother set out to subdue my wiry waves into Shirley Temple curls. She would pull a straight white kitchen chair close to the table, sit down, clench me between her knees, and go to work. She would slide a soft rag from the pile on the table, grasp a hank of my hair between her fingers, and wind it around and around, tighter and tighter until I could feel my ears and eyes inch upward. If I wiggled too much or strove too ardently for freedom, she whacked me on the shoulder with the brush. When I thinned her patience to a thread, she slapped my neck instead.

"Stand still," she'd say. "How can I accomplish anything with you fidgeting this way?"

"I hate curls. They're dumb."

"They're not dumb. And you don't hate them. What you hate is standing still."

"I do hate curls. And they are dumb."

She tried diversion. "There was a little girl who had a little curl right in the middle of her forehead," she chanted.

"I don't want a curl in the middle of my forehead."

"And when she was good she was very, very good. And when she was bad, she was horrid."

"Is that a proverb you're making up?" It was a fair question, given her talent for applying one to every situation.

"If the shoe fits, wear it," she said that day, and reined me in with a length of cotton.

"I hate shoes. They're dumb."

The Saturday evening ritual eventually ended, unwinding slowly, the way the rags came out of my curls on Sunday morning. My mother gradually let me go, consigning my rebellious nature to God and the future and Sister Fabian's eagle eye.

EXHAUSTED BY SCREAMING through the ear-piercing takeoff, Paul sleeps in my arms. I lean my head against the seat while the plane hurls me back to childhood. Fans whir against sticky Iowa air; I hear invisible crickets singing staccato songs. Above the dark lawn, fireflies flicker. Determined to know the connection between soaring and glow, I arm myself with a Mason jar and follow each blink. Around the blue spruce, over the grass, under the clotheslines, past the haw tree, across the path to Anna's garden, down the rows of knee-high corn. I stumble and scrape my knee against a rock. Blood sends me flying over the lawn, home to my mother's hand. Moments later, mended, I stalk again.

Now, over the wings of the plane, the sky flickers and goes out. We land.

In my mother's darkened hospital room, my eighty-eight-year-old father collapses into my brother's arms. He weeps and says he doesn't know what he will do without her. Over and over, John says, "I know, Dad. I know. I know." The deepened lines around his eyes testify to the questions haunting John this past year, the worried weeks of not knowing, the wrenching moment of finding out.

Through the night, while Paul sleeps in a crib nearby, Anne Marie and I take shifts sitting by our mother's bedside. I watch her body for signs of breathing. Each one comes with noisy effort. Her mouth gapes. Her body rises upward, ever so slightly, then falls in a quick, grateful motion. I stroke her hair, the soft, white curls strewn against the white cotton pillowcase. Fear clamps my heart tighter than my mother's knees.

WHEN IT'S MY TURN to sleep, I return to the home of my childhood, down the street I walked daily from school. I pass the scary spinster's house and the brick bungalow that always reeked of cigars. Set back from the street is the green-shuttered house with the thorny hedge I careened into when I was learning to ride my brother's bike. My mind chalks the sidewalk into hopscotch squares to my own front porch.

I start up the steps, then stop, my breath caught by the scent of lilies of the valley. But the pungent patch of unruly leaves has gone to grass; a tidy trellis hides the fertile earth beneath the porch. I crouch down and peer past the slats into the dank darkness where I once crawled in search of my lost kitten. The ripe odor of death breathes back.

I push open the door to an uneasy silence, as if the rooms hadn't adjusted to their hasty abandonment. The haunting smells of mustiness and recent baking pull me toward the pantry. There, lined up on cooling racks, are my mother's pinwheel cookies, a rich swirl of dough and dates baked for her birthday gathering. But the picnic in the park has been canceled. The few siblings left in her family will not be celebrating today.

Through the next days, I watch my mother's face. Two or three times her eyelids flicker, and I try to catch her gaze.

If I can make her look at me, really see me, maybe I can pull her from the darkness, pull *my* mother out of the stranger in this bed. What has become of her? Yesterday she was a woman sliding birthday cookies from a baking sheet; the day before, a mother fussing over curls. One moment, I pray; the next, I want to double up both fists and demand an accounting. What kind of God short-circuits brains and bungles chromosomes? Is there a design that requires broken things, or is it all happenstance?

I SEE MY MOTHER again in August when our family makes our scheduled trip to Iowa. She is conscious now. Her mouth droops to the left. Ned and I and seven children surround her hospital bed; she looks from face to face with suspicious eyes. Our children tell her their names and take her hand and glance anxiously at me. I put Paul down beside her. She reaches out her right hand and touches his hair. Her fingers linger on the soft, blond curls, and for a moment her spirit seems to soar. She smiles with the right side of her mouth and struggles for a word. Then she looks at me with wild, frightened eyes. As if she's changed her mind about death. As if she's no longer comforted by the thought of brothers and sisters who've gone before. As if years of Friday novenas to Our Sorrowful Mother and daily Masses and constant rosaries, as if none of this can save her. In fact, the woman I know is gone. My father is failing, too. This blow is too hard for an old man.

When we return to our home in Wyoming, I feel as dislocated as an orphan, a mother who needs a mother, someone to admonish me in letters and phone calls to "take care of myself," someone who counts the days until our summer visit, someone who pays attention to my children's birthdays, and to mine. Someone to convince me that "it's an ill wind that blows nobody good."

. . .

THE GOOD IS ALL around me. In my husband, my children, in the sheltered place we've called home for seven years. A row of Russian olive trees protects us from ill winds; a stalwart blue spruce stands sentinel on the front lawn. The man and woman who landscaped this yard and built this house came from Iowa, too. Like immigrants pulled by common roots to an oasis of irrigated land, we had walked together around the yard until we recognized home: our Midwestern garden in the foothills of the Big Horn Mountains. The other couple left reluctantly; his jaw was gone, his face devastated by cancer.

The vegetation they planted is lush and diverse, calculated to ensure something will survive spring: mock orange bushes, lilacs, languorous weeping willows, tulips and tiger lilies and daffodils and peonies and violets and startled poppies, an apple tree. And on the lawn's east slope, a whimsical garden of Peace roses, creamy pink-tipped petals thriving at four thousand feet. Hope born of nostalgia must have prompted them to plant the red maple tree, only four feet high after fifteen years. Seduced by winter's deceptive sun and stunted by spring's certain frost, the regal tree of Mississippi bluffs finally settled for being a bush, a bold bush, a passionate flame darting through the branches of fickle lilacs. Perhaps pragmatism is a virtue after all.

It's too late for us to be pragmatic. I'm pregnant again. Our eighth child is due in mid-October, around the time of Paul's second birthday. What would be welcome news is troubling in our present situation. The board of directors that hired Ned to develop a mental health program in this region now prefers a psychiatrist to run it, a man Ned himself recruited, envisioning shared leadership and an exemplary clinic in the rural West. Instead, a power struggle ensues: East Coast M.D. vs. Midwestern Ph.D., two young stallions vying for turf. Psychologists are easier to replace than psychiatrists, the board explains candidly, and invites Ned to resign. No, we reply, clinging to principle and our desire to stay where we've made our home.

It will be years before we understand that we were slaves to our own idealism. If we had been able to practice the pragmatism nature preached, if Ned had been able to compromise his role, if we had settled for being a bush when we hoped to be a tree, we might have avoided the humiliation and the uprooting that came a few weeks later with that letter of termination. Now, we will have to abandon the home we considered perfect and permanent and go wherever Ned's employment takes us. It's our turn to leave this place.

For the first time, I'm ambivalent about another child. Maybe we really *don't* know the cause. Maybe we're naive. Or greedy. Maybe we're megalomaniacal about replacing ourselves. I'm tired and discouraged. Tears spring to my eyes at random moments, at Sunday Mass, in the grocery store. Our future is too uncertain. The world itself is too uncertain. On May 4, the same day we celebrate Monica's fourth birthday, National Guard soldiers shoot down four students protesting at Kent State. I want to stay here where we are safe from this madness, where four of our children were born and I saw the lilacs bloom three times. Our roots are too sprawling to transplant intact.

Ned plunges into a job search, traveling for interviews, bringing home proposals that would mean relocating to unfamiliar regions. We lie awake late and wake up early. In midsummer, he joins the staff of the Mental Health Center in Miles City, a Montana prairie town two hundred miles away. He rents a room and commutes home on weekends. As soon as he finds a suitable house for a family of ten, we'll move. I feel like a child who's wandered too far from home.

All I can see is a hand waving in the distance. I want to grab it and hold on. Instead, I begin emptying closets and cupboards. I pack boxes and prepare to leave.

In September, our children return to school at Big Horn and all but our most essential belongings are stacked in boxes waiting near the back door, next to the window that looks toward the mountains. We wait, too, unsure what will come first, the signal from Ned that he's found a house for us or the baby due in mid-October.

Despite the swimming pool fiasco, I turn once more to Merton, who tells me that anxiety is the mark of spiritual insecurity, the fruit of unanswered questions. But a far worse anxiety, he believes, is to be afraid to ask the right questions because they might turn out to have no answer. I begin to glimpse the difference between optimism and hope. Optimism operates on the assumption that things will turn out all right. But hope, honest hope, watches things go wrong and trusts that there'll be a way through.

Paul doesn't worry that we're on the verge of upheaval. He simply asks now and then, "When movin', Dad?" He has been nicknamed Pla-goo, a variation on the biblical plague of locusts that his siblings learned about in summer religion class. He has descended upon their lives, crashing complicated Lego structures, reducing electric trains to manual ones, swiping pieces from nearly finished puzzles. He follows everything moving. Kittens. Dogs. Piglets. Brothers and sisters. Dire population predictions don't faze this kid. He has no clue that some people really do see him as a blight on the universe. He thinks he's essential to every task. When Dan goes to the barn to milk the cow, Paul bums a high sky ride. Twenty minutes later, they come into the kitchen beaming over a bucket full of foamy milk too heavy for twelve-year-old Dan to carry alone. When his dad weeds and prunes the strawberry patch, Paul plunks down beside him to dig in the dirt. Of all the intriguing places on our ranch, he prefers this spot. He's inherited his paternal grandmother's genes. She's happiest on her knees in the garden, too.

Years later, when Paul is an attorney in Missoula, he'll spade up a corner of his yard for a garden and plant vegetables as this grandmother instructed him to do: potatoes on Good Friday when the moon is waning; above-ground plants—tomatoes, peas, lettuce—by the waxing moon. What he did with the advice she delivered the day we visited her in the nursing home is another matter. "Now you use that," she said, dropping a pink plastic rosary into his palm and wagging her finger before his skeptical fifteen-year-old eyes.

Midmorning a couple of weeks before his second birthday, Paul and I are in the midst of making the cake he chose from the tattered book of animal cakes. Each stained page testifies to small fingers deliberating among Elly, the elephant; Douglas, the dog; Francis, the fish. If all goes well, Paul's cake will be Leo, the lion, with a coconut mane and licorice tail. We're baking it to freeze, in case we find ourselves moving on his birthday.

Paul drags a chair over to the counter and scrambles up. When I touch the blond curls I can't bear to trim away, I see my mother's hands. She is "better," if you compare her to the ravaged woman in the hospital, but her personality has changed. She writes letters in lines as erratic as an EKG. Her words stray up and down; they spread out and pile up; she adds extra loops to M's and N's. She's lost her sense of humor and righteous indignation. She no longer worries about making a good impression. Her hair goes uncombed. She shuffles all day in bedroom slippers. Twice she turned on the gas in the oven and forgot to strike a match. My dad is distressed. My sister calls and says we can't pretend much longer. Our parents will have to abandon the house where they lived out more than forty years of marriage. Everything comes to the same end: surrender to the rushing stream of life.

Paul raps on my arm with his knuckles, as if asking if anyone's home.

I laugh and touch his cheek, brush my fingers through his hair, twist a curl around my finger, and tell him I love him.

"I know." He sounds impatient, as if he wants to get on with the work in front of us instead of discussing the obvious. He's as sensible as the backyard maple bush, glad to be in the garden in any guise, while I've been lying awake nights reviewing my worries: How much longer can I survive these five-day stints of single parenting? Even if Ned does find a house large enough for our family, who but a fool would rent to us? What if I go into labor on a weeknight, when Ned is nearly four hours from home? What if the neighbor who's on alert doesn't answer her phone? Should I unpack the boxed-up newborn clothes? How do I convince five children that changing schools isn't fatal? How do I get through this night?

Another knock on my wrist.

I put Paul in charge of the flour. He dumps the first cup and lands most of it in the bowl.

"Good job," I say, and take a spoon to the mixture in the bowl. His eyes widen as the flour disappears into the creamy blend of butter and sugar. He dumps another cup and watches me stir.

"Good job, Mom," he says.

"I know," I say, emulating his confidence.

"Can I do that?" he asks, but already he's prying the wooden spoon from my hand.

. . .

BY THE TIME Paul is five, we will have moved twice and buried both my parents—my father in December 1970, my mother two years later. By the time Paul is ten, he'll be the official family gardener; his dad will help him prepare the soil and sow the seed, but Paul will take over from there, rototilling, watering, harvesting carrots and corn and beets and beans so fresh we can almost taste the moment of creation. Morning, noon, and night, he will ride his bike the quarter mile to the garden until he makes a path of his devotion.

MY MOTHER'S HAND touches Paul's hair; she twists cotton rags through mine; Michelangelo's Creator touches the human into existence. Perhaps Paul felt my hand the day I mourned the mare's dead foal. Maybe he learned to live on love in utero. *I love you, Paul.* But what is the echo I hear in his answer, *I know?* My brother's voice in that darkened hospital room, "I know, Dad, I know." What does he know? The answer to his anguished questions, *Why? What's the purpose?* Or did Merton get it right? Is it courage that opens the darkness, that helps hearts see a path minds may never know?

The Squeaky Wheel of Happenstance

·

JENNIE

T he ghost of my fertile past haunts this darkened theater. As my husband, Ned, and I sit listening to the Billings Symphony perform *Carmina Burana,* I scan the faces of the musicians onstage. The silver-haired woman singing in the chorale was a young brunette when she taught our son Spanish. The petite woman next to her gave piano lessons to four of our children. The rapt violinist in the third chair directed our youngest two children in high school chorale; the bearded cellist was another son's band director. Something about the white-haired man in the top row is familiar. The broad forehead, the boyish mouth, the angle of his ears. Intrigued, I watch his lips shape the notes. A gaping C, a rounded D, a strenuous E that ripples into a frown. The frown gives him away. The man who was my doctor twenty-five years ago.

·   ·   ·

I'M ON MY BACK, pinned to the narrow table by a draped sheet that turns me, waist up, into a Cézanne still life. Waist down, I sprawl like a Schiele nude, legs wide, my heels in the grip of cold steel stirrups. His face soars above my knees. He leans over and peers. I feel the clamp and turn of metal against my flesh. His voice is muffled: "Hmm. Hmm. Cervix maybe a little red. Uterus seems back to normal. Everything looks healthy." He straightens, picks up a clipboard, and scratches a message to himself. His pale eyes brush over my face. "You're breast-feeding, aren't you? Good. Helps uterine tone." He studies my chart. "Now, let's see, how many children is this?"

"Eight," I say. "Jennie is our fourth daughter." The telltale flicker moving across his brow provokes me to flippancy. "The perfect planned family. Four daughters and four sons."

He frowns. "What are you using for birth control?"

"Nursing." I nod soberly. "Nursing works for me."

"Works?" His eyes probe like a sharp instrument into my frail argument. He clears his throat. "Mrs. Tranel, have you considered another source of fulfillment beyond children?" A pause. Then, "Has your husband considered a vasectomy?" He is a vociferous community leader for Planned Parenthood, a zealous advocate of Zero Population Growth. He is the doctor to whom I have come for my six-week checkup in Miles City, the Montana prairie town where we moved in mid-October 1970, when Jennie was two weeks old. "You can go ahead and dress," he says. "I'll be back shortly." I watch his white coat retreat.

Fulfillment? Vasectomy? This doctor is unsettling me when I've just unpacked the last box in the rambling rented house we reluctantly call home. We've reclaimed five bedrooms from the apartment carved out upstairs. For the first time, six-year-old Alane is sleeping apart from four-year-old Monica, whose room formerly served as the kitchen. We've disconnected the gas range and camouflaged it with a length of flowery fabric, but there's nothing to be done about the ungainly sink. Or the two doorways that yawn arrogantly, problematically, without doors. The other day when her dad banished her to that room for some misdeed, Monica stomped off like a diva. "And close the door," Ned called after her. Halfway up the stairs, she halted and yelled back, "My room doesn't have a door." Ned snickered; I smiled; we looked at each other and laughed. "My room," she'd shouted. "*My* room." Her spunk had survived the move! Maybe there was hope, after all, of transplanting our protesting progeny and hesitant hearts from our cherished country place to a lot in town.

The doctor's "shortly" stretches to ten minutes, then twenty. His time means money; mine has no price. Maybe he's busy dealing with someone else's fulfillment, or deliberately stalling while I consider mine. Would it relieve his mind if I told him what this baby means to me, to our family? But I can't, because it will be years before even I fully realize what her birth has brought: trust in happy endings, light enough each day to guide us through the dark.

IN THE BEGINNING, the pregnancy felt like insult added to injury. Carrying a child through those long months of upset when Ned worked Monday through Friday in Montana and the rest of us remained in Wyoming was a bleak prospect. I spent the days doing what was in front of me, shopping for groceries, making meals, doing laundry, bandaging knees and hurt feelings, reading bedtime stories while gradually packing up to make a move that represented loss and defeat. I longed to call my mother and hear the consolation of one of her proverbs—*It's always darkest before the dawn*—but the stroke she suffered last year had robbed me of her solace.

On the night of October 1, two weeks before my due date, my labor began as I feared it would, in the middle of the week when Ned was two hundred miles away. I bundled up in a confusion of self-pity and resentment and imagined driving myself the ten miles to the hospital. A few hard pains later, I summoned the neighbor woman on call. My doctor met me in the maternity ward with a warning: He was leaving town at eight a.m. for his son's football game; I should select an alternative physician. But our considerate baby came with dawn—eight pounds of squealing, squirming girl. Across the room, nurses cleaned the remnants of birthing from her and chatted with the doctor about weather and football scores, while I lay alone, alternately longing for Ned to share my joy and astonished by gratitude and the sun rising on this new day.

On Paul's second birthday, October 11, we baptized our infant "Jennie Christa" at Holy Name Church, where, in the past six years, we'd baptized three other babies—Alane, Monica, and Paul. Four days later, a Mayflower truck overshadowed our back door, a cruel behemoth gobbling up furniture, dishes, clothing, toys, intent on turning seven years of our lives as well as the future we'd envisioned into leavings on the bare floors. As we drove away from our place in the foothills of the Big Horn Mountains, I wondered if we could have poured so much labor and love into making that house our home if we'd foreseen ourselves now, packed up and moving on, seven children strangely subdued in the backseats, Ned taciturn behind the wheel, Jennie somber-eyed in my arms. But as I looked at her, her tiny pink fists flailed like promises: we can put our life back together; we can figure out how to be a family on a city block.

THE DOCTOR'S FOOTSTEPS pass my door. His disregard is making me mad. Anger is giving me ideas. I fantasize telling him when he comes back that it's impossible to consider *anything* in this windowless room. I'll explain to him that the word *consider* is rooted in the Latin, *con*—"with," and *sidus*—"star group." Therefore, to "consider" means looking to the heavens for guidance, charting one's course by the stars. There is no heaven in this closed-up room reeking of disinfectant. Next, I take up *fulfillment,* the byword of the era and the bane of women like me raised to imagine children as a suitable filter for ambition.

When he finally returns, I'm dressed, but still shivering on the edge of a straight-back chair. He leans against the table where earlier I sprawled, looks down at me, and examines my conscience with his eyes. "So, what do you think?"

In the two or three minutes he'll grant me, there's little hope of explaining my thoughts about anything. I'm fair game in his anxious world. I forgo linguistic vengeance and say simply, "I think we don't agree."

I *know* we don't agree. Constellations he wouldn't recognize have steered my course: light slanting through stained-glass windows, the solace of my mother's proud soprano when I knelt as a girl at her side during the Friday evening novena to Our Sorrowful Mother. The prayers were obsequious and saccharine, the songs sappy. "Good night, sweet Jesus, guard us in sleep," we warbled in a waft of incense at the close of the ceremony. "Our souls and bodies, in thy love keep." But the yearning engendered was real. So was the Thomistic philosophy fed into my young brain like the steady drip, drip, drip of glucose into a vein, its effect so powerful that, in the year 2000, I will continue to write "Catholic" in blanks asking for religious preference. Never mind that I attend Mass irregularly or that I bristle at papal pomposity, the answer is truthful. The scent of sacrament is embedded in my bones. I'm Catholic in the way that I'm Irish and Iowan, a circumstance I accept and sometimes celebrate.

But here in this clinic in Miles City, the doctor has made his point. Bad enough that I'm adversely affecting the world with my Catholic fertility; now I've found out that I'm also abdicating responsibility for my own life by remaining morally and existentially asleep. Like the dreamy heroines of fairy tales, I'm destined to wake up and wonder what I want to be when my children grow up. His prying has exposed a nerve where the message of the decade begins to strum its tune. Do your own thing. Find your own space. Liberate.

I watch for opportunities. A few days later, as I fill out a magazine subscription, I puzzle over a blank requesting my professional title. I decide to create one, something that will describe the multifaceted work I do. "Psycho" I print on the line, thinking of the psychological components in child rearing. Then "bio," referring to the care and nurturing of young bodies. And finally "geneticist," meaning the traits donated by ancestors that both help and hinder my daily tasks. "Psychobiogeneticist." Perfect. When the *Harvard Newsletter* arrives addressed to "Virginia Tranel, Psychobiogeneticist," I smell sweet success and hunger for more.

I invest in oil paints, brushes, and canvases, sign up for my first formal art class, and set out to resuscitate my potential. As a child I drew constantly, but in our parish school, religion was the fourth R, and art was a costly frill. In col-

lege, when art classes were available, I passed them up, pre-
ferring at seventeen to *be* ignorant rather than to *show* it by
studying a subject I knew nothing about. But now is my
hour. When I'm not nursing Jennie, I'm becoming an
artist. Alas, my narrowed focus produces mostly burnt stews
and neglected chores. When a childlike Picasso with dis-
torted eyes and mislocated ears appears on the dining room
wall beneath a scrawled "Mom," I recognize Monica's de
Kooning–style artwork. "She'll adapt," Ned consoles me as
I scrub off the paint and blame the mischief on my
negligence.

But the handwriting is on the wall. We return from
a Thanksgiving holiday spent in Colorado with Ned's
brother and his family to a FOR SALE sign planted in our
front yard. An ultimatum: Either move or buy this house.
We open the door to a ringing telephone. Elizabeth races to
answer it. "Mom! It's Uncle John." My brother tells me
our eighty-nine-year-old father has died. I must return to
Iowa. Another winter car trip is too much for everyone, so
I take the train and a select group. My infant, of course, and
Mike, who appreciated my dad's tales of mules and wagons,
and Ned Anthony, who appreciates any chance to skip
school.

A few days later, on a steel-gray Midwestern day, I
kneel next to my mother during my father's funeral Mass.
Whatever she might feel is hidden behind the curtain of
expressionless eyes. At the cemetery, as my father's body
is lowered into the earth, my heart reels with the echo of
his promise. *Someday you'll be sorry.* I study Jennie's face as
she sleeps in my arms. The fringe of lashes against her ivory
cheeks, the grimace verging on a smile. Enfleshed in her
is the hope impressed upon my childhood: Life triumphs
over death. Afterward, at the funeral dinner, my spry

ninety-two-year-old uncle Joe demonstrates his version of that belief. He defies gravity and old age by standing on his head.

The funereal scent of gladiolas follows me home to Miles City. On Ash Wednesday, the priest traces a cross of ashes on my forehead and repeats the words I heard at the start of every Lent throughout my childhood: "Remember man that thou art dust and unto dust thou shalt return." That reminder, a bell that inevitably begins to toll in one's mid-thirties, combines with our dislocation and the doctor's tantalizing, "Mrs. Tranel, have you considered . . ." to form in me a sense of unfocused urgency.

More and more often I pause before the mirror to study the vertical line forming between my brows, the age gathering around my eyes. I study the ways of other women. Are those stylish office workers "fulfilled" or simply dressed up? I buy one of the wiglets popular at the time, a cluster of coy curls meant to ride atop my head like a beauty queen on a float. It does—out of the salon, across town, into the house, past Ned reading in his chair. He speaks, glances up, and does a double take. With all the delicate curiosity of a man oblivious to fashion, he asks, "What's that thing on your head?" Obviously, *that* thing is not his idea of *my* thing. What *is* the thing that will unleash my potential, or at least preserve my youth?

I'm submerged in relationships and mired in responsibilities, but I'm also a college graduate with a degree in English and Spanish who should show a semblance of intelligent participation in society, who should find some "thing" to fulfill her beyond the children in her life, the infant in her arms.

When spring comes, I strap my sweet, fat baby, Jennie, into a backpack and ride my bike through the neighborhood, speculating about other people's lives. I avoid the steep hill to the airport where, on any given day, I might be terrified at the sight of my husband and two of our kids careening down on a contraption they call "the three-seater," a welded-together homemade bike Ned found discarded in an alley. Three handlebars and pedals and seats wobble atop two wheels. The lead rider holds 90 percent of the power in his handlebars, the middle person 10 percent, while the third, depending upon his attitude, is either giddy passenger or terrified captive. What could be a tame, communal ride is, in Ned's hands and my mind, a reckless plunge to prove something. Our disparate bike rides are emblematic of our attitudes. Even so, neither of us can roam long or far. Jennie's weight nags at my back, and the Miles City mosquitoes keep six legs pedaling hard.

Town life and traipsing after youth encourage Ned and me to socialize in ways foreign to our country lifestyle. We go to nightclubs, where we dance and drink with the lonely crowd. We try out roles beyond mother and dad. But coming home to a houseful of children keeps ruining our act.

Or maybe responsibility enabled our long run. We were yoked together like workhorses sharing a load. Forward now, pull, pull, pull. A backward slip, four feet lost, now forward again, pulling always toward some nebulous summit where we would find our children grown into adults who yearned for something beyond their own comfort, who saw past their own reflections to a larger meaning in life, who had the courage to ask questions that might not have answers, who were developing their gifts and giving them, freely, recklessly, entirely. Having been raised on existential "shoulds" and "oughts," we endeavored to pass them on to our children: *What ought I to do with my life? How should I behave in this situation?*

Often enough, our greatest struggles involved each

other, as documented in the anniversary card our youngest daughter, Adrienne, sent to Ned and me this year. A grim couple arm wrestles at the kitchen table. "Give up, wimpy," the woman snaps. "No way, Tinkerbelle," he snarls back. Inside the card is the heart of the matter: "Another anniversary and still holding hands."

Sometimes, looking back, I count us among the lucky survivors. We were simply too busy onshore to board the boat that sank in the seventies, all those marriages that went down, perhaps many of them unnecessarily, men and women and children thrown into strange, lonely waters to flounder and cry out and sometimes drown.

In a world where things fly apart, what *does* it take to make the center hold? Experience has led plenty of people to suspect that hanging loose doesn't work, that being true to yourself might involve being true to others, that instead of being regressive and repressive, morality—the effort to discern the good and live with conviction and responsibility—may be the glue that holds society together after all. At the same time, life's lonely lessons, fraught with struggle and failure, make us more hesitant to judge others for the glues they use out of desperation. Maybe the seventies illuminated that message by default. Or maybe by design, some mysterious design visible only in hindsight.

Perhaps the strongest glue of all is compassion.

"WELL, I CERTAINLY do feel sorry for myself," says three-year-old Jennie at the breakfast bar. She slumps, elbow on the counter, chin in hand, and gazes forlornly at the row of cereal boxes in front of her.

All this introspection so early in the morning, so early in life, catches my attention. "Why?"

"Because the cereal is all gone."

It's 1973; Miles City is in our past; and I hope the disheartening self-scrutiny incited there is, too. But self-pity seems to linger on in our youngest child, here with Paul and me and the slim pickings left by six older siblings gone off to school at St. Labre. She's disposed toward inclusion, toward receiving her share of the bounty and the Cheerios, toward the world as an enthralling place. If a vehicle leaves, she expects to be in it.

Ned, who learned to fly in Miles City, now pilots a single-engine plane to the far-flung Montana communities where work calls him. When he takes off from the airstrip below our hill, Jennie looks out the kitchen window and pouts. Why isn't she in the other seat, traveling with him? And one day, he does invite her for a ride. Paul, too, since he's the other half of the self she refers to as "Jen-Paul." Soaring over the raw red hills and determined pines, they giggle and gain a larger perspective. It surfaces a few days later when Danny scolds her for crying. She rubs her eyes with a small fist and listens for a while. "But Danny," she whimpers, "when I get hurt, I *have* to cry."

Her desire is simple—to be in on everything—but impossible to carry out. She drops over exhausted at random moments: at the dinner table; stretched out on the bathroom floor, overtaken by sleep in the midst of her toileting task; curled up in a corner of the sandbox; occasionally even in her bed.

She gives me rhymes and good-night kisses in accordance with her age: at four, *One-two-three-four, now I love you all the more.* That's the year her brother, Ben, is born. *One-two-three-four-five, I'm so glad that we're alive.* That's the year we move to the ranch north of Broadview. She's old enough for kindergarten and counting on it, but it's a day-long affair and she's already receiving more education and socialization from her siblings than she can absorb. *One-two-three-four-five-* but nothing seems to rhyme with six. It's time for school and first grade and for Jennie to explore a world beyond home.

Looking back, I think this daughter occupied an enviable position as eighth child. She was part of the "main group," the family continent, but also the youngest child for four years, twice as long as anyone else basked in that limelight. She ran with a lively herd of siblings while reaping the harvest of parental experience. She knew that she belonged, that she was safe and loved. On this foundation, she could build the courage to risk and care.

Now, here in the dark of another place and time, a piece from my past has surfaced, the venerable doctor of the condescending questions, singing his heart out on the stage before me. But *condescending* is my word. Maybe he was striving sincerely, as I believed myself to be, to understand his obligations, to act on what he thought was true. Maybe his reprimand was a courageous act done with a fast-beating heart, out of conviction and a dry-mouthed duty to speak his conscience at my naive turn down a dead-end path.

I'D BEEN to Europe before. Two brief trips to Rome and Florence; a ten-day trip through Prague, Vienna, and Budapest, where, if it's true that when you're lost you're found, Ned and I are irrefutably found. On those narrow, spiraling streets, his rural compass whirled while I scanned the signs for vowels, an *A* or *I* or *U* that would make sense of those densely consonanted words.

But this trip to Spain in 1996 is our first. Jennie, who moved here last fall to teach in the American School of Madrid, invited us to join her, along with everyone else in the country, for Semana Santa in Andalusia. It's here that the Holy War between Ned and me erupts.

Or perhaps it began months ago, the night I realized that there we were, two cradle Catholics propped up on pillows reading side by side in bed but worlds apart. He was engrossed in the Bible. I was reading Marguerite Duras's *The Lover.* Only the *Song of Solomon* could have redeemed the scene.

I was in the midst of a developmental task I'd skipped in college, that spree of atheism or agnosticism that treats tradition like the contents of a dresser drawer, dumping it out, rifling through it to see what's there of value. I was questioning credos and catechisms and the immutable bind God had created for Himself. After all, shouldn't the "Father of Lights, with whom there is no change, nor shadow of alteration" (James 1:17) know that he could escape that dilemma by going female? No longer would *he* be incapable of change; change was *her* prerogative. *She* could flow with the rest of creation, in a state of flux! In the process, the absolutes that bred conquistadors and crusaders might give way to awe.

"Maybe you should put the Bible on the shelf for a while," I said to Ned, wooing him in words borrowed from eco-theologian Thomas Berry, whose writings I'd recently discovered. "Maybe it's time to study the book of nature, including our own human nature." Never one to refuse a good offer, Ned abandoned his meditation and turned toward the nature nearest him. But my persuasion took a different turn.

"We need a new story," I said, launching into Berry's version of hierarchy. Fish are best at swimming. Birds at flying, and humans at reflecting. "So, if reflection is the unique human contribution to diversity," I went on, "shouldn't we make time for it?"

Ned scratched his head.

"But there's that bad word 'should,'" I said. "Besides, contemplation takes time. We'd have to set aside a day for rest and recreation. What would become of the GDP if we shut down malls and whiled away our Sundays?"

"Maybe we could start gradually. With an hour in church," said Ned, drawing his sword and pointing it at my unholy Sabbath.

"Faith doesn't depend on time spent in church," I replied, and snapped shut my book.

"That notion of worshiping in the woods is fine as far as it goes. But I fail to see how we can pass down faith and values if there's no structure for doing it. If there's no place or group to support you in your belief, how's it going to keep going?"

"Faith and belief are two separate things," I said. "Belief is a means to an end. Something to hold on to until we can let go. Faith is about being open to whatever turns out to be true."

"And how would you go about teaching . . . *whatever?*"

"Through word. Example. Stories."

"Stories? You think there'd still be a Christmas story if no one went to church? There'd be Santa Claus. Which is about where we are now."

"I'm not saying we should *never* go to church. I just don't want to be a slave to it. Going out of habit or anxiety, a vague fear that some boom will be lowered on me if I don't show up every Sunday morning. I thought Christ came to set us free."

"I go to Mass to pray," said Ned, turning over. He reached for his Bible and found his place.

Our religious disagreements intensify, ironically on Holy Thursday, more ironically in Cordoba, where tenth-century Jews, Christians, and Muslims lived side by side in open-minded tolerance. The effects are ever-present, especially in the city's mosque, famous for its innovative architecture and sumptuously decorated mosaics. But carved into the heart of the mosque is a cathedral. Gothic-style transepts and apses document the seductive search for grandeur. Inside, a crowd gathers for Mass; Ned joins them. Jennie and I roam the streets, sniping at Christians and their bad historical habit of killing off dissidents.

The more I resist Ned's religious fervor, the more he seems compelled to worship in every church in southern Spain—Trujillo and Caceres and Toledo and Cordoba and Sevilla and Granada. He stays to the end of every service, a plethora during Holy Week in a country as flamboyantly Catholic as is Spain. Pragmatically so. During the Inquisition, ostentatious religion was the glue that kept body and soul together.

Night after night during Semana Santa, solemn processions clot the narrow streets. In Granada, we wait with throngs of enthusiastic Spaniards while hooded, white-robed Catholics make their way down the steep wooded hillside from the Alhambra, the famous Muslim fortress overlooking the city. Walking slowly, deliberately, the barefooted penitents emerge in pairs, their faces eerily lit by the flickering candles they carry. As they enter the city through the ancient Muslim arch, years of treacherous religious warfare seem to disappear into one transcendent moment of harmony.

On our way home, somewhere over the Atlantic, Ned and I make our own peace.

WE'VE TRAVELED, but we're not the types to fly off on a whim. But opportunity lures us, such as this spring's chance to join Jennie again, this time to travel north into Asturias, through the Picos de Europa and along Spain's northern coastline into Basque country. We plan the trip for late

March 1999, then notice a bargain airfare—round-trip, Billings to London, three hundred dollars—and can't resist. So we schedule that for the last of February, leaving a four-week interlude between trips.

In late January, Jennie calls to tell me her apartment mate will be away for those four weeks. "This is the perfect chance, Mom. Come to Madrid from London instead of going home with Dad."

"Instead of going home?" I parrot.

"Sure. Why go home for four weeks? Spend the time here."

Four weeks. My heart races with excitement. Or is it dread? Often I have trouble telling the difference.

Jennie interrupts my thoughts. "It's the chance of a lifetime. That's what you'd tell me. Take it."

It was. I would. I will. But first there's the requisite Irish suffering.

Two people from my past begin waking me up in the middle of the night. One, a tiresome eighth-grade girl, enacting the same strange scene night after night. She's making a costume for the school Halloween party, spending arduous hours cutting and drawing and coloring the complicated image of the Queen of Spades onto a long, narrow box that she intends to wear. But the moment she finishes the project, doubt sets in. Boxed up as the Queen of Spades, she won't be asked to dance. At the first coed party, the boys will prefer girls masquerading as glamorous vampires and cute Cinderellas. The girl makes a swishy grass skirt out of crepe paper and donates her box to a desperate friend.

I might have dismissed this dream more easily if I didn't know the outcome. Not only did the Queen of Spades dance all evening, but she also won first prize for the most unusual costume. The foolish girl walked home slowly, combing unhappy fingers through her drooping grass skirt.

The other middle-of-the-night intruder, a ruby-lipped, cigarette-smoking college senior, maddens me more with her flashy engagement ring and suitcase full of vague plans and worst-case scenarios. Night after night, she wakes me up with stories about the bad things that happen to good women who travel without a man at their side. Early one morning, this woman anxiously dials Spain and hands me the phone.

"I don't think it's a good idea for me to come," I hear myself telling Jennie. "A month is a long time to be away. You'd be at school all day. I'd be alone. You know me; I'd get lost walking. Subways scare me. I've forgotten all my college Spanish and—"

"My apartment's ten minutes from everything." She begins naming art museums. "The Prado. The Reina Sofia. The Thyssen. It's easy to find your way anywhere from here. You'll be surprised how quickly your Spanish will come back. And you'll have time to yourself to write. Isn't that what you've been longing for? Plus, I've found an art center with live models where you can go to draw. Monday through Saturday, four to ten. And only a twenty-minute walk from my place."

"Ten? At night? You mean, walk home alone in the dark?"

"Ten in Madrid is like six there, Mom. Everyone's out. Having tapas. Walking. The street is busy, lit. Or come home earlier if you want."

She's doing exactly what my mother accused me of as a child—refuting and rebutting until I'd exhausted both her and her arguments. "Every hole I dig, you fill," she'd sigh. But often enough, she'd add, almost enviously, as if secretly she admired my persistence, "The wheel that squeaks gets the grease."

Jennie employs my silence. "Mom, remember how scared I was leaving for New York that first time?"

I see the two of us sitting side by side in the Billings airport waiting for the flight that would take her, at twenty-one, to New York to teach in a private high school for inner-city girls. All morning, she'd been strangely quiet, refusing conversational bait while her silence fished for something I sensed but didn't name. At the airport gate, she told me she was frightened. The previous evening, her boyfriend, with a saboteur's shrewd timing, had spun a horror story about a friend of a friend who'd been shot to death moments after getting into a New York City cab. She imagined her own bullet-ridden body sprawled in the backseat of a taxi.

"Remember what you told me that day?" she prompts into the receiver now. "'Stay in the present,' you said. 'Pay attention to right now. Each step of the way, remind yourself that at this moment you're okay.' That's what I did. All the way to my apartment. And I made it. The cabdriver didn't pull a gun."

As she talks, my blushing thoughts leap to the following fall, when I visited her in New York. Huddled in the backseat of the cab, I ignored my own advice, my heart nearly stopped by a vicious duel between my driver and the female cabby in the next lane. They pitched and darted and charged in front of each other until finally, with a triumphant, obscene gesture, she took an exit ramp. I arrived at Jennie's apartment pale, but alive. I went with her to the Matisse show at the Museum of Modern Art; I saw those vibrant, joyous canvases blooming in the city gray. But more significantly, I was sitting in one of Carnegie Hall's plush red seats the evening the Oratorio Society performed the Fauré Requiem. And there onstage was my daughter singing her brave heart out.

One day when Jennie was about four, we were stopped at a traffic light, motor idling as we waited for red to switch to green. An elderly couple shuffled across the street in front of our car. Jennie studied them from her backseat perch. "Who are they?" she asked. One of us replied, "Some old people." Her eyes grew somber. Finally she spoke: "Are we new people?" Yes, yes, new people. New people notice what old eyes no longer see; they question fears and prejudices that masquerade as thought; they wonder at every turn. I liked looking at life through that clear lens.

In a foreign land, I would be a new person. It was time to grease that squeaky wheel again.

I TOWEL MYSELF dry in Jennie's fourth-floor apartment in Madrid. I've just emerged from a brief, capricious shower—warm, hot, tepid, brutally cold—to the sound of a woman singing on the floor directly above me. The tune haunts me. I hum along until the words come. "Midnight. Not a sound from the pavement. Has the moon lost her mem'ry? She is smiling alone." I may be humming "Memory," but this is my Buddhist moment. I'm paying as much attention to peeling the orange as I do to eating it. And a new day has begun.

I've been in Madrid nearly a week now, basking in solitude and time and my daughter's generosity. Happenstance has reversed our roles.

"I feel like I'm the kindergartener and you're the mom," I told Jennie my first day here as we rehearsed my route to the Circulo de Bellas Artes, the center where I would spend time drawing each day. We were walking arm in arm, in the style of Spanish women. Every so often we stopped while I mapped streets and turns. Jennie's four years in New York had given her nerve and an intuitive sense of city direction. But I'm a Midwestern naïf with an uncanny ability to get lost. That's an understatement. I'm straight out of the little house on the prairie. Iowa, Wyoming, Montana, that's where I've lived. I enjoy cities, but I'm as jittery riding subways as a New York driver dodging tumbleweed on a stretch of open range.

She laughed. "It's *my* turn to walk *you* to school. Except you're forgetting. I didn't go to kindergarten. You didn't believe in it."

"You didn't need it." Both statements were true.

"At least you could have taught me the ABCs," she says, feigning humiliation at being sent to first grade ignorant of basic kindergarten skills.

"It took you ten minutes to learn them," I said, and impulsively put my arm around her waist. "In fact, I've been reading an interesting book on that very subject. The authors argue that—"

"Mom, what did I tell you about quoting authorities?" But she laughed and hugged me back.

What she'd told me was to say things for myself. If I read something and believed it, I didn't need to attribute it to someone else's authority. On the other hand, my scientifically trained oldest son flinches at my undocumented statements. He wants footnotes.

"Anyway," I'd gone on, "they cite studies showing that kids who aren't taught to read before age seven are better readers at age twelve. And the brighter the child, the more time she needs to explore before being confined in an academic setting. Too often, that's where kids experience failure for the first time. Which, of course, takes a toll on self-confidence. See," I gloated, "that's what I've been saying all along."

"That's why you should say it for yourself. Wait," she said suddenly. "We missed our turn." We'd been lost in conversation before, on trails in Yellowstone Park, on the campus of Notre Dame, in Central Park, and now here in Madrid. Two short, sixtyish Spanish women slowed to gaze up at my tall daughter. Wide-eyed, they looked at each other and then at me as if hoping for an explanation. I considered quoting Jennie's brother, Ned Anthony, who pitched in this two cents' worth when coaches courted her to play college basketball: "Just remember, you're smarter than you are tall." From oldest to youngest, our children have grown progressively taller, as if affected literally by the space and time we allotted them.

We backtracked a half block and turned onto a street bustling with cars and pedestrians. "We're on the Paseo del Prado now, "she told me. A couple strolling past stopped to kiss, tenderly, at length.

"That's a familiar sight here," Jennie said. "People live with their parents forever. With no privacy." She sighed. "Seeing them makes me want to fall in love again." Her sigh told of a broken heart, the trip home to mend, then leaving to begin again, this time in Madrid.

Cars danced past in a crazy choreography of honking sambas and raucous rhumbas. An ambulance screamed; I caught my breath, but the flashing lights wove miraculously through the pandemonium. "Spain is the noisiest country in Europe," I announced. "Second in the world only to Japan." This was something I'd read this morning, but I cannily omitted the reference.

"And did you also read in that book that Spain has more holidays than any other country?" she teased, then pointed. "There's the Prado." I followed her finger pointing to an elegant building behind an arch of trees across the street. People were lining up at the main entrance. "I'm sure you've read about that place, Mom. It's probably the world's greatest gallery of classical paintings. The Spanish collection is fabulous. You'll love it."

How had it happened that I was here, pausing on the sidewalk, able to anticipate coming back tomorrow to stand before El Greco, Velázquez, Goya?

A few blocks farther on, a woman with a red scarf tied gypsy-style around her head thrust a pamphlet into my hands. It announced an El Greco show opening at the Thyssen-Bornemisza Museum. Near the wrought-iron railing, a man with scabbed shins sat cross-legged beneath a cardboard shelter. He might have been invisible except for the clink of an occasional coin into the cup at his feet. This unfamiliar scene troubled me for blocks.

"Pay attention here, Mom," Jennie said, noticing me drift into my habit of watching people and missing landmarks. We'd come to a busy traffic island. "This is the Plaza de Cibeles," she said. A finely sculpted fountain displayed the Roman goddess Cybele sitting in a chariot drawn by a pair of lions. "That's the Calle de Alcalà on the left. We turn here for your school." My school. I was as giddy as a baby on a swing.

We were walking uphill now. As we went up the wide marble steps of the Circulo de Bellas Artes, my college Spanish yawned and stretched in a cranny of my brain. I tried a few words on the dark-eyed woman behind the polished cherry desk. She listened patiently, then smiled and said, "I speak English." My heart sank.

Jennie supplied verbs and nouns as I filled in the blanks of the registration form. I abstained from my title of "psychobiogeneticist." It seemed irrelevant to the artistic thrust of the Circulo and absurd next to my daughter's real accomplishments.

In the art studio, I risked a question I'd been practicing.

"¿Donde puedo conseguir el papel para la pintura?" The man behind the counter raised his eyebrows to Jennie. She repeated my question. Soon, he was ignoring me and talking to her, gesturing elaborately as he explained where to shop for drawing paper. But she wouldn't be here to interpret for me tomorrow. Or the days after that. What then?

Two robed models emerged from the studios into the hallway, then the artists, men and women of assorted ages, some with telltale signs of charcoal on their hands, each with a cigarette poised to light. I resisted wrinkling up my American nose in a hypocritical disdain of public smoking. I recognized a few words in the rushing conversation. *¿Cuándo? ¿Pregunta? Lapiz. Americanos.* They were talking about Americans. No, they were talking about me, the looming *Americana*. Tomorrow I would be standing here alone, a mute foreigner lost in a cloud of Spanish smoke.

I STAND AT the window in the morning sun and sip café con leche while I gaze four floors down at the drama in the heart of Bourbon Madrid. Last night, Calle de Atocha was a commotion of chanting, marching women carrying banners announcing the Week of the Woman. Yesterday afternoon, all the streets off the Paseo del Prado were filled with enthusiastic, garrulous people waiting for some unfathomable event. Last Saturday morning, farmers jammed the street in front of the Ministry of Agriculture near the train station. Some were costumed as cows and bulls. Others hoisted signs painted with heavy-uddered cows and the slogan *"Galicia, la leche,"* their way of saying "Galicia is the cream of the crop." Obviously, the dairy farmers from that milk-producing region are as discontent with prices as American dairymen.

This morning Calle de Atocha is astir with cars and

buses and men and women hurrying to work. Across the street, housewives chat on third-floor balconies abloom with red geraniums, yellow pansies, purple petunias, and the ever-present orange bombona, the container for bottled gas. *Quaint* is the harmless-sounding word I use for the gas pipes meandering through the kitchen. *Hazardous* and *leaky* are the thoughts lurking in my mind.

Madrid is switching to natural gas, but state-operated utilities move at the same snail's pace as the Roman Catholic Church. Jennie's landlady, Clara, has endured this laborious process for more than a year now. The other day, out of patience with the utility man's hopeless tangle of red tape, she shouted hysterically in Spanish that if he didn't connect the gas tomorrow she would fling herself out the window. He went off shaking his head and waving his arms. Clara dropped into a chair in the living room and delivered in English a tirade on the *mañana* philosophy. Of Italian-Hungarian descent, she is married to a Spaniard and operates a language school in Madrid. "We are all a mix, too, as Americans are," she told me over tea. She described the Soviet occupation of her home in Hungary. "They simply sent letters to the people in Hungary saying the government now owned all of the property. Everyone had to go to work. Mothers, too. We had to sell our grand piano. They divided up our home and allotted each person only so much space. Russian men and two women from some religious sect lived with us, walking through our dining room, using our bathroom. Our previous life was over." She had lived in a world I had only read about. No wonder some Europeans bristle at the spoiled younger sibling across the ocean who tends to take good fortune for granted.

Jennie left an hour ago for the subway ride across town to the American School, where she teaches high school English and creative writing. My pattern is to sleep in until she leaves, a luxury for me, an hour's privacy for her. On the tiny table in the corner of the living room lies her morning note. In these daily messages, she tells me her schedule, suggests activities I might enjoy, lists produce we need from the market, and challenges me with an assignment in independence. Each evening, at nine-thirty or ten, we meet here for our Spanish dinner hour. We share news of our day, her anecdotes as a teacher, her pondering about work possibilities after she completes her master's at Bread Loaf next summer, my adventures in the marketplace, my drawings. At eleven p.m., hissing trucks and crashing cans tell us the garbage collectors have begun their late-night show and it's time to go to bed.

These days spent alone are graced: retrieving my college Spanish as I buy *manzanas* and *plátanos* with housewives at the morning market; exhilarating hours in the art museums, working silently alongside *madrileños* at the Circulo de Bellas Artes, our hands and eyes our common bond, the scratch of pencils and charcoal substituting for words; the leisurely walk home through streets aglow with people; the stop in a pastry shop to select our evening dessert.

Because I feel safer walking Madrid streets than hiking Yellowstone Park trails, where my imagination meets a bear at every bend, I begin to wonder if I'm a misplaced person. I've adjusted quickly to the rhythm of the Spanish day, which revolves around living, not business. I delight in the way people of all ages congregate and revel in ordinary moments. They remind me of figures from Matisse's *Joy of Life,* except that in this scene everyone is clad in the finest clothes. Old couples stroll arm in arm; young couples chat over drinks in the plaza while their children race in abandoned play, dodging balls and bikes and one another. I admire the attention Spaniards pay to family meals. The corporate culture has begun to challenge the siesta concept, but surely the country that refused to let the European Union take the tilde from their keyboards will resist this rude awakening.

In her note this morning, Jennie has escalated her challenge. She would like me to have copies made of her door keys. She has written down the phrases that will help me accomplish the task, but she's not sure if the shop is on Antòn Martìn or Calle Santa Isabel. I will have to ask for directions. And explore. I may get lost. She's a mother bird daring the fledgling to fly.

As I eat my orange and yogurt, I study verb conjugation and try to remember the distinction between the Spanish forms of "to be," *ser* and *estar*. One can make embarrassing mistakes by confusing them. Jennie hastily corrected me the other day when I meant to tell someone I was warm, but instead implied sexual heat.

The buzzer on the street rings in the middle of my study. *"¿Cómo se llama?"* I ask the intercom. Of the torrent of words tumbling back, I recognize *fuga*—"leak." The man is here to check the gas stove and the phantom leak that prevented the utility man from hooking it up. A few minutes later, a rotund, mustached man huffs and puffs at the door. He mutters something about *la cocina* and looks around. I gesture to the door on the right and pull out a phrase from college. *"A la verdad."* He tinkers with the stove for a few minutes, shrugs a few mysterious words, and leaves. I'm beginning to sympathize with Clara's dramatics.

I dress and go down the shadowy, uneven stairs. Now and then, I hear voices behind the doors and catch scents of food. A fish stew, perhaps, already simmering for the midday meal. A burst of March sunlight greets me on the street. I turn up Calle de Atocha, hurrying past the sex shop, Mundo Fantástico, and the dazed men coming out of its depths. I take my fragmented question—". . . *una copia de estas llaves?*"—to the clerk in the variety store. She nods and points. *"A la esquina."* At the corner, I repeat myself to a thin-lipped man. He launches into an explanation translated by a gesture toward the right. I am on a treasure hunt, and I've found the words to make myself clear.

When the shiny new keys are tucked into my pocket, I join the Spanish housewives gathering at the Mercado Antòn Martìn. The narrow cobblestone street is pungent with odors of fish, apples, cheese, bread. Today, the olive-skinned man behind the stand lifts his eyebrows to a stooped old woman critiquing the pear in his hand. *"Dulce,"* he tells her. *"Muy buena pera."* Then he nods toward me. *"¿Y tú?"* I glance at my list: *"Naranjas,"* I say. *"Seis naranjas. Y cuatro limones. Y seis manzanas."* I count out pesetas and drop them into his hand. Satisfaction surges through me. I've said everything in Spanish, and he's understood.

I tote plastic bags full of heavy produce up four floors and put the fruit into the small refrigerator, then go down the steps again, this time taking the street to the Centro de Arte Reina Sofìa, rehearsing a question along the way: *"¿Hay oferta especial para persona de la tercera edad?"* Is there a special rate for someone of the third age? "Third age" is the Spanish equivalent of "senior citizen." I prefer this phrasing. It seems more accurate than being cast into a class about to graduate from the earth. Indeed, as a person of the third age, I cherish the gift of time as I once did the afternoon hour when children napped.

A weary-looking woman stands in a dark doorway. Her hair is brown, short, practical. She wears a blue utility coat and sturdy brown oxfords. The mop she leans on declares her work. A young woman, impeccably dressed in a short-skirted black suit and black hose, strides by in Prada shoes with a matching attaché slung over her shoulder. Her black hair is fastened in a sophisticated bun. The cleaning woman purses her lips and studies her as if comparing their lives. If she had been born of wealthier parents, she seems to wonder, if she had gone to college, hadn't married so young, hadn't had children, would she be cleaning the steps of this apartment? What might she have been?

Her daydreaming sets off mine. What might *I* have been?

I might have been the old woman crossing the street instead of the mother driving the carful of new people.

I might have been on the way to New York myself that morning in the airport instead of waiting with my frightened daughter. I might have had a manuscript tucked inside my attaché, a meeting scheduled with my agent, a publication date for my latest novel. I might have been riding subways with the closed face of a city sophisticate.

I might have danced in the Queen of Spades costume I designed instead of anxiously handing it off to a friend.

I might have married the boy I was engaged to at twenty; I might have been a carefree single looking for love in all the wrong places.

I might have been a disgrace.

Or a nun. As high school girls, we were summoned periodically across the hill to the convent to hear a talk on vocations. A vocation was a call from God to the religious life: priest, monk, nun. Marriage was the default vocation of the masses. There in the convent, as we listened to glowing accounts of life as the bride of Christ, the lusty odor of gingerbread rose from remote ovens. Now and then, a young woman flitted down the shadowy corridor, scurrying close to the walls, glancing furtively our way. The recruiting nun handed us a list titled "Signs of a Vocation." I scanned it with relief until I came to the last item: "Not wanting to be a nun is often a strong sign that God is calling you and you are resisting His grace." The contorted notion haunted me. Nun. The very word sounded like negation. None. Never. Nonesuch. No one. No home. No passion. No sex. No children. I dated defiantly, entangling myself with boys to prove I did *not* have a vocation. I didn't want to marry Christ and eat gingerbread baked in ghostly ovens; I wanted to marry a flesh-and-blood man and sleep with him (in that order, as I'd been taught); I wanted to have children with him and open my body to a world of creation I believed was good. Otherwise, why would my mother plant dozens of geraniums in the earth every spring? Why would my father turn half our backyard into a garden where tomatoes and raspberries and corn could grow? Fulfillment meant planting and cultivating and nurturing and rejoicing in the harvest of your labor.

I pass a ubiquitous kissing couple and think about my husband, our marriage, the years we've spent looking, not at each other, but in the same direction. How have our choices as a couple affected our children's marriages? Our eldest son's is faltering. Last week, Jennie phoned him to say that he no longer had to be the big brother, that everyone else was grown-up, too, that he could lean on them sometimes now. And cry when he was hurt.

"*¡Es gratis!*" Free admission, smiles the red-haired woman at the museum admission desk. She hands me a card that pronounces me a full-fledged member of the third age. I can walk the ten minutes to this museum daily, stay for an hour or two, come back at my leisure. I live in Madrid! For three more weeks, I live here! Today I am here to see the famous *Guernica*. The elegant glass elevator glides from the street to the second floor. I find Room Six: Pablo Picasso. In spite of the crowd, the room is hushed. Critiquing has changed to meditation before Picasso's overwhelming wall:

the fragments and dislocations, the mother and her murdered child, the dead fighter's hand clutching a broken sword, the brutal human-headed bull, the dying horse, the black-and-white horror of civil war. I imagine May 1937. I hear the roar of German bombers called in by Franco. Mothers weep. Children wail. And old men prophesy the agony of World War II.

Other walls hold Picasso's preparatory drawings, curiously colorful. As I study the dates of his work, I realize an intriguing fact: my father and Picasso were born the same year, 1881; my father died in 1970, Picasso three years later. What different lives they led: Pablo Picasso, the astonishingly gifted artist, and Charlie Holmberg, the weary man in his sweat-soaked workshirt who seldom traveled beyond the borders of his birth state, Iowa. The struggles and failures, achievements and disappointments of two very different men have brought me here. Only chronology and my thoughts connect them.

Picasso's world was a passionate mix of art and women, wives and children, tradition and avant-garde; my father spent his energy as husband and provider, working to pay bills and educate his children for lives he hoped would be better than his. Because of my father's effort, I am standing in this room full of Picasso's art.

Because of my daughter's effort, too. Jennie, who is always on the lookout for good things to share, who hauls shopping bags full of Spanish cheese and sausages home each Christmas, who had the nerve to go to New York and the heart to tell her high school students to forget weaves and cornrows for a while and think instead about words. Jennie, who, on college break, sat with me over coffee all morning as we talked about books and possibilities and the shared indecisiveness we call broad-mindedness, who risks and fails and struggles and succeeds and cries when she's hurt. Jennie, the child whose birth was so ill-timed that surely she would have been aborted by logic's hand.

Because of Jennie, I am standing in this room with the *Guernica*.

That evening, when I tell about today's episode of the gas man, Jennie explains that the proper word to indicate the direction "right" is *a la derecha*. The "right" I'd used—*verdad*—means "correct, true, in accordance with fact or reason." Essentially, I had told the man the kitchen was "on the side of truth."

I like the idea: a kind of magical kitchen whispering answers to me as I open cupboards and chop garlic, a kitchen that will act as in-house consultant clarifying things I don't understand. Why, for example, do people gobble obscene Big Macs in the McDonald's restaurant that blasphemes the corner of Calle de Atocha? Are they Spaniards seeking adventure or Americans avoiding it? Have they considered other sources of nourishment? Why not *paella* or *sopa de pescado*? Tomorrow I will ask the magical kitchen if there is a difference between *verdad* and *derecha*, or if they come down to the same thing, choosing the direction one believes is right.

No, I will ask no one. This I know for myself. Tomorrow I will walk to the Circulo to draw. I will turn when I should and follow the path prepared by my father's faithfulness and my daughter's courage. During breaks, I will talk with José, a man my age who knows a little English. We have agreed to practice our skills by talking to each other while the *madrileños* smoke. I will look out the window at the mountains to the north and think of Montana. But I will not be lonely or wonder why I am here. Never before have I felt so sure that my direction is both *verdad* and *derecha*.

The Presence of Absence

·

BENEDICT

*O*n this rainy September 5, 2001, Ned and I are delighting in the tundra of Denali National Park. Because of the rich root system and poor drainage, walking on it is a little like hiking across a waterbed. We bounce along, savoring Alaska's feast of autumn color— scarlet dwarf birch, burgundy blueberry bushes, blazing yellow scrub willow, patches of deep green alder. Above all, we're cherishing the company of our son, Mike, who works for the National Park Service as park planner for Denali. It's the first time we've visited him on his Alaska turf and the first time he's spent three days in the role of only child.

As we make our way up Blueberry Hill, Mike's eyes turn continually toward the horizon in search of the mountain he knows is there—Denali, the High One, hidden behind a curtain of iron-gray clouds. Hidden, in fact, seven days out of every ten. If we hadn't seen the elusive peaks clearly from Anchorage a few days ago, acknowledging their presence would be an act of faith. Mike, with a pride akin to parental, wants to show off the mountain from this impressive proximity.

We stop often to pick blueberries or simply to listen to the silence. My glance strays to the brush around us. I rehearse what to say and do if a bear or moose should crash through and discover intruders. Mike tells us Denali is home to one of the greatest concentrations of wildlife in the Northern Hemisphere. The Park Service challenge is to protect their refuge while providing human access to this splendor. Entrepreneurs envision building a railroad to Wonder Lake and a hotel with a view; others worry over this invasion by the rowdy masses with their pollution and plumbing, their golf clubs and machines. As he talks, Mike glances persistently toward the absent mountain peak. Anxiously, I scan the path ahead for bears.

The next day, as we're leaving the park, we do, in fact, encounter a grizzly family. Ambling along the road bank, digging for roots and snooping for squirrels, are a sow and two cubs. We watch from the shelter of the truck cab, mesmerized by the rippling power and deceptive speed of brute muscle. The sow moves on; her cubs tug and yank a few more times, then scramble after her.

The heavy mist enshrouding the mountain dims our prospects of seeing it. We drive slowly over the narrow road, glancing up, watching, waiting, hoping. Finally, the sun begins to melt away the fog. The clouds drift and scatter. A patch of blue breaks through. Another and another. And then, there it is—the wondrous white presence that is Denali. We stop and this time get out to stand on the dirt road in silent awe, that mix of amazement and respect and reverence that seems instinctive before realities we don't understand.

Fear, never far from me in these wild places, shivers through me as I imagine men and women struggling toward that bitter summit. Who is the shadowy being of the mountaintop, I wonder, who summons us toward its grandeur, then lashes out with furious wind and brutal cold, turning back most of those who try?

"Be still," the mountain seems to reply, "and know that I am God."

The clouds close, and the vision disappears.

Forty-eight hours later, our plane lifts through the clouds over Anchorage and into the sunlight. There, clear and soaring, is Denali. Ned and I gaze, godlike, imagining all the earthling eyes striving to see.

We land that night on the sandstone shelf atop the rim-rocks that shelter Billings. Against a clear sky, the Beartooth Mountains appear amiable, almost diminutive, as they beckon us home.

THREE DAYS LATER, on Fifth Avenue in New York, our youngest son, Ben, stands with his office mates, looking south. Like Mike, he is searching the cloud on the horizon. But there is no Denali behind the black fury on Manhattan's skyline. It is September 11, 2001. Terrorists have plunged planes into the World Trade Center towers. Ben turns north in anguish, south again in hope. The second building falls. Under the exploded rubble lie thousands of human beings. Brothers, husbands, friends, sisters, mothers, children, people from eighty nations. A great city is suddenly a massive crematorium.

"Oh my God, oh my God," people cry instinctively into the blackened streets of New York. "Oh my God, oh my God," cry the rest of us huddled in disbelief before the destruction on our television screens.

One by one, throughout the day, my children call home. Have I heard from Ben, they ask from Alaska and Iowa and Spain and Virginia. Is he okay? I reassure them that he called early this morning from his office a mile north of the disaster, unharmed but distraught. His girl-friend, Karen Seong, works in a building near the stricken area. He hasn't been able to contact her; he doesn't know where she is.

Is any place secure? asks Ned Anthony, father of three young sons. How can I explain hatred to my children? asks Alane, mother of a two-year-old daughter and four-year-old son. Do we dare to look toward the mountain and hope? all of our hearts ask. The mountain itself can't be trusted.

Later that day, Ben calls to tell me that Karen's there with him. She exited the subway just before the first building fell, took refuge in a phone booth, then walked the long blocks north to his office. She arrived bathed in ashes, but safe.

THROUGH THE NEXT DAYS, Ben's e-mails home describe the eerie aftermath of destruction: New York streets emptied of cars and taxis; people walking, covered with ash and dust; parts of buildings and lampposts and stoplights going by on huge trucks; smoke pouring out of lower Manhattan as if the entire city had gone up in flames; his own desire for retribution.

> *To see the second building collapse was an unbelievable reality . . . this is my home, where I live and work, and we've been at-tacked. . . . I hope that our retaliation is soon, exacting, accurate, thorough, and totally debilitating to the countries that harbor these terrorists.*

While understandable, his angry hawkishness is completely out of character. He was the six-foot-four football lineman who drove his high school coach to frenzy because he lacked a killer instinct. As the coach barked, "Kill 'em, hurt 'em, put 'em out of the game," Ben loped down the field like a curious bear cub, unaware of his raw power.

In junior high, after we had moved to town but before his adolescent growth spurt, Ben was the vulnerable country kid pegged by the school bully as a target for torment. Karate lessons taught mental stamina, but ultimately, it was Paul, Ben's eighteen-year-old brother, who made the convincing argument. He posted his six-foot-two self outside the junior high school door. When the bully appeared, Paul grabbed him by the arm. "If you hurt my brother," he said, "you deal with me."

Throughout childhood, Ben's modus operandi tended toward empathy and gentleness. One afternoon, he came home from first grade in tears because the teacher had severely scolded a fellow classmate, a boy Ben described as "too little to get yelled at." Another day, as he was building with his blocks in the playroom while I sewed nearby, I heard a sniffle, then a sob.

"What's wrong?" I asked, assuming frustration over a failed project.

Without looking up, he said, so softly I had to strain to hear, "I wish I had a grandfather like the other kids around here."

"Here" was Broadview, the wheat-farming community six miles from our ranch home. At basketball games and band concerts and potluck suppers, everywhere families gathered around children, Ben saw weather-beaten retired farmers beaming over the progeny of their daughters and sons, the generation now living in the "main house" and running the farm, often with a good deal of advice from the couple in the small, new house nearby. But the potential problems of extended family weren't Ben's concern. He longed for the security of a grandfather's hand clamped around his. It was four years before Ben was born that my dad died. Ned was just past four when he lost his dad.

Four. Half the age of the misty-eyed boy in front of me on the playroom floor. Ned has told me he was too young to realize his father's death, that he felt protected by siblings and their shared chores and traditions and by the big-sister reminders that began with his footstep on the porch: *Leave your muddy shoes outside; take off your cap; comb your hair; say grace before you fill your plate; keep your elbows off the table.*

Still, I wonder at his claim. Recently he reported a dream in which he and his brother were little boys again. It was haying season, and they decided to put up their own crop, all by themselves. They cut it and then built a small hut to store it in, but the hay was too green and rotted. Discouraged, they sat wondering what they'd done wrong. But along came our children, out of context, to reassure their dad, the little boy Ned, that it wasn't his fault, that he didn't know how to harvest properly because he had no dad to teach him.

No dad to stretch out on the sofa every evening as Ned did with Ben astride his chest demanding the story of the little boy and the dog, an impromptu, meandering narrative of a boy remarkably like Ben and his dog, Gretchen. No dad to ride next to on the front seat of the pickup, no one to answer the questions popping into a young boy's head. "Dad, what do roads do?" Older brothers, like Paul, riding on Ben's other side, emit ready exasperation. "That's the stupidest question I ever heard. They just lie there."

Dads tend to be more merciful than brothers. They dignify curiosity with answers, albeit vague. "What do roads do?" Ned repeated, stalling. "Well, they take us from where we are to where we're going to be."

And sometimes little boys have answers for dads. When Ned grumbled over a fallen fence, Ben took a philosophical tack. "Dad, don't worry about things you can fix."

OUR FAMILY E-MAILS to Ben argue for a peaceful approach. He responds:

> *I am not a proponent of violence or rage, but a nonmilitary response to these attacks will send a message that we've been crippled and we accept it. A peaceful response is negligent. We have a responsibility to stop the distortion of the Islamic religion and the oppression of millions of people in those nations. That is our war.*

"Write to your grandmother," I proposed to Ben that afternoon in the playroom, "and ask her about your grandfather." Promptly, he sent off a one-sentence letter to his only surviving grandparent, Ned's mother in Illinois. "What was my grampa like?"

She responded with a long letter: "Your grandfather was tall and handsome with a long, straight nose. He had dark hair and big, dark eyes. I met him at our little country school. He grew up on a farm next to my family's farm. Sometimes when we worked in the fields, we stopped our horses to give them a rest, and then chatted across the fence. We were friends and sweethearts for seven years and married at age 23."

Ben replied with more questions: "Did my grampa wear a cap? What size shoe did he wear? Did he like pizza?" He was constructing a grandfather, an image to tuck inside his heart and take out whenever he encountered other boys with flesh-and-blood grandfathers in tow.

Ben's imagination heightened his vulnerability to both joy and pain. He was five the fall we delivered Ned Anthony to Gonzaga University in Spokane, Washington. When Ben realized we were returning home without his big brother, he grieved for two hundred miles, the first time I'd seen a child that young cry inconsolably for reasons other than frustration or injury. Perhaps the story of *The Fox and the Hound* alerted him to the meaning of loss. No matter how often he listened to it, when the baby fox, Tod, lost his mother, Ben cried.

> *I went to a prayer service at noon. The two men next to me were crying so hard. We prayed for our leaders, for peace, and for those who lost someone. I dedicated a candle. I had every intention of working today, but once again, I'm sitting here listless. It's hard to go back to work when more buildings are collapsing and the smoke and dust continue to rain down the dead.*

IT HELPED TO TALK over his concerns with God, Ben told me one night during those boyhood years, because "God won't tell the world and he'll understand." He'd just read aloud a Helen Steiner Rice poem, "Daily Prayers Dissolve Your Cares," selected from a booklet sent by his grandmother. His bedtime ritual was this: I would sit on the edge of his bed and listen, first to the concerns of his day, then to his inspirational poem. Next, he kissed me good night, told me he loved me, and with a contented sigh, settled under the blankets with Doogan, the floppy-eared stuffed hound that was his birthday gift from Elizabeth. If Doogan languished in another room, or I was distracted and impatient, or Helen Steiner Rice was incarcerated in the dark beneath

Paul's nearby bed, the division between day and night blurred.

Confiscating his six-year-old brother's bedtime book was twelve-year-old Paul's revenge. Ben didn't just talk in his sleep, griped Paul, he delivered loud, long-winded, incoherent speeches. Eventually, Paul gave up and moved to the barn to sleep.

In retrospect, I think Ben's nocturnal eloquence was his way of catching up. Shortly after he'd begun to talk in earnest, a troop of siblings returned for the Christmas holidays and surrounded him with more noise and confusion and speech models than any toddler could decode. To make matters worse, Mike continually drummed along to "Christmas with Shirley and Squirrelly," a record featuring a chorus of squirrels and a stuttering chipmunk named Melvin. By January, two-year-old Ben's speech was an indecipherable mix of chipmunk and sibling and squirrel.

"You don't really have to tell God you're glad he gave you a certain gift, do you?" Ben asked during one of those bedtime chats. "I mean, he knows, if you use it every day." If this logic holds, the hours Ben spent on the playroom floor, day after day, year after year, creating with wooden blocks houses and barns and towers and corrals and airports, surely convinced God that this boy appreciated his gift as a builder.

"Mom, what do you think I'll be when I grow up?" he asked one day, looking up from his building project.

"Oh, maybe an architect," I answered offhandedly, too engrossed in my own thoughts at the nearby sewing machine to propose anything but the obvious.

"What's an architect?"

"Someone who makes buildings."

He pondered this, then picked up a block and went back to work.

As an architect, my passion is to build and create buildings where people can live and work and enjoy their environment. We are well aware that our biggest projects symbolize a society's accomplishment. To see the buildings destroyed carries a special pain, in addition to all of the unnecessary and brutal loss of life. They don't expect to find any more survivors in the wreckage, but thousands are still missing. Giuliani ordered 6,000 body bags.

A few days later, over the phone, Ben struggles to put into words the terrible confusion and discouragement he feels at the sight of the gaping hole on the Manhattan skyline, the stench of air polluted by hatred. He tells us that the plazas where last weekend he "was just hanging out on a bench" are filled with heavy construction equipment. Bus stops normally posted with fliers for apartment seekers are plastered with signs of the missing. Spontaneous candlelight vigils are constant. Like everyone else, New Yorkers are grappling for a framework on which to rebuild their lives, but they see only twisted remains. What was important on September 10 is suddenly meaningless. The woman who runs an art gallery questions the relevance of paint and canvas; the chef at a gourmet restaurant no longer sees any point in trying to make perfect carrot soup.

Now I am back in the office and trying to get back to a semblance of normality. My boss is here and working, even though I think he knows people who perished. We are working on a lot of towers throughout the world. It's strange to see all of these drawings of huge buildings on our desks. But I know that I will keep building, because that is what I do.

I KNEW LABOR was imminent that November morning in 1974 when I woke to vague aches. Ned was preparing to drive the seventy miles from our home in Ashland to Miles

City, where he was scheduled to see clients at the Mental Health Center. It seemed prudent and convenient for me, nine months pregnant, to ride along. Because nothing specific occurred on the way, I checked into a room in the Olive Hotel, where I was close to both my husband and the hospital and could wait comfortably for the birthing process to move in its own time.

As usual, I'd brought enough books to last a month, but the one I chose was optimistically slender and oddly irrelevant given the significant process under way in my body—*Man's Search for Meaning* by psychiatrist Viktor Frankl.

I settled into a comfortable chair. Frankl described three years of suffering and degradation in Nazi concentration camps. The question besetting most of the prisoners was, "Will we survive the camp?" But for Frankl, who'd lost everything that mattered to him—his family, the manuscript of his first book, all the familiar goals in life—the question was, "Has all this suffering, this dying around us, a meaning?" If not, he could only conclude that life itself had no meaning.

Now and then I stood up and considered going out for a walk. We'd lived in this town for two years. Perhaps I'd encounter a friend for an hour's conversation. But the minute I got to my feet, a clamping pain forced me back into my chair.

My pain subsided before the horrors of Auschwitz. Frankl had no escape from his suffering. Somehow he had to transcend it. He began to see that even though he was a prisoner, he was still free to take a stand, to choose his attitude toward his circumstances. This *choosing,* he realized, was the one way human beings could satisfy their need for meaning. Pursuing happiness is elusive and unfulfilling; meaning is created by doing the work set before you that only you can do, the meaningful task at hand.

The task at my hand that November 15 was obvious. When Ned returned to the hotel room at the end of the day, we ate dinner—for me, tea and Jell-O—then walked the snowy, cold blocks around the hotel. Finally, the contractions grew regular and strong. Shortly before midnight, we checked into the hospital. Half an hour later my doctor arrived.

"You should have come here much earlier," he snapped when he learned that I'd been in town all day experiencing erratic contractions. *You should have been considerate,* his tone implied, *and checked in at noon when I could have ruptured the membranes and accomplished the whole thing by midafternoon with no one losing a moment's sleep.* Instead, I'd frittered away the day in selfish pursuits, then pulled him from a warm bed in the middle of a cold November night. I'd rousted his wife, too, I learned later, because her duties included scraping frost from the windshield of his car. Clearly, he preferred compliant women. For birthing purposes, he also preferred them unconscious. But I was insisting on minimal medication and maximum awareness. After all, this was my ninth trip into this particular setting. I knew more about what was happening inside my body than did this swarthy doctor looming at the foot of my narrow bed.

"No," I protested, "I don't want to be 'put under.' I want to be involved in this." His eyes darkened like an approaching storm. His words, heavy with a Middle Eastern accent, ground through clenched teeth. "Mrs. Tranel, you are a very stubborn woman."

Stubbornly I labored while he sulked, his anger like a threatening cloud darkening the room. He brandished forceps and at one-twenty a.m. applied them as if deliberately testing my resolve. Just then our child emerged, howling, howling before fully born, before we could even tell that it was a boy, a nine-pound boy, our ninth child announcing what would be the theme of his childhood: hunger and wonder. The nurse laid him on my chest, and, skin to skin, he settled into the attentive tranquility peculiar to newborns.

Minutes later the doctor bore down on me with a needle in his hand. "It is time for you to rest," he declared. Before I could claim this transcendent moment mine, he injected his venom into a vein and sent me into the pliable place he had in mind for me all along. Thus, he cheated me of that hard-earned postbirth ecstasy, the sense of merging with the universe and creation and every other woman who's arrived safely on this ineffable shore. He deprived Ned and me as a couple, too, of precious moments of intimacy, shared amazement, and gratitude. Our son was whisked away. I was a limp sprawl under a heavy sheet. Ned decided he may as well go home to the two-story house on the hill above Ashland, where eight other children, ages four to seventeen, awaited the news.

Swaddled in a blue blanket in the bassinet, our son was the biggest bundle in the hospital nursery, this ninth child whimsically weighing in at exactly nine pounds, perhaps sticking out the day with me in the Olive Hotel for the sake of another quarter ounce.

Two weeks later, on Thanksgiving Day, in the seclusion of our hilltop home, we baptized our baby "Benedict," after the beggar-saint Benedict Labre, for whom the Capuchin mission to the Cheyenne people was named. In a sense, our son owed his existence to that mission. My desire for another child, the child who would be Ben, awakened as I cared for a two-week-old Cheyenne infant, rescued from a drunken party by our parish priest and left with us until a safe alternative could be found.

Although baptism is intended to be a community ceremony held in church, where people can pledge their support toward forming this child in faith, a series of unsettling phone calls kept us home. Daily, for over a week, someone had been calling with a whispered message: "Mrs. Tranel has too many children."

The name Benedict comes from the Latin word *benedictus,* meaning "blessing." No amount of hateful, anonymous whispering could alter the enormous blessing of another healthy baby, another bundle of possibility to open slowly with awe and care.

What kind of hate would make somebody want to do these things to our beautiful city? Imagine waking up tomorrow to go to work and it's gone, all gone, nothing at all to go to, nothing to pick up. They want us to be scared. But this is my home and I will not be terrified in my own home.

HIS ALLEGIANCE to New York was obvious in February 1999, when Ned and I stopped for a weekend on our way to London, that impromptu trip sparked by bargain airfares. Ben, a graduate student in architecture at Columbia, immediately took us to the woodshop to show us where he spent many hours each week, "quite a few of them daydreaming," he confessed. Wood scraps and shavings littered the concrete floor beneath sharp-toothed saws and wicked blades. He showed us his half-finished model of a ferry terminal, another of a library, then fanned through a portfolio of architectural exercises, sketches articulating forms, relating mass and volume. Next, he picked up an elegant chessboard made of alternating squares of maple and walnut and pointed out the factors that went into his choice of wood and the process of designing and crafting it. I'd seen the absorbed play of the boy but not the craftsmanship of the man.

"I didn't know you had these skills," I said. "Except for the daydreaming part."

"I kept them secret so Dad wouldn't put me to work building corrals."

In an upstairs classroom, large printed letters on the blackboard announced a critique at two p.m. on Friday.

"Everybody sweats those," Ben said. "Putting your stuff out there for other people to take apart. Trying to explain what you had in mind. Hoping your brilliant idea will make a little sense to somebody else."

A professor strolled in and defended the ordeal. "These young minds whirl with lofty ideals. They imagine being the one who'll discover the new forms and patterns that will restructure the world. But on Friday morning, they're challenged to connect that imagining to reality, the here and now. Which, of course, is the task of genuine creativity."

During the subway ride downtown, Ben noticed my wide-eyed fascination for New York bizarre. He touched my arm and warned me to be careful. In Manhattan, staring attracted weirdos. In Montana, Ben was the one stared at. His shoulder-length curly hair caught in a bushy pony-tail once provoked a cowboy to exclaim, "Jesus Christ!" which inspired Ben to raise his hand in a blessing and reply "Peace." Here, he was run of the mill, except for the friendliness surging beneath big-city brusqueness.

As we walked along Park Avenue, he explained the significance of various architectural decisions. Setbacks, he told us, were the traditional solution for allowing sunlight into the canyon of buildings. But the Seagram Building was a steel-and-glass skyscraper set on a plaza, the first of its kind. "Thirty-nine stories," said Ben. "I'd like to figure out how to get up on that roof."

"Why do you want to go up there?" asked Ned.

"C'mon, Dad. Don't act so naive. You know why. You're a rooftop kind of guy."

In Billings, Montana, one seldom sees lumpen piles of humanity on the sidewalk. But in New York, outside St. Patrick's Cathedral, passersby appeared indifferent to the black bundle huddled behind the cardboard sign with its crudely printed letters: FOR THE LOVE OF GOD. Their faces closed with a Malthusian stinginess as they averted their eyes and hurried by. As we passed, the bundle stirred. A shriveled old woman struggled to lift her head and focus her faded eyes. The hand she held out revealed a purple finger that appeared to be rotting.

Waiting at the curb a short distance away from her was a festooned bridal car. The driver was tapping the steering wheel and watching the elegantly garbed guests collecting on the steps in front of the church.

Ben dawdled at construction sites, stopped to admire scaffolding or to poke around brass pipes and plastic tubes. He photographed piles of stuff that I made the mistake of calling "debris." As he showed us the city from his architectural perspective, the same parental pride glowed in his eyes that I would see later in Mike's when the clouds opened to reveal Denali.

On our way to the New York Public Library, he slowed before Rockefeller Center. The most remarkable aspect of this building, he told us, was the fact that someone had the wherewithal to construct it during the Great Depression. We stopped for a while in the library's third-floor reading room, that elegant wood-paneled oasis of quiet.

"I'm not ready to leave," I sighed as we dropped onto a bench in Bryant Park, outside the library. I meant this city and the comforting presence of my son. But I meant something else, too, something evoked by the haunting sign, FOR THE LOVE OF GOD, and the old woman behind it. The wind exhaled a chilly breath. Ben saw me shiver, slipped off his wool scarf, and wrapped it above my collar.

THIS GOOD-NATURED penultimate child lived up to the name given to him on his Thanksgiving baptismal day. Benedict was our blessing and, in turn, was blessed. He reaped the harvest of our parental experience while basking in the affection of eight older siblings. Fourteen-year-old Elizabeth nestled him in her arms and danced to the current hit "Feelings." Eight-year-old Monica wheeled him about in the stroller, the happy king of our hill. He attended to the discordance of after-school piano practice as if it were Mozart. He bounced to the pandemonium of Mike's drumming. He went along to basketball games and track meets and church. In August, when he was nine months old, he traveled to South Bend with Ned and me for Dan's freshman orientation at the University of Notre Dame.

We returned to a house teeming with noise and activity but ominously empty. When I scanned the jam-packed bedroom Dan had shared with his brothers, I saw only the missing quilt, the cleared-off desk, the empty hangers in the closet. The exodus had begun. Soon it would be Mike, then Elizabeth, then Ned Anthony. No longer could I avoid the question raised by the Miles City doctor after Jennie's birth: *Have you considered another source of fulfillment beyond children?* If having children was my hedge against oblivion, would meaning be stripped from my life like posters from the bedroom wall when our last child went off to college?

The myriad details of caring for my family filled my days, but a lonely restlessness haunted me. I was not a rancher or Native American or Capuchin monk, although the isolation of this place weighed on me like a grim, unspoken vow. I agonized day and night, giving myself pep talks, romanticizing reality, trying to survive on sunsets. I told myself our life was "interesting," but I knew the word was a coverup.

In early January 1976, I packed away clothes that in another setting I would have worn to holiday parties. As I folded dresses into the cedar chest that once stood in my parents' bedroom, I thought of Beret, the disconsolate wife in Rolvaag's *Giants in the Earth*. Unable to take root in her sod house on the South Dakota prairie and desperate from loneliness and monotony, she would open an old family chest and put away things that represented the life she longed for. One time, certain she was about to die in childbirth, she emptied the chest so it could serve as her coffin.

Isolation burdened me, too. Our holiday season was filled with traditions designed for children: a hike through the woods to find the perfect tree, the Christmas Eve drive over gravel roads in search of Santa (who invariably came while we were gone), sledding and skating, cookie baking and ice-cream making, music and singing, Chinese checkers and charades. But I longed for adult festivities, an evening of dancing, dinner at an elegant restaurant.

The next day, Ned and our older sons set out for Lemonade Springs, a ski hill a few miles east of Ashland. Hoping to avoid Beret's extreme, I put Elizabeth in charge of the younger children and went along. I hadn't been on skis since I was a kid in the Midwest, where skiing meant sticking your feet through straps for a short trip down a steep hill. I felt imprisoned and awkward in the huge, clamped-on boots. When I lunged for the rope tow that carried skiers to the hilltop, I fell, scrambled up, fell again. Something disconnected in my right ankle. Three hours later, in a Billings hospital, an X ray revealed a broken tibia; surgery was scheduled for the next morning. I awakened from it to a leg entombed in a full-length cast and the gloomy prospect of three months on crutches while mothering a one-year-old son.

Brought to a halt in the backwoods of Montana while January gray melted into February dun, I propped up my unhappy leg and faced by the stark light of day the questions tormenting me at two a.m., the "What's it all about, Alfie?" angst we label midlife crisis, in many ways an adult version of adolescence.

I began reading anything that promised an answer: Louis Evely's *Suffering;* Paul Tournier's *The Whole Person in a Broken World;* the writings of C. S. Lewis, Thomas Merton, Erich Fromm. Then I remembered those stolen hours with Viktor Frankl in the Olive Hotel and turned again to him. Concern over the meaning of life is a spiritual distress, not a mental disease, he told me now. The existential vacuum that doctors too often bury under a heap of tranquilizers is a widespread phenomenon of the twentieth century. Just as there's no such thing as the best move in a game of chess, there's no point in searching for the abstract meaning of life. And he said again the words I'd read on November 15: instead of *asking about* the meaning of life, *answer for* your own life. Respond to your responsibilities. Solve the problems life puts in front of you, and your life will have meaning.

At the kitchen sink, as I balanced on crutches and washed knives and forks and spoons, I began to understand. My responsibility was to heal, both my leg and my self-regard. Responding to the needs of others had been bred into me by my culture, but recognizing my own honest interests, mastering skills important to me, imagining meaningful activity when there were no longer any children in our home, felt wrong and too hard.

The proof of my dismissed self was in the kitchen.

We'd built this house in 1972, when a dishwasher was a standard appliance and ten people ate at our table every day. Yet I'd stoically denied myself that convenience. In 1968, it took a threatened pregnancy to justify owning a clothes dryer. Now, in 1976, my well-being was at risk.

On every airline flight, the attendant warns adults traveling with a young child to put the oxygen mask first on themselves and then on the child. If I intended to care properly for my children, my needs had to go into the mix that composed our family life. While my leg mended, my malingering soul began the work it alone could do: discovering the desires embedded there and deciding how to respond.

I needed a dishwasher. Our entire family needed a community. We were round pegs forcing ourselves into square holes and chafing against the ill fit. Wobbling on one leg, I telephoned a Miles City appliance store and ordered a dishwasher. Then I picked up the newspaper and began scanning real estate ads.

We'd moved a dozen times before we found our way from Miles City to this hill overlooking the Cheyenne reservation. We'd paced this land for a prime location, dug down through shale to pour a foundation, gone up through ponderosa pines until we had our three-story house with a view, the only home we ever built. A boys' dormitory downstairs. Large windows to the west. An enormous kitchen and dining room with the sunset our dinner guest all winter long. Moving would mean abandoning everything we'd made here: house, shed, fences, windmill, rock wall, even the sandbox, structures that defined our lives, places that sheltered our traditions and routine. The thought overwhelmed me.

But more disheartening was the notion of staying. And so we began again, taking pictures from the walls, clothes from the drawers, books from the shelves, emptying the rooms, one by one, until the home we'd created on that hill of red shale was reduced to an empty house.

The work of rebuilding our lives had begun, and although I couldn't have known it then, it was uncannily appropriate that Ben was the child born into this process.

When I first saw the buildings burning and then collapse, there was no doubt in my mind that we were at war, a new kind of war, involving strategy and long-term foreign policy. To overthrow the Taliban is to interrupt the flow of history and redirect it. There is no solution. It's a process and we have to start the process. The world will be okay when we realize we're all in the same boat.

President George W. Bush declares war between freedom and fear. He urges Americans to get back to work, to go shopping, to carry on with their lives in the usual way lest too much power be given to the irrational forces at work among us. If we quit waving the flag of economic bravado, the GDP might topple and with it our security.

But sometimes carrying on in the usual way *is* the irrational force. Sometimes we need the silence of the mountain, not the bustle of the marketplace. Sometimes freedom means the ability to pause empty-handed and wait for understanding. Anxiety—that diffuse feeling of dread and helplessness we suffer when "there is no solution"—feels intolerable; it can propel us into a reaction that's neither accurate nor judicious. Political and religious groups vying for power exploit it with promises, harangues, shrewd premises set side by side to engender an illogical conclusion that puts us in their camp.

Anxiety might be more tolerable if we understood it as an opportunity to make a choice. The anguished interim between provocation and response can teach us what we care about, prompt us to name our fear, and help us determine if our actions will break through our bonds or fasten us more firmly to them. "He therefore who has learned rightly to be anxious has learned the most important thing," wrote philosopher Søren Kierkegaard. The technological age has trained us to be spectators unnerved by silence, which is the worst of combinations because it eliminates both the pause conducive to creative insight and the action that brings insight into being.

THE FIRST TIME I descended the spiral staircase of the Spanish ranch house forty miles north of Billings, I felt light-headed with freedom. Two hours earlier, the full-length cast on my right leg had been replaced by a walking cast. After six weeks on crutches, that easy mobility lent an auspicious air to the day and the venture of buying a house. More: a ranch backdropped by the Snowy Mountains seventy miles to the north, and in between, wheat fields, rangeland, the pine trees and coulees of the rambling Bull Mountains, all drenched in sunlight and possibility. Here was authentic Montana. Here was our next home, this white stucco ranch house situated on a north slope with a view.

A few months later, that spiral staircase was the center of our lives, the connection between the main floor living area and the downstairs playroom that was surrounded by bedrooms. From the kitchen, I could look down and assess the tenor of my children's play, whether a tone of voice communicated a routine row or impending war.

When I think of that house now, I think of the staircase, the mundane circling down and up, down and up, down and up, the evenings when I descended exhausted to

bed, the mornings when I hurried to the kitchen to orches-
trate breakfast and schedules and the exodus to school, the
afternoons when I went down to sew on the periphery of
someone's play, that middle-of-the-night trip up in labor,
back down a few days later with Adrienne in my arms.

In the summer of 1989, I followed our two youngest
children up those stairs, Adrienne toting her bedtime
friend, Fievel; Ben clomping in size-twelve tennis shoes—
awkward, innocent country kids on their way to life
in town.

PICASSO SAID EVERY ACT of creation is first of all an act
of destruction. Every significant insight alters our world
and changes our relationship to it. A family confronts a
loved one's alcoholism and upsets the equilibrium; the tumult of pubescent hormones overturns the simplicity of
childhood; the naive ranch kid discovers town's mischief-
making possibilities and ruins his parents' peace of mind.

One of those first summer evenings in town, fourteen-
year-old Ben arranged a late-night tryst with the girl next
door. Long after we were sleeping—having assumed he
was, too—Ben, unaware of the city curfew, crept out of the
house. We woke to the doorbell. There stood our son, as
miserable as a molting penguin, shifting from one foot to
the other, in the company of a policeman.

Ben's next foray was mailbox bashing, a ritual of man-
hood for high school boys, who equip themselves with
baseball bats, pile into the back of a pickup, and drive down
dark roads to swing at mailboxes. But one irate owner spotted their license number and tracked them down. Police
ordered the boys to face their victims and fix the mailboxes.

And there was the memorable midnight in spring when
the sheriff telephoned and identified our car as one aban-

doned on the county road where high schoolers had staged a kegger. When the kids saw the law approach, they raced off on foot through the borrow pit. "Man, was I worried when I looked up and saw our car going down the highway on a tow truck." Ben laughs whenever this story surfaces. But invariably, a moan follows. "Every time I tried anything, I got caught."

Sometime during those years, he declared he was tired of traditional scales and compositions, quit his piano lessons, and, ironically, began to spend more time at the piano. He sat absorbed for hours, rewinding and fast-forwarding tapes by pianists George Winston and Phil Aaberg, picking out notes and mimicking their melodies, removing the music rack from our grand piano as he'd seen George Winston do in concert in order to reach in and pluck strings. After a Phil Aaberg concert, he brought home three signed CDs and played them around the clock. His compensation came the day a brother yelled into the living room, "Hey, how about playing something besides Phil Aaberg? That's the seventeenth time for 'High Plains.'"

The piano stopped. "Hey!" Ben yelled back. "The last four times it was me."

The "me" he was creating was a mixture of the hopes and dreams, models and metaphors and myths thriving in his imagination. Now he had begun a sorting process, choosing what to keep and what to throw away, identifying, in a sense, the false gods of society in order to reject them. Adolescent passion is on the lookout for truth, a tumultuous search that can bring new insights and perspective. With it, growth and creative potential emerge. Defiance can become wonder. This process is hastened, and the danger of youthful enthusiasm going berserk diminished, when consequences come on the heels of actions. In Ben's case, Phil Aaberg and George Winston endured. The late-night trysts? Well, he's older now.

THROUGHOUT THE FALL of 2001, family concern focuses on Ben. He expresses gratitude for e-mails as well as telephone calls of support. He asks people to keep writing. "There's strength in numbers," he tells us in early October. But his tone begins to take on an impatient edge. "I don't care too much about liberalism or peace right now," he retorts to siblings who continue to advocate a peaceful response. "Please wake up to the reality that there are over five thousand dead in lower Manhattan." It's as if his anger at the terrorists has spilled onto a family he's begun to perceive as a naive group cosseted in the pastoral oblivion of Iowa and Montana.

A flurry of rebuttals informs him otherwise. A few people drop out of the e-mail fracas. In late October, Ben announces that he has cleared from his e-mail list the name of anyone who doesn't write or who only provokes fighting that causes others to quit writing. "Funny that we have to fight about peace," he says.

In a phone conversation, Ben tells his dad that he's begun attending Mass on Sunday again, sometimes even on weekdays, at a Jesuit church near his office. He describes St. Francis Xavier as a "progressive" parish with an eclectic congregation and an outspoken priest, ingredients missing in high school religion classes when his brimming questions were too often dismissed as captious or insolent.

Adrienne, who's living in Madrid this year, worries about flying home for Christmas. It's time to schedule a flight. That thought troubles me, too. Christmas without our family gathered would be grim. But so is the daily news.

"Me—I'm going home for Christmas," Ben's e-mail

replies. "And maybe even for Thanksgiving, too." He reminds her that the terrorists are the ones living in caves, that here we're free to go where we want as long as we don't let fear overcome us.

Longing like many other New Yorkers for the reassurance of a pristine horizon, Ben and Karen schedule a flight to Anchorage to spend their Thanksgiving holiday with Mike and Jane and their daughter, Kelsey. Mike advises them, as he did Ned and me last summer, to reserve seats on the right side of the plane coming and the left going in order to maximize the coastline view. And if luck is along, they might glimpse the peaks of Denali as they land.

But the reclusive mountain has something more spectacular in store. On the day Ben and Karen drive to Denali Park, the sun slants low in a crystal sky, and throughout their trip, the peaks of the High One glow.

THE TEARS SPRINGING to my eyes when I greet Ben surprise both of us. "It's been a whole year," I say, to account for myself. He's the last traveler to arrive; the others pounce on him in the entry room. But he seems distracted and wary as he walks into the living room and glances around. "No Christmas tree?"

"We're cutting it tomorrow," Adrienne explains. "We waited for you."

He stands at the window, looks toward the Beartooth Mountains, and describes the view from his apartment window in Harlem, the canyons of shadow created between buildings by the setting sun. Then he turns to ask his dad if there'll be a chance to go to the ranch and ride Bess, his strawberry roan mare.

At dinner, Ned Anthony reports on the status of Ben's cows. The heifer he bought in high school has multiplied into a small herd. Ben says he's thinking about selling them.

I take it as a sign that he means to break his ties here. But after we finish eating, he hunts down Yurii and bundles up to churn ice cream in the driveway. And later on, he comes into the kitchen and asks if I'll teach him to make whole-wheat bread.

The next day is Sunday, two days before Christmas. Downstairs, everyone else is sleeping, but upstairs in the kitchen, Ben is finishing an espresso and preparing to leave for early Mass with Ned. At the last minute, greedy for time with this son, I abandon my kitchen tasks and go along.

As we enter the church, he glances about, taking in the structure and contemporary design—a semicircle of pews surrounding a simple altar, no statues, no stained glass, no suffering Savior nailed to a crucifix, just a large, unadorned freestanding wooden cross. I tell him this reflects Vatican II theology: Christ is risen; the people are the church.

Ben nods, then catches my eye. "Simple is nice, but my vote's with Gaudí." He means the architect Antoni Gaudí, and the dramatic cathedral, La Sagrada Familia, that he designed for the city of Barcelona. Ben visited it a few weeks before Ned and I were there in March 1999.

"But this church is *finished;* you have to give it that," I reply.

Throughout the murmuring prayers and intermittent song, Ben's eyes lift to circle the ceiling and study the wooden beams, but when I look up, I see the soaring spires of Gaudí's cathedral. And it's spring in Spain.

AS NED AND I approach La Sagrada Familia, I don't ad-mit it, but I'm as eager as he is for the quiet repose of a church. We're grouchy after a futile morning of circling busy streets but never gaining access to the one that would take us from where we were to where we wanted to be, atop seven-hundred-foot-high Montjuïc, where the Museum of Catalonian Art is located. Now we stop to admire the beautifully sculpted nativity scene on the facade of the cathedral, but our weary bones and spirits coax us inside. We open the door to a discouraging scene.

Instead of the hoped-for refuge, we encounter a vast construction site humming with activity. Cranes reach heavenward right along with the spires. Workers in yellow hard hats ramble about an enormous space. This church, begun in 1882, is less than half finished. Only eight of twelve planned towers are complete. But when we learn that the top of the east one is accessible and offers a magnificent view, our mission is clear.

We take an *ascensor* partway up, then climb steep stone steps through a passageway so narrow that two people passing must turn sideways. Ned's claustrophobia flares, but his longing for an eagle's privileged perspective pulls him upward. This time, the reality exceeds the promise. Not only can we see beyond Barcelona to the Mediterranean Sea, but also we can observe the astonishing sight below, more thrilling to me than the static grandeur of a completed church.

There, workers are engaged in what Ben's professor had called the "genuine task of creativity," translating Gaudí's vision into reality. Day after day, year after year, for more than one hundred years, Barcelona's people have been transporting wheelbarrows full of cement, hoisting steel beams, chiseling stone, hammering, consulting, making decisions, doing the work in front of them. The sheer scope of the project is evident in the evolving technology and materials. Smaller, irregular, less expensive stones date to the Spanish Civil War; large, quarried blocks distinguish work done since the sixties. When—*if ever*—it's completed, the church will form a Latin cross. There will be four more bell towers, one for each apostle, and a soaring central tower.

Looking down at La Sagrada Familia, the Sacred Family, I see a reflection of the human family. I think of our family, of our persistent search for the perfect place, the ideal refuge we imagined finally calling home, where year after year our children could return to the same room, the same furniture, the same trees, the same view. But below me is the reality of earthly life: flux, imperfection, some places patiently attended to, others half done, projects begun and abandoned and begun again, problems only partially solved, everywhere disorder and uncertainty.

BACK IN MONTANA in December, sitting between my husband and youngest son in this modern, completed church, I realize how much we long for our lives to have meaning, for the things we create to count. Yearning to outlast death and decay, we build families and towers and temples and cathedrals. But all the while, we sense that our creations may not survive; we may not succeed in carving out our human niche in nature.

I think of the cruel summit of Denali, of the fierce breath of Alaska's glaciers, the grinding journey of ice through rock, the huge boulders and debris dumped into braided rivers and terminal moraines, as if some formidable force lurked unseen, heedless of life-forms in its way.

I think of the afternoon Ned and I walked with Mike and his wife, Jane, and their daughter, Kelsey, to Exit Glacier, north of Seward. The trail wound through fireweed, Sitka alder, birch, cottonwood, and spruce, a successor forest springing from gravel deposits left in the glacial aftermath. Along the way, small signs dated the glacier's earlier reach. The trail ended in a roped-off area at the base of a cliff of blue ice. GO NO FARTHER, warned a sign. The ice could not be trusted. Heedlessly, several people stepped over the rope and trudged across rocks and snow to frolic at the glacier's base. They posed for photographs near a yawning blue crevasse. A woman was killed here a few years ago, Jane told us. She dared the glacier, too.

What's behind this drive to assert our power over nature, I wondered to Jane that day. Is it defiance that goads climbers to challenge the summit, to plunge, like Melville's Ahab, into the heart of mystery? Or awe, the wondering, wandering soul of Ishmael that strives not to conquer, but to see? Or is it anxiety, the fear of a cold dark we don't understand but try to dispel by overpowering some Thing or some Other?

This is our unique human challenge. The mountain can only surrender to the glacier; the cub becomes a bear instinctively. But we achieve human dignity through choice. Anxiety, and the plight that prompts it, is what reminds us to pause and choose.

The heedless ones among us—the dogmatists who terrorize others with their hard gods, the Dr. Lauras who interrupt doubt midsentence with their shrill certainty, the merchants of pleasure who silence wonder with noise—are dangerous because they're out to destroy the anxiety that, used rightly, can make hearts bold and solutions humane. When we find the courage to open our minds, we glimpse truth extending far beyond a mere moment on earth. And then, realizing we might be wrong, we can decide to offer something anyway, however small, toward a future we can't know.

DURING OUR VISIT to Alaska, as we drove back to Anchorage from Seward, Mike suggested a side trip that puzzled his wife, Jane, and frustrated his daughter, Kelsey, who was eager to get home. Tomorrow was her first day of junior high school; still on her list of essential items were two No. 2 pencils and a pair of white-soled gym shoes. Mike promised to keep the detour brief. We turned off the main highway and drove a two-lane road through a lush coastal forest, then turned right onto the gravel main street of a ramshackle town set against the mountains on Cook Inlet. HOPE, ALASKA, said a sign at the side of the road.

We parked and walked through town, past a building proclaiming itself bar, café, hotel, and information center. On the porch, a few people clustered, talking and laughing in the crisp air of a landscape as formidable as it is majestic. FOR SALE signs curtained the gaping windows of several haggard-looking houses across the road. In the center of town stood a worn-out building wearing a tattered coat of white paint and a sign above the door: HOPE SOCIAL HALL. We peered through the dusty panes at a vinyl-covered orange sofa and a chrome table.

Desolation Point, False Pass, Resurrection Bay, Wonder Lake: these are the poignant place names we encountered during our days in Alaska. And now here was Hope, gasping for breath in the chilly shadow of a mountain, its name cheerfully denying its predicament.

"So why are we here?" I asked Mike.

He smiled. "I just wanted you to know Hope exists."

HOPE EXISTS in the struggle to break free of our bonds. It exists in Michelangelo's slaves writhing upward from their stone prisons; it exists in the people of Barcelona striving to realize Gaudí's dream; it exists in the dreams of little boys who decide to harvest their own crop of hay; in the empty-handed plea "For the Love of God"; in the paradox of joy and sadness at the core of human life; in those who one day cry, "Oh my God, Oh my God," and the next emerge from the ashes to make carrot soup; it exists in poetic insight, and in these words of Seamus Heaney:

> *History says, Don't hope*
> *On this side of the grave,*
> *But then, once in a lifetime*
> *The longed-for tidal wave*
> *Of justice can rise up*
> *And hope and history rhyme.*

Hope exists in our desire for children, in the commitment to nurture and teach them, in the vulnerability that is the inevitable price of loving them. And hope exists in the e-mail messages of a young architect endeavoring to find meaning in the midst of ruin and grief:

Architects feel a kind of helplessness in the aftermath of these events, wondering, "Is there something we could have done to keep those buildings standing, even for ten more minutes?" And in the longer term, "What does it mean for our cities when buildings that symbolize society become targets?" But right now, it's 8 a.m. in New York and the jackhammers are having a field day in the street below as they continue their work constantly upgrading the infrastructure of the city. With the sounds of building and the sight of steel towers under construction in midtown, somehow I know we are going to be okay.

On Being a Ten

ADRIENNE

I LOVE MY BROTHERS, proclaims the hand-lettered sign traveling on a broom handle held high above the mortarboards of the Class of 2000. As the graduates enter the outdoor quadrangle at Washington University, my Montana bones, accustomed to sun and drought, shiver in the chilly mist of this St. Louis May morning. I draw my jacket closer and strain to see my daughter's face. There she is now, the bearer of the sign, striding with the same erect confidence that took her up the sidewalk to first grade: Adrienne, with her jubilant, dimpled smile, her green eyes searching the crowd for us. We wave furiously until she locates us, Ned and me, and the three brothers so flamboyantly loved, Dan, Ned Anthony, and Ben.

Nature has done her best to keep those brothers away. Dan and his daughter, Courtney, drove from Iowa City, five hours through hard rain over drenched, sometimes hail-slicked roads. Ben's flight from New York was grounded in a downpour in Detroit, where he rented a car and drove the remaining five hundred miles through the night, arriving at dawn to sleep for a couple of hours on the sofa in Adrienne's apartment. Ned Anthony anxiously left behind his wife and two young sons for a simple flight that became a trial of turned-back planes and long waits on storm-lashed runways.

Being there when it isn't convenient is the hallmark of parental love. Even for moms and dads, whose hearts inevitably stir at the first chord of "Pomp and Circumstance" and the first glimpse of a beloved child in cap and gown, graduation ceremonies are tainted with duty. This brotherly devotion impresses me. Especially when I consider Adrienne's prickly history toward their unsolicited presence and advice.

She was six months old when Dan graduated from college and came home to spend the summer, the only time all ten children lived together. But he has a habit of showing up at regular intervals, as if Montana weren't a sixteen-hour drive from his home in Iowa City, as if he actually belonged to our family, as if his archaic opinions were relevant to her life.

After Ned Anthony took over the management of our ranch, he was on the scene routinely. He provided Adrienne with a Yahtzee opponent and a listening heart, but his patient solutions tended to collide with her need to set things straight.

Ben was a constant in her growing-up years, her playmate, adversary, irritant, and friend. He was the first sibling to see her after she was born, to hold her in his arms while his four-year-old eyes rounded in awe. They shared trucks and dolls and books, the same piano teacher and astrological sign. He "watched over" her outdoors as they rode horses or tended Butch, his well-loved calf. Indoors, he often sent her to the sidelines to watch him, the little sister forbidden to touch his electric train and the puzzle always in progress on the coffee table. They were ten and fourteen when we moved to town and suddenly became a typical family, mom, dad, and two kids living near a park and a school. And Ben was an adolescent, a condition that bound Adrienne, in the way peculiar to younger sisters, to watch over him. Observing his agony of awkwardness prompted her to conclude that she "never wanted to be a teenager." They suffered teenage chicken pox together; they entertained each other with imitations of an eccentric teacher; she made him cookies; he fixed her bike; they cared about each other with fierce fraternal ambivalence; they gave Ned and me a chance to amend our parenting mistakes.

As she proceeds past, Adrienne pauses and waves her sign, making sure we understand. Her childhood method of soliciting my attention was to take hold of my chin and turn my face toward hers. Now other people turn to track our rambunctious response. They smile, perhaps surmising that she's the doted-upon only girl in a four-child family, not knowing that usually there's a whole row of us cheering our graduate into the world. I see a tremulousness beneath my daughter's smile, a question behind the happiness in her eyes. Where are her other six siblings? Isn't her graduation worth their while?

They're busy with work and families, of course. They're in Alaska, Spain, Montana, Iowa. Monica is in Philadelphia training to row in Sydney in the fall. This winnowed booster section is the lot of the youngest child.

Adrienne's graduation, however, is not simply one more college commencement, but the last such event in our family. An opportunity, then, because so often we don't know when something occurs for the last time. The last

Christmas with one's family, the last coffee klatch with a friend, the last afternoon spent with your mother before a stroke changes her into someone else, the last time a husband and wife sleep together in their marital bed. When I change the sheets on the bed Ned and I share, I'm haunted by a scene from a short story. In it, a woman laments that diligent routine because the same day she put on fresh sheets, her husband died. His scent was gone forever from his pillow and her life.

Today is a landmark for Ned and me, too. We're completing twenty-five years of children in college, an era beginning in 1975 when Dan entered and continuing until this millennium year. We've had kids in school since 1962. We've survived phonics, sight reading, cooperative learning, open primary centers, and closed administrative minds. We've put up with sex education programs that patronized parents as either mute, absent, or incompetent. We've consoled losing candidates for class president, chaperoned hayrides, and deferred to childless teachers twenty years younger than us. We've beamed at our progeny through speech meets and track meets. We've applauded fifth-grade cacophony presented in concert. My heart reached with Jennie's voice when she climbed every mountain as Mother Superior in their high school production of *The Sound of Music*. It contracted with fear when fourteen-year-old Adrienne slammed headfirst against the gym wall as she dove for an errant basketball.

Perhaps our proudest moment occurred the evening Adrienne volunteered to solo—a cappella—"The Star-Spangled Banner" before her high school volleyball game. As the packed gym stood at attention, she began, confidently, on key, our brave, talented seventeen-year-old daughter. Ned and I preened. But somewhere between the "proudly we hail" and the "broad stripes and bright stars," she stumbled, stopped, glanced hopefully at her teammates on the bench. One of them whispered something about "the twilight's last gleaming" and she set off into it, but darkness quickly enveloped her. She stammered out a phrase or two, paused, found a few more words, then slapped her right arm across her chest, straightened her shoulders, and began, loud and clear, "I pledge allegiance to the flag . . ." "of the United States of America," joined in the wide-eyed audience, on cue and on through "liberty and justice for all." The starting buzzer sounded. Unruffled, our daughter took her position on the court while Ned and I gaped in admiration.

Beyond all of the sentiment embedded in this commencement lies another argument for sibling perfect attendance: justice. From 1979 when Adrienne was an infant sleeping in my arms as Dan graduated from the University of Notre Dame, through 1997 when Ben received his diploma in this same place on a morning much like this, her faithful face is in every graduation photograph. She's attended raucous cork-popping affairs and straitlaced events forbidding the most innocent shenanigans. (I'm thinking of the "I love Mom" message Ben taped across his black high school mortarboard. I recognized the disarming defiance of school rules, but when the solemn principal ordered it stripped away, I felt like a deflated Goodyear balloon.)

She was with us at Notre Dame in 1981 when Ronald Reagan, rebounding from an assassination attempt six weeks earlier, sprinted onto the commencement platform to assert his invincibility and the efficacy of his code of the cowboy: rugged individualism heedless of marginal voices, including the students outside protesting with signs and black armbands his callous undoing of the civil rights efforts of the sixties and seventies.

Another spring, Adrienne leaned wearily against me

during a high school graduation while a coach-speaker tried to convince us that life was like a game when anyone past thirty knows better. Games, played by rules as black-and-white as a referee's shirt, end with a clear winner. Real life is gray, a tie between muddle and mystery, its wins and losses as ambiguous as middle age and purgatory and "We'll see."

Now, the sign marches forward into the section designated College of Arts and Sciences, where it sticks out throughout the ceremony, announcing the presence of an English/anthropology major who refuses to sink into the anonymous crowd. There is my daughter, my youngest child. And here am I. Today is our mutual commencement.

ONCE, I WAS SITTING on a park bench with my infant on my lap while my other children scattered to nearby swings and slides. My two-year-old clung momentarily, then joined the others for a burst of play. But soon, she returned to the bench and me. After a few minutes, she went off again for another venture with the others, but before long, she bounced back, as if she were tied to me by an invisible elastic band that stretched only so far. This, of course, was typical two-year-old behavior, the desire to run off and investigate, but the confidence to do so dependent on a secure home base. Soon enough, my baby would be testing that leash, too.

Not so for the mother-baby dyad in the portrait on our wall. The woman sitting there is quaintly serene, as if she were fantasizing growing old within that frame. Or perhaps the tables have turned, and her security is fastened to the babe upon her lap.

When I pause before the portrait, I see the low light of November drifting with the snow across afternoon fields. I see myself sitting in the kitchen nursing my newborn, my tenth child, my last, a sweet reward after dark months of waiting. An idea simmers. A portrait, I want a portrait of my baby and me, a bona fide artist's rendition, my swan song to mothering. I pick up the phone and schedule the first sitting, explaining to the artist that the painting will be my husband's Christmas gift. As if I need to rationalize the cost or legitimize the gesture. As if I need to justify my song by making it his.

Through the tranquil postpartum weeks, I care for my baby and ignore the hullabaloo, the newspaper ads counting down shopping days until Christmas. Instead, I count down the six weeks until our three oldest children, in college in South Bend, will arrive home. But as the days dwindle toward a grinchlike season, my anxiety grows. Too pregnant to waddle through the stores before my baby's November birth, I'd cast my lot with my youngest kids, who imagined a sleigh full of toys spilling from the midnight sky. Now, in early December, reality rears its head. I live in a house full of believers, a few of them pragmatists aware that the faithful get the goods, others willing to suspend their disbelief, and the youngest few who know a miracle happens each year in exactly the same way. I must come through. I'll do the dreaded shopping on the day I plan to be in town for the portrait sitting, December 10, my baby's one-month birthday, my forty-fifth.

The sun rises on new snow, six inches unevenly distributed by a caterwauling west wind. A ten-foot drift here, three inches there. A glimpse of freedom, a wall of despair, a mile from our house to the highway. A day to stay home by the fire if it weren't for those fervent lists. And so it's off to the mall with the other visitors, the frenzied masses out to get and spend and lay waste to one another if need be for the sake of a Cabbage Patch doll or a Play Station or Hogwarts Castle or whatever TV deems essential to the happiness of this year's children.

My daughters, Alane, fourteen, and Monica, twelve, are my chosen helpers, even though I'm concerned that seeing will ruin their belief. We drag through the overheated stores in boots and heavy coats, country folk dressed for drifts. When Adrienne cries, I retreat to a department store dressing room or the back booth of a darkened restaurant lest someone be offended at the sight of a female breast put to practical use. Whatever can go wrong, does: one package is stolen, another lost; we emerge from the mall to a missing car key, then a dead car battery. A young male savior appears, raises the hood, and rescues us. But there's still a final trudge over our road through drifts. Somehow, in the midst of this, I managed to sit for the initial drawings, but the snow persists through winter, and it's Father's Day before the portrait is finished.

Now, when I ponder the canvas where my daughter and I dwell, I see past the tranquil Madonna to the off-canvas reality, a model for Murphy's law. I see snow and drifts and hectic shopping. But I also see ardent days of waiting, a joyous homecoming, Adrienne's Christmas Eve baptism celebrated on the anniversary of my own, Mike and Elizabeth serving as sponsors, the infant in our midst serving as a profound reminder of the season's meaning: innocence, rebirth, renewal, rejoicing, the return of light and hope to a darkened world.

"O BEAUTIFUL FOR SPACIOUS SKIES," sings the confident soprano voice under the hovering gray St. Louis sky. Adrienne's sign bounces like a boat tied to a shore of black caps and gowns. Suddenly I'm a vessel without a port, adrift at sea with no lunar month to guide me, no stars on charts, no Monday music lessons, no birthday cakes, no random encounters in the kitchen with my youngest child asking for a hug.

"NEXT FALL when I go to school, you won't really be alone," six-year-old Adrienne assures me. She's just awakened on this June morning and come into the kitchen, where I've taken her onto my lap and told her I loved her. "I know." She nods. "I love you, too. We love each other and that's sorta like telephone wires. We're hooked up." Two months later, she skips up the sidewalk toward school without a backward glance.

Once I watched a sow give birth. She screamed with frightened incomprehension and threw herself against the earth, rolling and writhing in frenzied rhythm to the pulsating lives within crying *let go, let go, let go,* her body their sole escape into a wider, necessary world. She grunted and lurched to her feet, sank again, twisting and moaning. Again she stood, this time shoving her snout against the wooden rail, grappling and gnawing in openmouthed agony until at last, one by one, the piglets oozed from her into mud-deep freedom. This labor is too hard. My mouth reeks with dread. I want a rail to sink my teeth into, wood to gnaw through this birthing pain.

Ah, but there'll be no moaning for me. My liberation is at hand. At last, I can "have it all," a life of my own between eight and three, motherhood from dusk to dawn. I turn toward town, where I've scheduled a full day. At nine, a Jungian discussion group where I hope to gain insight into a book I've been puzzling over alone, Marion Woodman's *Addiction to Perfection;* lunch with a friend puzzling over her sullen fourteen-year-old son; and in the afternoon, a water-color class. But I must be back in Broadview, waiting outside the school, at three-twenty, when Adrienne's first-grade classmates prance down the sidewalk like restless colts bound for green fields. I leave town ten minutes too late and try to cover thirty miles in twenty minutes. As I round the only bend on Highway 3, I come into full view of two patrol cars headed my way. Immediately, one spins around and catches me in a whirl of light. Fifteen minutes later, ticketed and reprimanded, I pull back onto the road and realize I'm on the verge of tears, a naughty child caught in wrongdoing, Saint Augustine stealing pears.

But the story Augustine tells in his *Confessions* is one of rebellion. At sixteen, he steals fruit he's too full to eat and throws it to the pigs. What fascinates and repels him is his lack of motive. He's committed a crime for the sheer joy of doing evil, a way of imposing his own will, of playing God.

I *can't* play God; I'm female. And in trouble at every turn. My tears flow because I'm caught. Where do I belong in this patriarchal culture that idealizes motherhood for its emotional virtues—nurturing, providing care, tending human relationships—but pays no wage for the work? I must stretch beyond the frame that contains my daughter and me. The culture warns me to beware of this Judeo-Christian pose, mother and child cocooned in domesticity, confined to a world of food and feelings, without influence or power, protected and supported by a man who isn't in the picture. He's off making money and decisions, gaining prestige, flexing his muscles, riding his horse. He's autonomous while she's dependent and vulnerable, unsure whether to trust the intuition that tells her concern for others is what makes souls grow, or the world's version of truth that denigrates caring work by assuming it involves no intelligence or skill.

. . .

FOUR YEARS LATER, still a fringe feminist but now living in town, I attend an all-day conference titled "Women, 1990." At two-fifteen that same afternoon, at a school assembly, eleven-year-old Adrienne will receive a presidential award for academic fitness. I'll juggle my schedule, a theme woven throughout the day as speakers discuss careers, family, the search for self. They praise children who've adjusted to a working mother, husbands who've learned to cook and clean. One speaker concedes that if she were doing it again, which she won't be, she'd take off more time after childbirth. Another proclaims that mothers should stay home only for the sheer joy of the moment, not because of some imagined benefit to the child. Obviously, I'm missing something. I've had my moments of sheer joy, but they were buried amid long hours, months, and years on the scene, where I imagined my presence made a difference.

At five after two, on the brink of a promising talk called "Who Gets Ahead and Why," I reluctantly leave and hurry across town to my daughter's school. I join parents on bleachers at the far end of the gym, and sit, without a program, through awards in P.E., math, spelling. Adrienne receives several; I clap, we exchange smiles, but I'm concerned about falling behind the women at the conference. My flourishing future is vanishing into a long list of awards, one indistinguishable from another. I ask the woman next to me for clues. She scans her program and shrugs. Surely, I decide, somewhere in the midst of that batch, Adrienne has received her academic fitness award. I return to the conference in time to hear a final hint on business negotiation: don't let the use of "we" pull you in.

When I return home, Adrienne is in the kitchen. She turns to me, tears brimming her eyes. "Why didn't you stay to see me get the president's award?"

I'd missed it, after all. Trying to arrange my day for success, I'd let her down and cheated myself of that proud shared moment.

"AMERICA, AMERICA, God mend thine every flaw, Confirm thy soul in self-control, thy liberty in law," concludes the triumphant vocalist. She's navigated shining seas and thoroughfared wilderness without forgetting a single word. No emergency pledge will be said today. Even so, I put my hand over my heart and keep my eye on the little boat with its cargo of brotherly love.

"DO YOU KNOW what it's like to be the youngest of ten?" came Adrienne's plaintive childhood plea. Whenever she tried to explain her heavy burden, how boring it was to live with two old-fogy parents, how tough it was to break new ground, how humiliating it was to be the passenger in an older sibling's car, how tired she was of unsolicited opinions, she met a chorus of discordance, brothers and sisters comparing her life of luxury to their own saga of deprivation.

Her brothers and sisters loved her not always wisely, but so well that they implanted deep in her being the trust that is born of care. The result was a mixed blessing, a confident little sister insistent on her rights, fiercely devoted to them but with her antennae always up for hints of domination or injustice.

One moment she felt essential to the happiness of her siblings, the next, like a nuisance, someone to fetch and serve. "Sometimes I feel like the flour in a cake," Adrienne summed it up, "but other times I feel like the wooden spoon that mixes it."

She gravitated naturally to a style Ned's mother recommended to me as sound parenting strategy: Speak with authority even when you're not sure you're right. But embarking on this feat with nine older siblings is a bit like trying to enter a rush of highway traffic from an uncontrolled intersection. Even when Adrienne saw an opening, there was always someone ready to cut her off with a rude reminder: *You're too young to drive, to go along, to understand.*

"I hate being told I'm too young," she fumed when she was five. "I hate people saying, 'You're too young to answer the phone, you're too young to . . .'"

"Well, you're not old," I interjected.

"At least they could call me middle-aged."

Surely this was the first documented case of someone volunteering for a life stage most of us try hard to swerve around. Indeed, Adrienne's existence may be evidence of an unconscious swerve on my part, an unplanned conception at age forty-four, after I put away all the things of a child and considered my reproductive phase accomplished.

"An unplanned conception" . . . an intriguing comment coming from a woman of my ilk, implying, as it does, that the other nine *were* planned. And they were, although not in the rational mode of abandoning pills and sheaths and diaphragms. Nor were Ned and I bullied by the official Catholic stance on artificial birth control—*it frustrates the natural God-given power to generate human life.* What inspired us was a more symbolic understanding of being "open to life," also woven through Catholic teaching: a couple's willingness to do the work life reveals to them. The best-kept secret in all of this is that the Church recognizes individual conscience as the ultimate guide, the right of couples to make decisions based on the truth of their experience, the reality of their lives, the desires in their hearts. For us, that translated into children. And life opened us. Even, perhaps *especially,* at those trying times when we felt neither willing nor able to stretch any further.

Maybe five-year-old Adrienne was observing what so

many of us miss in the presbyopic anxiety of middle age—the power of maturity. I'd like to think she saw competence developing in me, the strength of a woman coming to accept herself and the import of generative work. When she told me at age four that it was "boring to be a girl," I assumed she meant a momentary lull in the afternoon, not some observed stagnation intrinsic to females. Inevitably, the act of "staying" appears mundane compared to the romance of setting forth on a journey of risk and adventure. In fact, stay-at-home child rearing may be the high-risk occupation of contemporary life, a daily balancing act on a high wire, your sense of competency often on the line, critical decisions about the children you love made with no net of certainty, your equilibrium assaulted by the skepticism of an anxious culture.

Surrounded by student siblings, a psychologist dad, and a middle-aged mother eager to sink into a plump chair after lunch to read Dr. Seuss, often reading myself to sleep first, Adrienne had only one recourse if she wanted the whole story—to become literate early. She quickly discovered the might in a sharpened pencil.

She outlined her predicament in this childhood message: "Mom and Dad, I love you but I don't know about my brothers and sister's. I do like it here but nobody treats me like it. Sorry about the bad complaments. I love you lots. Adrienne."

When she was eight, she tacked up a notice of her employment availability, as well as her charges for various chores: "Setting table: one nickel; Making bed: one nickel; Cleaning room: one dime; Folding clothes: (depends on how many)" and on through dishes and laundry and cleaning the car.

Ben penciled in an addendum: "Other people do this stuff because it needs doing, not for pay. Your pay for doing those jobs is a beautiful ranch to live on, an enormous and luxurious home, plenty of food and a nice family."

She posted this rebuttal: "Things that drive me nuts: my brother! Loud noises. Gross things. Beans. Pigs. Ben. Today went great until he came home. He's just a 12 year old jerk."

Her righteous indignation extended to the classroom. Beneath the row of A's on her fourth-grade progress report, her teacher stated this concern: "I would like to see Adrienne 'settle down' and do less 'visiting' so as not to distract the other students and teachers, so as to provide a more suitable learning environment."

Adrienne responded: "Dear Mrs. M: I hate school so I'm trying to make it a little more fun. Plus if the other students don't want to listen to me, they don't have to. I'm beginning to think I can't have any fun in fourth grade. Very unsincerely, Adrienne."

As Adrienne's industrious traits emerged, so did her managerial skills, labeled less charitably by her siblings as "bossiness." She'd heard rumors of my previous life in the kitchen, and there were blackened cookie sheets and aged pans around as evidence, but the mother she came home to after school often was absorbed in paint at an easel or immersed in tapping out a fiction world on her computer keyboard. My apathy toward meals and mixing bowls astounded her. *Some people like to cook,* she would say indignantly, rifling through recipes and flinging open cupboard doors. And then, *Hand me that measuring spoon.* It was a domestic version of the ranch motto, "If you're going to hang around, make a hand of yourself." So I handed her measuring cups and wooden spoons, and, by the time she was twelve, I was the one who turned on the oven and greased the pans and lined up ingredients on the counter as she'd once done for me.

But my past actions told her more than my current disposition. She knew I respected the work that went on in the kitchen. She wore the chef's hat, but I was still on the scene, buying groceries and figuring out menus and fixing more meals than I got credit for. Together, we cleared away books and newspapers from the table and set it nightly for dinner. Properly. A tablecloth. Napkins. Forks on the left, knives and spoons on the right, because it matters. Because when families come together with their hungers at the end of the day, more than bodies are fed. This is the place where we can sit and talk and be nourished and known.

But the frenzy of our days has devoured the family dinner hour. Even though people seem to recognize intuitively the powerful symbol of dining together—we celebrate with banquets, carry food to bereaved families, preserve our holiday meals—contemporary schedules no longer honor the day-after-day coming together that bonds souls. Families straggle home at unpredictable hours to poke around the refrigerator and eat cafeteria-style, that efficient refueling process that has nothing much to do with anyone else at the table. As I shifted food in and out of the oven and reheated casseroles, maintaining enthusiasm for preparing meals *did* become more difficult.

Fortunately, some people still "like to cook." Adrienne has executed complex menus. She's also made miraculous order in the midst of family chaos, planned complicated itineraries, implemented a family newsletter by assigning one person to each month, and called the crowd home to celebrate our fortieth wedding anniversary. When I visited her in Toulouse, France, where she studied during her junior year, I depended on her for language and direction.

And last year, she surreptitiously gathered up a batch of my recent paintings, took them to the local art gallery, and urged the proprietor to schedule a show of my work. The surprised woman handed her the standard application form, and, as Adrienne swung around to leave, asked, "By the way, who are you?" My agent, my daughter, myself. With chutzpah.

BECAUSE COOPERATION, not competition, is the required course in large families, such families are natural schools of democracy, especially if parents limit themselves to the role of firm advisers. What Ned and I gradually learned was that a firm advisory capacity is the only sustainable energy policy. Democratic collaboration among brothers and sisters is inefficient and boisterous and sometimes drifts toward a Darwinian free-for-all. It's tempting to avoid open friction with preventive measures—separate teenage phone lines, individual television sets, a room per child. In a large family, this is impractical; siblings have to work things out and learn to distribute privileges and obligations fairly. Doing so gives them a chance to experience the power of making choices and exerting influence. They develop a sense of responsibility to the group and can relate in ways impossible to parents. I think of snippets of advice overheard in our home:

You don't have to drink at parties. Or make a big deal out of it. Order a blue dolphin. People don't know it's ice water.

Don't worry too much about not having a best friend. Sometimes it's better to make lots of friends you like for different reasons.

Sibling truth telling can nip in the bud annoying habits and obnoxious behaviors a spouse might have to endure later. They're quick to spot the log in a brother's eye and eager to dislodge it. Younger children, candid if not always kind, provide a reality check for teenage fantasies. "You look like a lion," a five-year-old blurts at the sight of a sister's untamed hairstyle. A three-year-old beating on the bathroom door, screaming, "I have to go NOW," simultaneously abbreviates a twenty-minute leg-shaving shower, lowers the electric bill, and does the Earth an environmental favor.

Throughout Adrienne's childhood, there were siblings, siblings everywhere, but not a drop of awe. Been there, done that, they told her, in actions and in words. Had she been Paul's only sister, surely he would have been impressed when she and her date went off in a stretch limo with two other couples, six nervous freshmen decked out for dinner and the high school homecoming dance. But the indulgent father who rented the car for one flamboyant hour failed to have a backup plan, an oversight a father of many could never afford. Alas, all the elegant restaurants were full, and searching for one idled away the limo's hour. The couples settled for Big Boy, where they crammed into a booth and ate hamburgers. Afterward, Adrienne sent an SOS to Paul, who chauffeured the humiliated group to the dance in the family's ten-year-old Ford Escort. To his credit, he didn't address her as Cinderella until the next day.

Perspective is perhaps the greatest gift to be gleaned from a sibling group that spans two decades. Someone's always passing through a stage—from the two-year-old practicing "no," to the eighteen-year-old asserting herself with a pierced tongue, to the aging couple in their midst struggling to understand what it's all about. But just as naive parents tend to hurry the first child developmentally and emotionally, brothers and sisters, especially when they're twelve, sixteen, twenty years older, sometimes tread thoughtlessly on youthful idealism. Jokes about high school crushes aren't funny to a fifteen-year-old in the throes of one. And zealous agnostics, i.e., college freshmen who dump their doubts on the holiday table, can squelch the light burning in hopeful hearts.

"Dad, I know why I got a lot at Christmas," Adrienne confided when she was six. "It depends on how much you hope. You have to hope and hope and hope. You have to start hoping about at Easter."

Night after night throughout her childhood, I sat on the edge of her bed and listened to those hopes. Fears, too. The leftovers from her day that needed mulling over. In high school, whenever she asked if I was coming to her room to say good night, it usually meant she wanted to talk about a problem. Or, every so often, to make amends after the battle of wits and endurance we'd fought that day, mother of ten and her last child, tangled in wires that wouldn't let go, our weapons words, glares, and tears.

My hope is that out of her tribulations as youngest child, she's salvaged some enthusiasm to pass on to the possible children in her own future. I want her to remember the hot July afternoons Jennie took her to the ranch swimming hole, the crayoned notes with sticks of gum inside that Alane sent from graduate school, the embroidered sunbonnet Elizabeth brought from Rome to tie under her baby sister's fat chin, Mike's faithful birthday cards.

"YOU GRADUATE at an auspicious time," commencement speaker Julian Bond advises this millennium class. "You are about to officially join an elite within our nation."

Elite? My eyes go straight to my daughter. I imagine her bristling at the word with its suggestion of smug superiority. I remember her consternation last year as we toured Windsor Castle outside London. The extravagance there aggravated memories of the month she'd spent in Tanzania the previous summer. But when we strolled past Queen Mary's Doll House, where the opulence was replicated in miniature—dainty portraits of royalty, gleaming chande-

liers, exquisite furniture, exotic carpets, even plumbing—
Adrienne went mute with anger. In strategic locations on
the castle grounds stood clear plastic bins soliciting contri-
butions: a restoration fund for a bedroom ceiling damaged
by fire while some royal nose snored in another room. An
hour later, outside the railroad station, we encountered this
sign: DO NOT ENCOURAGE BEGGARS BY GIVING THEM MONEY.
Adrienne sizzled. Begging, it seemed, was permissible only
for an elite with at least a partial roof over their heads.

But Bond is referring to the elite "community of educated women and men" that these young people are now
joining. He summons forth their potential. He urges them
to do well, but also to do good. To offer not just love, but
justice. He tells them how important they are to their
nation and to their world.

"NOBODY PAYS ANY attention to what I say or think,"
Adrienne cries, bursting from the group gathered around
the holiday table. She dashes to her room and whams the
door emphatically behind her. I push back my chair, then
change my mind. She's twenty.

"Whoa! What was that all about?" asks Dan, the mysti-
fied, well-meaning brother Adrienne has appointed as her
adversary in her search for a place in this disputatious group.
Coming so late into her unwieldy family, Adrienne is a
little like a newly independent country, intent on having a
vote, but unsure about the dynamics of this democracy. So
far, her human rights reforms have been aimed primarily
at Ben.

"She has a point," Elizabeth argues. "After all, she spent
the past semester studying the evolution of *Homo sapiens*."

"Why are we discussing *The Bell Curve* on Christmas
night anyway?" Ned Anthony wants to know. He glances

apologetically toward his wife, Dana, who no longer expects relevancy in our table talk. Or under our roof, for that matter.

"She brought it up," Ben says, and finishes off his White Christmas pie.

"Actually, Dad did," Paul says with a lawyer's flair for tracking down culprits. "When we were talking about the Olympics. And he said Monica told him not to conclude blacks were better athletes than whites just because they're overrepresented in track events. And Danny said . . ."

Dan cocks his head, listening carefully for misquotes, then finishes Paul's sentence. "I said there were definite racial differences in the way biological variables are distributed. That's what set her off."

Actually, the trouble started before dinner. Even though three of our children weren't home this year, there were still sixteen people to accommodate at a table that, fully extended, seats fourteen. While I tended to details in the kitchen, Paul and Adrienne worked on the seating arrangement in the dining room. I heard him suggest putting the younger kids at the kitchen table. Adrienne, aware of my convictions about including children with the group, let him know that wouldn't do. They resorted to the usual solution, adding a small table to the end, then covering the two tables with one enormous cloth. Adrienne returned to the kitchen to help me while Paul set the table.

When she went back into the dining room a little later, a protest went up, followed by Paul's exasperated reply, "So I'm supposed to take off *all* these dishes?"

Silence. Then the sound of plates being stacked up. Then Paul's frustrated, "Okay, okay, okay. I'll *do* it. If it's that big of a deal, I'll *use* the good china. Just *mellow out*."

The expression in her eyes when she came into the kitchen told me she hadn't taken his advice. To the contrary, she'd gone on high alert for slights, the raised eyebrow or interrupted sentence that discounted her opinion.

Later, as the turkey waited to be carved, Jennie lit the candles, I dimmed the dining room lights, and we gathered around the table, laden with bowls and platters holding our traditional Christmas fare. Ned led grace, then turned to his carving task. Someone picked up the dish of cranberries and passed it left.

"Shouldn't you pass the other . . ." Adrienne began, but Elizabeth, next to her, said softly and wisely, too, since more bowls had set out on the journey around the table, "Just let it go." The commotion of passing tapered into conversation, and, toward the end of dinner, the stories began. Antics dredged up now that everyone had survived, always prompted by the same words, "Remember the time . . ." I've learned to pay attention. This is where I find answers to questions asked years ago. And where younger children refight battles lost in earlier years but now meant to be won.

This evening's session of nostalgia was provoked by a question from Ned Anthony. "Paul, remember when Mike built that wooden fort for our Johnny West guys? Then had the Indians attack it with flaming arrows?"

Paul laughed. "Oh, yeah. We lit matches and threw them at the fort. But when that grass fire started, I was scared. We did some fast shoveling that time."

Ben chimed in on behalf of the younger kids. "Adrienne, remember that night when we went sledding by moonlight? And you gave Mom a ride down the hill? And went flying under the rail fence? Trouble is, Mom was sitting up."

Adrienne grimaced, then grinned at me. "You bailed fast. Huh, Mom?"

"You would have been in trouble on your paper route

without your mom," said Elizabeth's husband, Jim, which prompted me to tell the story of the fall when fifteen-year-old Adrienne, chafing against her financial dependence, took on a paper route. She rose daily at three a.m. to roll and band papers, then stumbled through the dark on foot, pitching papers onto porches before five a.m. The monetary reward was minuscule, so I counted on its character-building aspect and discounted my own lost sleep as I lay awake weighing the risk of predawn rapists and drunk drivers against my own remembered hazard, being an over-protected youngest child. Two weeks into her route, she sprained her ankle in volleyball. And there I was, walking the sidewalks and tossing papers, but with no mother to disempower the dark with worry.

The conversation meandered through talk of ski trips and family bike trips up the Cooke City Highway and then to the '96 Olympics and the feats of black track stars. That brought up a recent report someone had seen in which several scientists used studies of IQ test results to argue that whites are more intelligent than blacks.

Adrienne simmered. "IQ tests are inherently biased. It's not fair to ask someone who's never seen a pig where bacon comes from."

Dan replied that those questions were taken into consideration. Her eyes shot hot sparks. "So you agree with the guys who wrote that book?"

"I'm just citing the research," he said, then launched into a lesson on biological variables and the influence of education and socioeconomic status. But what her fury heard was bigotry: her oldest sibling claiming intelligence can be determined by brain size, that some people are genetically smarter than others, that social policies might be set accordingly.

"Have you ever heard of Lucy?" Adrienne demanded. "And the theory that the human race can be traced to her?"

"Adrienne, don't be so intense," suggested Ben.

"We have one genetic mother," she flared. "We're all the same color."

Dan smiled and asked calmly, "Would you agree that there are shades of color?"

His amusement was the spark that ignited the explosion. She turned to her oldest brother. "Have you ever been to Europe? No! Or Africa? No! Or studied anthropology? No! I'm the one who went to Tanzania last summer."

"You were there when the U.S. Embassy was bombed," Ned added, trying to affirm her and defuse the argument, but instead, resurrecting those anxious hours.

"Danny doesn't even know where I was last summer. Or care. Nobody pays any attention to what I say or think. Ever." And then she was gone.

"People could be a little more gentle with her," says Jennie. "I remember how it feels to come home with new ideas. I got skewered one year because of my so-called religious fervor."

Paul laughs. "You were ready to join the convent."

"I lit a candle and said a prayer."

"Should I go down and talk to her, Mom?" Elizabeth asks, gesturing toward the stairway Adrienne descended.

I get up. "I'll go down."

I knock on the door of her darkened room. No answer. "Adrienne?" Silence. "Can we talk?"

"Why?" Tears float beneath the anger in her tone.

"It's Christmas. This isn't the time to—"

"To what? Say what I think? You're right. Nobody's interested anyway. I hate my brothers."

"Sometimes people forget you're grown-up."

"*Sometimes?* Nothing I say ever makes any difference. To anyone."

"Of course it does. To me, for one . . ."

A sigh, then silence.

I try again. "I don't think anyone meant—"

"Oh, Mom, what's the point? You're the only one who cares."

"Don't I count?"

A longer silence. Then the knob turns. She opens the door, and I open my arms. I hold her, stroking her hair, wishing I could shield her from hurt, wishing I could lift her the way I did when she was three, wishing I could carry her to bed, wishing I could read the worn-out stories that took her down the path to dawn. A moment later, she wrenches free and wipes her eyes. "I really don't care"—she sniffs and lifts her chin—"what *they* think."

Together, we go upstairs to where *they* are, past the portrait on the wall, a union fused on canvas twenty years ago. In that isolated moment between my daughter and me, I'm reminded of what matters most: human connection, the flesh-and-blood relationships that are the ground of all our trouble and pain, joy and healing.

Later on, as people wander wearily off to bed, she comes to me. "Mom, will you come down and tell me good night?"

THAT NIGHT, a fire rages through my dreams. I'm standing on the sidewalk watching helplessly as flames leap toward the upstairs of my childhood home. Suddenly, on the lawn, the giant blue spruce bursts into flames. This is the tree that served as background for every family photograph, where my mother sent us to stand when she emerged from the kitchen with her old box Kodak in hand. With the tree gone, what will become of our family history, the common fund of memories that tells us we belong? Will we forget the soldier-cousin pulling his girlfriend close as they smile bravely into each other's eyes (1942)? Or that other soldier, the fiancé I didn't marry, with his arm around me before he left for Germany (1954)? Who will understand the two grumpy girls in their grade-school uniforms, my sister frowning because she hates school, my frown meant to tell my mother that I'm tired of posing in front of this tree? In fact, the blue spruce isn't even in our yard. It belongs to our neighbor, Anna. Her German tree in all those Irish photographs; my mother's purloined setting now consumed by fire.

The flames leap higher, hotter. I'm worried about something upstairs, something I'm impelled to save. Fire flashes across the roof. I must go into the house now or it will be too late. A spurt of courage pulls me onto the porch, through the door, past the flames, up the stairs to the hall where a portrait hangs. I unhook it and carry it down the steps, outside to safety. I've salvaged what I treasure most from my childhood home, the portrait of Adrienne and me.

MY MOTHER, that other tenth child, would have cherished the portrait, too, the tribute to the bond between a woman and her last child, inevitably different, as it is with her first child, not because of preference, but because of its impact on her life.

In my mother's generation of Irish Catholics, being the youngest *daughter* was the tie that bound. She was the designated caretaker for her aging parents, the one who put off marriage until her thirty-eighth year. Throughout her life, she was the center around whom her siblings revolved, our house the place they stopped by for homemade cookies and a compassionate ear, our kitchen table where they ate impromptu meals and shook their silver-haired heads over the plight of the world and their own reluctant joints. The Sunday I was born, her oldest brother, Mike, sat at that table. While she prepared his supper, he delivered one of his monologues of regret about a wife who died young, a son who moved to California and never returned. She listened, then set his plate before him, put on her coat, and got into my dad's black Chevrolet for the ride to Mercy Hospital. That's what she told me, but what I heard was that everything depends on the woman in the kitchen, what she believes about herself and her work, whether she experiences her role as one of constraint or connection, and if the man waiting at the table pays attention to anything she says.

Now and then, I tease Adrienne about this youngest-daughter tradition, as if threatening to hold her to it, but when she commands the kitchen to cook a gourmet dinner for a festive occasion or to bake an enormous batch of cookies, I sense my mother's kindred spirit. And when she takes my arm on a slippery street or steers me through city traffic, I sense our singular bond.

At the same time, I hope that her keen sense of responsibility won't tempt her to try to shield me from the anxiety of old age, the dread of being left behind in a society on wheels. Children need to let go of parents, too. I confronted this fact from a distance as my parents grew old and died while I spent my energy on the life going forward around me.

Ned's mother once told me how much she cherished solitude in her later years. How much, in fact, she needed it. After decades of hard work and obligation, she longed to reflect, to have time to take hold of each thread woven through her life in order to appreciate the pattern that emerged. Watching her face death with courage helped those around her face life.

. . .

THE FIRE CLARIFIED something. The immeasurable moment between mother and child is not a representation of
some outdated cultural misunderstanding. Mothering is
a commitment of body and mind and soul, a day-by-day
responsibility *to* and *for* an "other." Connectedness is not
restrictive but enriching and liberating and necessary to
humane living. An irrational force sent me into my burning
childhood home, intent on rescuing some unnamed treasure there. Only afterward, when my fear subsided and I was
safe again outdoors, did I recognize what I held in my
hands.

I admire the youngest-child traits that make Adrienne
irate over injustice. But I worry about them. What fires
will she face? Will her youthful compassion survive in a
merged world where connection is so often an 800 number
answered by a recorded voice, powerless, unaccountable,
anonymous, speaking only of corporate efficiency? An
abstract approach to human needs won't hold our loyalty or
infuse us with passion enough to spend our talents. We
pledge our allegiance to particular people and places inte-
gral to the ongoing narrative of our lives.

Last summer, as Ned and I were leaving Iowa after visiting family there, we drove slowly, slowly, one last time
down the street in Dubuque where I grew up, past the two-
story white house on South Grandview. The front lawn was
well kept but eerily barren. The house now wore an unbe-
coming coat of yellow and sprawled into the backyard
where my mother's clotheslines had been. My swing was
missing, too; there would be no more soaring over my dad's
garden or spying for hints of red in the raspberry patch.
The single garage, that cluttered home to shovels and hoes
and rakes, to my Flexible Flyer and beloved red bike, was
now three times the size and attached to the house. Buried

beneath it were the peony bushes that bloomed so triumphantly along our property line. I imagined my mother
walking down the sidewalk that was no longer there, and,
when we pulled away, I turned to wave good-bye, as I had
the summer before her stroke. That day, a vague foreboding
ing had gone through me, and I'd regretted my backward
glance. She hadn't turned, but kept her focus ahead, on the
steps and the porch that led into the silent house and the
shelter of her kitchen. But this time, when I looked back, I
was astounded by what I didn't see. The tree. Anna's blue
spruce was gone.

FACES HOVER in the background of the canvas containing
Adrienne and me: grandparents and uncles and aunts who
depended upon one another and reached out to one
another for answers and sometimes heard "no." Brothers
and sisters who knew the continuous give and take of relationship. People whose lives we learn over a grave, at the
kitchen table, beside the creek that winds through the
family picnic ground; men and women affected by mountains and plains, weather and work, money for bread,
and whether the garden grows. Vignettes of a grandmother
who went west to teach at nineteen when other young
women stayed home, of an aunt burned to death when a
wood stove exploded, of the sister who took her children
in, of Charlie and his two Anne Maries, the second who
lived out her marriage in a house haunted by the belongings of the first, a detail I learned only years later. What I
saw was my mother rankled by random things, the worn-
out leather chair always in her way, a picture of the Sacred
Heart bleeding on the dining room wall, a celery dish, a
plant table, ghosts she couldn't throw away.

"That old thing is an eyesore," my mother would say in
a tone of disdain each time she passed the blackened hall

rack standing inside our front door. Years later, when I scratched through the varnish and found oak, I refinished it for the front entry of our home. And for my mother, too. When my brother saw the restored piece, he told me it belonged to the first Anne Marie. Now I own the hall rack and the story.

ONE DAY my youngest daughter will own the portrait. She knows the story. Every year on her birthday she hears about the storm of 1978, when winter came in like a lion after a long mellow autumn, and November 10 headlines screamed "Blizzard." In the middle of that night, I waited in the kitchen while her dad warmed up the Suburban, then the pickup, anxiously scraping ice from both wind-shields, deciding finally that the car was warmer; we set out, lonely pioneers trekking into the unknown, driving the forty miles to the hospital over dark roads emptied by the storm. I describe to her the wailing wind and the snow swirling into drifts beneath the hospital window while I labored with her, my last child, for the first time fully con-scious and frantic with unmedicated pain. And at noon, I heard her cry and then, there she was, my daughter, and I held her, still bloodied by our bonds, and she quieted instantly in my arms. But the part I haven't told her, because I've never understood it, is that this time I wasn't trans-ported by the usual postbirth euphoria to some transcen-dent place. This time, I lay there earthbound, touching her.

THIS SAME HAPPY exhaustion embraces me now as the orchestra strikes the first joyful recessional note and the graduates, boisterous and hopeful, begin filing into their future. My daughter passes by, still lofting her sign of love. Satisfaction pours through me, the sweet relief of a woman who cringed beneath the cultural glare and the tight-lipped judgments on her rampaging fertility, who donned bifocals to sign into the maternity ward and later cried out in anguish as her tenth child came through her body into the world.

Today I'm yelling inside: *I've made it! I'm on the finishing line!* No one is cheering; I haven't won any blue ribbons, not even a yellow one, but I'm here, and so is our last child, and Ned just reached for my hand. I feel contented, tired, grateful, grown-up, glad, amazingly graced. *Fulfilled.* Is that the word I'm searching for?